n and so.
and—b

an
led

D1221862

John Adair, MA, B Litt, PhD, Fellow of the
Royal Historical Society, lived in
Buckinghamshire near Hampden country
during his youth. After national service he
became successively Senior Lecturer in
Military History at Sandhurst, Director of
Studies at St George's House, Windsor
Castle, and Associate Director of the
Industrial Society. Since 1970 he has
worked as an author, lecturer and
management consultant, and his books on
management training have a world-wide
reputation. His historical writings include
*Roundhead General: A Life of Sir William
Waller* and *Cheriton 1644: The Campaign
and the Battle.* In 1969 he founded the
Roundhead Association which, as part of
The Sealed Knot Society, re-enacts English
Civil War battles throughout Britain.

JOHN HAMPDEN

The Patriot

Other books by John Adair:

History
Hastings to Culloden (with Peter Young)
Roundhead General: The Life of Sir William Waller
Cheriton 1644: The Campaign and The Battle

Training and Management
Training for Leadership
Training for Decisions
Training for Communication
Action-Centred Leadership
Management and Morality

A LIFE OF

JOHN

HAMPDEN

The Patriot (1594-1643)

John Adair

MACDONALD AND JANE'S · LONDON

© John Adair 1976

First published in Great Britain in 1976 by
Macdonald and Jane's Publishers Limited
Paulton House
8 Shepherdess Walk
London N1 7LW

ISBN 0 354 04014 6

Printed and bound in Great Britain by
REDWOOD BURN LIMITED
Trowbridge & Esher

CONTENTS

List of Illustrations

Between pages 88 and 89
John Hampden, with facsimile signature *Private Collection, England*
Visscher's View of London *British Museum*
Sir John Trevor and Family *English Life Publications* (Reproduced by kind
   permission of Mrs Humphrey Brand, Glynde Place, Sussex.)
The House of Commons *British Museum*
The Trial of Strafford *British Museum*
Sir John Eliot *Private Collection, England*

Between pages 186 and 187
John Pym *British Museum*
The Earl of Essex *British Museum*
Arthur Goodwin *Devonshire Collection Chatsworth* (Reproduced by Permis-
   sion of the Trustees of the Chatsworth Settlement)
Etchings of London by Hollar *British Museum*
Engraving by Houbraken of John Hampden *British Museum*
Oliver Cromwell *National Portrait Gallery, London*
The Statue of Hampden in Aylesbury

Maps
South Midlands p. 90
The Battle of Edgehill p. 190
The Battle of Brentford p. 197
The Battle of Chalgrove Field p. 228

Drawings are by P.S.W. Beck

Truly, Jenny (and I know you may easily be persuaded to it), he was a gallant man, an honest man, an able man, and take all, I know not to any man living second.

ARTHUR GOODWIN *writing to his daughter about* **HAMPDEN**

INTRODUCTION

Hampden whose Spirit mov'd o're the goodly frame
O'the British world, and out this Chaos came;
Hampden a man that taught Confusion, Art;
This Treason's restless, and yet noiseless Heart.

ABRAHAM COWLEY, 1643

It is strange that for more than forty years no attempt has been made to present a picture of John Hampden in relation to his times. In 1933 two biographies of him appeared in one year, written by Hugh Ross Williamson and John Drinkwater. Both authors acknowledged their indebtedness to the pioneer work, Lord Nugent's two volumes of *Memorials of John Hampden: His Party and His Times* published in 1831. Nugent based his book upon several years of research. Indeed he literally left no stone unturned, for in 1828 he disinterred a body from a coffin in Great Hampden Church which he believed (quite wrongly) to be the corpse of John Hampden. Mr Williamson and Mr Drinkwater had an obvious advantage over Lord Nugent in that they could draw upon a hundred years of historical research into the seventeenth century by such scholars as S.R. Gardiner and C.H. Firth. Since then another forty years of historical studies have produced further crops of books, monographs and articles. What is needed now is an interpretation of Hampden's life in the light of this increased knowledge of the period. In this book I have attempted to paint a fresh portrait of Hampden against the rich background of his times. In addition I have been able to add some new evidence from original sources, including some hitherto unpublished letters.

Perhaps Hampden suffers from the same disadvantage as

a modern television actor who has become famous in a role: it is difficult for the public to see him playing other parts. All that most of us remember from our schooldays about Hampden is that he opposed the royal demand for Ship-Money in the reign of King Charles I. Hampden and Ship-Money go together like eggs and bacon. Yet there is more to Hampden than his refusal to pay a tax. On the eve of the Civil War, the country looked to him for direction much as it turned to Winston Churchill, exactly three hundred years later, when a far more formidable tyrant than King Charles threatened the peace and welfare of this island.

In a remarkable passage Lord Clarendon describes Hampden in November 1640 thus:

> The eyes of all men were fixed on him as their *Patriae pater*, and the pilot that must steer their vessel through the tempests and rocks which threatened it. And I am persuaded his power and interest at that time was greater to do good or hurt than any man's in the kingdom, or than any man of his rank hath had in any time: for his reputation of honesty was universal, and his affections seemed so publicly guided that no corrupt or private ends could bias them.

Thus men turned to Hampden as a great patriot in 1640 just as their descendants looked to another in 1940.

The word *patriot* entered the English language from the French tongue during Hampden's youth. It described the man who exerts himself to promote the well-being of his country by maintaining and defending his country's freedom or rights. The minting of this word tied up with the heightened Puritan love of England and the English. 'Whoever considers England', wrote Hampden's contemporary Mrs Lucy Hutchinson, 'will find it no small favour of God to have been made one of its natives, both upon spiritual and outward accounts. The celebrated glory of this isle's inhabitants, ever since they received a mention in history, confers some honour upon every one of her children, and with it an obligation to continue in that magnanimity and virtue, which has famed this island, and raised her head in glory higher than the great kingdoms of the neighbouring continent.' Both Shakespeare and Milton wrote their plays and verses for audiences who shared this basic sense of England's history, value and destiny.

Only by understanding the social and religious background of his day can we begin to appreciate why his contemporaries saw John Hampden as such a significant person. Besides his patriotic action in resisting a king's tyranny in defence of the democratic element in the constitution, he personified many of the virtues which the Puritans admired and sought to practise. Even among 'one of the most truly noble nations in the Christian world' (as Lucy Hutchinson called her England) Hampden became a byword for nobility of character.

The Civil War left among its legacies the paper war between two different interpretations of English history under the Stuarts. The Tory sons and grandsons of the Cavaliers obviously gave a meaning and significance to those events which were poles apart from the interpretation of their Whig counterparts. Dr Samuel Johnson unwittingly summed up the Tory view of Hampden by his Dictionary's definition of a patriot as *a factious disturber of the government*. For the Whigs, the image of Hampden came to them bathed in the aura of martyrdom: he was their equivalent to the Blessed Royal Martyr. But paradoxically the most glowing account of Hampden comes from the pen of Clarendon, quoted above, who began his *History of the Rebellion* in exile on Jersey after the Civil War. In 1647 he wondered to a friend if his view of Hampden was too eulogistic for Royalist taste, yet he added magnificently: 'I am careful to do justice to every man who has fallen in the quarrel, on which side so ever.'

How far Clarendon's estimates of Hampden as a person and as a statesman are true I shall leave the reader to decide. Certainly he seems to have glimpsed in Hampden a greatness in the making. Moreover, the other available evidence supports Clarendon's conclusion that Hampden was 'a very extraordinary person, a man who enjoyed a universal esteem'. He was the first great commoner in English history, the first member of the House of Commons to be hailed as a popular leader by the nation at large. Thus he deserves not to be so much overshadowed by his more illustrious cousin, Oliver Cromwell, who took up the work that an early death wrenched from Hampden's hands on Chalgrove Field.

Chapter One

EARLY DAYS

In his entrance into the world he indulged to himself all the licence in sports and exercises and company which was used by men of the most jolly conversation.　　　CLARENDON

The Hampden family had lived in Buckinghamshire since before the Norman Conquest. King Edward the Confessor first granted them the hill of beechwoods in the Chilterns south of Wendover which bears their name to this day. Domesday Book recorded this estate as belonging to Baldwyn de Hampden. His descendants in the direct male line acquired an impressive holding of manors in the home counties. In Buckinghamshire itself they were lord of the manors of Great and Little Hampden, Stoke Mandeville, Prestwood, Kimble, Dunton, Hoggestone, and Hartwell, while in addition they owned lands in Oxfordshire, Berkshire and Essex.

Besides being active in county administration, many of the Hampdens sat in Parliament. An early adherence to the House of Lancaster cost them dear in confiscated lands. But Edmund Hampden survived to become an Esquire of the Body and Privy Councillor to the first Tudor monarch. Indeed the family prospered under that dynasty. Sir John Hampden 'of the Hill' rode in the train of the English Queen at the Field of the Cloth of Gold in 1520 and later commanded *The Saviour*, a ship of the royal fleet. His daughter Sybil, an ancestress of William Penn of Pennsylvania, acted as nurse to the future King Edward VI. Brass portraits of him and his two wives and three daughters, dated 1553, lie in the chancel of the parish church of Great Hampden, in company with that of his father John (who died in 1496), also resplendent in armour, with his wife and ten children.

Griffith Hampden sat in the Parliament of 1585 and also became High Sheriff of his county. He enlarged and partly rebuilt the family manor house, and entertained Queen Elizabeth and her Court in sumptuous style. For example, he cut a long and stately avenue through the beechwoods from the road up to the house, in the process levelling a section of rampart and ditch of Grim's Dyke, which crossed his estate. The opening in the woods made by this avenue where it breasted the Chiltern hill near the house is known to this day as 'The Queen's Gap'.

Griffith Hampden died in 1591 and was succeeded by his eldest son, William, who followed him to the grave only six years later on 2 April 1597 at the early age of twenty-six. By that time, William had sat in Parliament in 1593 as Member for East Looe, then a flourishing port in Cornwall where the Hampdens obviously had some influence. More important, he had married Elizabeth, the second daughter of Sir Henry Cromwell of Hinchinbrooke in Huntingdonshire, who bore him two boys – John and Richard. Elizabeth's brother Robert Cromwell was the father of Oliver Cromwell, born in 1599, who was thus a first cousin of the Hampden brothers.

The language of William Hampden's will suggests that he was a man of Puritan convictions: certainly the vicar of Great Hampden who witnessed it stood in that tradition. About the man the will tells us little, except that probably he loved horses. He left 'his best ambling gelding in special signification of good-will' to his uncle Warren, and to another uncle, Weston Hampden, 'a baye mare called Baie Peter'. He bequeathed a grey mare to one of his friends, and also forgave him a debt of £4. In all he assigned ten horses to the male members of his family and friends, with rings and bracelets (or money to buy them) for the women folk. Elizabeth, his twenty-four-year-old widow, could have 'such apartments as she shall chuse' in Hampden House, and her dowry money of £140 to furnish them.

John was born in 1594. The exact date and place of his birth are unrecorded, but an early historian gives the latter as London. His mother sent him to the Grammar School at Thame in Oxfordshire, not ten miles from Great Hampden and only three from a family manor at Emmington, where

Richard would live in later life. According to Anthony à Wood, himself probably a pupil at the school a few years later, 'the Hampdens while young had been mostly bred in the said school of Thame and had sojourned either with the Vicar of the Master'. Although they were wealthy land-owners who could have sent their children further afield, the Hampdens rooted their sons in their native Chiltern country.

Thame is a small and ancient market town, typical today as then of so many others throughout the shires of England. Its immensely broad main street, flanked by old buildings, betrays its main function as a market-place. Here traders set up their booths and shouted their wares, while horses, cattle and sheep changed hands nearby amid much noise, dust and heat. Thirsts were quenched in the old inns which fronted the street, like the 'Signe of the Birdcage', which has not seen fit to alter its timbered visage much since Hampden's day. The local Cistercian abbey, founded in 1138, had been dis-solved in John's great-grandfather's time, and parts of it had been incorporated into Thame Park. Prosperous burgesses and cloth merchants built almshouses in the town, and improved their venerable parish church with monuments to themselves.

Thame Grammar School was established shortly after Lord Williams' death in 1559. Unlike rather similar founda-tions of that period, such as Sir John Gresham's Grammar School at Holt, Norfolk, it was not destined to evolve into a great public school but it might have done so. By 1601 or 1602, when John Hampden's schooldays began, it had estab-lished a good reputation for scholarship under the master-ship of Richard Bourchier. The Tudor school building still stands, alas no longer a school, its Cotswold stone walls pierced by square Elizabethan mullion windows and crowned with tile roof and brick chimneys. Here, in the large schoolroom on the ground floor, Hampden struggled with those tiresome Latin and Greek verbs. High among the gables there is an attic which tradition declares he occupied, which used to contain the frame of a solid oak bed, four feet wide and nearly six feet long, upon which he is said to have slept.

Hampden's predecessors among the scholars included

George Croke, who would sit one day as judge of the King's Bench in his Ship-Money trial. Henry King, a notable poet whose love lyrics did not bar him from becoming Bishop of Chichester, almost certainly was a school-fellow of Hampden as well. but he was two years senior in age – a wide difference among small boys. Less sure tradition names other celebrated pupils of Thame: William Lenthall, later Speaker of the House of Commons, born at Henley-on-Thames; Arthur Goodwin, Hampden's friend and fellow soldier in the Civil War; and another poet, Edmund Waller, a kinsman of Hampden's, whose family had lived at Beaconsfield in Buckinghamshire since the fourteenth century. The initials and date 'E.W. 1617' are among those carved upon the headboard of the oak bedstead, which is now on loan to the Buckinghamshire County Museum in Aylesbury.

The lessons each morning began with the reading of twelve verses from the Greek New Testament, and the day's work ended with the customary recitation of a chapter from the Bible in English 'for inculcating piety or for checking the frivolity of the young, to be clearly and distinctly repeated by one of the pupils who is best able to read it with ability and proper articulation'. On Sundays the boys attended the morning and evening services in the parish church, and were expected to discuss the subject matter of the sermons on Monday mornings. Before going to bed, they all knelt again, and John may have come to know by heart the founder's prayer said each night (which aptly sums up the purpose of the school):

> O Lord Jesus Christ, eternal wisdom of the Father, Thou who hast added to man's nature the benefit of teachableness, memory and understanding, hear our prayers. Give the help of Thy grace to our own natural endeavours, that we may more the readily learn true knowledge and sacred learning, which shall serve Thy Glory.

We can well imagine Master John Hampden, say fourteen years old, rising at five o'clock on a dark winter's morning for prayers and breakfast, and then taking his seat on the school benches at six o'clock, a spluttering candle from his chest upstairs adding its light and odour to the other candles in the room. Perhaps Richard Bourchier had a warm log fire blazing for them in the massive arched fireplace which stands so cold and empty today. Then, until five p.m., the boys studied their ancient Greek and Roman texts, and perhaps – according to Bourchier's taste – later Latin works: such authors as Erasmus, Melanchthon and Linacre. They learnt Hebrew on three days of each week. Besides regularly composing some Latin verse on set subjects, Bourchier made them write epigrams, eclogues, epitaphs and epithalamia in the three ancient languages as well as in English, and he practised them in oratory by getting them to speak in public after the models advocated in Cicero's *Orations*, Pliny's *Panegyrics* and Quintilian's *Declamations*. Such exercises made Hampden's schooldays arduous, but they brought to him in later life the fruits and pleasures of scholarship.

Hampden left Thame Grammar School in 1609 at the age of fifteen, and entered Magdalen College, Oxford, probably in the Michaelmas term that year. For Magdalen enjoyed the patronage of several prominent Buckinghamshire families at the time, including the Goodwins. The Lollards had once flourished in the Chilterns, and their influence lingered long. Under Queen Elizabeth, the gentry of Buckinghamshire developed a distinctive Puritan tradition. Yet they continued to send their sons to Oxford, a university somewhat behind its sister on the Cam in embracing the new theological orthodoxy of the Reformation. Magdalen still stands today by the river on the eastern side of Oxford, the red fallow deer grazing in the park as they did in Hampden's undergraduate years. It is on the edge of the university, on the road that leads from London through Buckinghamshire. This geographical position prompts a picture of the college as a bridgehead of the continuing Reformation in Oxford: in the reign of James I it had been referred to as a 'very nest of Puritans'. To the Anglican mind of Clarendon it was an unfruitful place, 'the discipline of that time being not so strict as it has been since, and as it ought to be'.

At Oxford University the undergraduates enjoyed considerable freedom over the use of their time. Thomas Hobbes, who matriculated a few years after Hampden, seems to have spent many hours reading travel books and snaring jack-daws in the deerpark, a comparatively harmless pastime by the standards of the day. Yet the college Fellows did not neglect their duties. John Crowther, Ralph Verney's tutor at Magdalen Hall, sent him a sheaf of astronomical notes, which he had compiled especially for his pupil. In addition Crowther prepared for him a general scheme of the Arts and a genealogy of the kings of England, and exhorted him 'to devote to logic and divinity from three to four hours a day'.

One relic of Hampden's studies during his first year at Magdalen College has survived. It is a vellum book of copies measuring three by ten inches. Contained within it are thir-teen kinds of hands written by James Davies. On the flyleaf there is the inscription: 'For his kinde friend and loving Scholar, Mr John Hampden, anno 1610.' Although the uni-versity and college records yield no mention of James Davies, he was clearly one of Hampden's tutors. The brief dedication hints at two important later characteristics already present in the sixteen-year-old boy: his natural kindness and gift for friendship, on the one hand, and his marked interest and diligence in scholarship on the other.

John Hampden matriculated on 30 March 1610, and gave to Magdalen a silver cup inscribed *Cantharus ex dono Joannis Hampden, Buckinghamiensis* to commemorate the occasion. By one of those ironies of history, the college donated it, along with other silver plate, to the King in 1642. Perhaps coins minted from that very cup may have lined the pockets of the troopers who killed John Hampden on Chalgrove Field the following year, but such a possibility could not be even imagined in 1610. That year King James paused on his way to hunt at Woodstock in order to refresh himself at Magda-len. On that occasion the college authorities paid for some repairs in the road in front of the tower, as well as giving £2.10s. to purchase a present of gloves for Prince Henry, £2 to men who brought a stag for the King, £1 to the royal trumpeters and twelve shillings to the Magdalen bell-ringers. The Fellows may well have groaned inwardly when the King chose to visit them again in 1612, again while on a journey to Woodstock.

Hampden and Goodwin both wrote verses in a Magdalen collection entitled *Luctus Posthumus* to commemorate the death of Henry Prince of Wales in 1612. The following year some Latin verses by John Hampden on the marriage of Princess Elizabeth, the lovely daughter of King James, to the handsome and equally young Elector Palatine, on St Valentine's Day, appeared in another university anthology in honour of that occasion, published at Oxford under the title *Lusus Palatini*. A fellow contributor to the volume of two hundred and forty poems in Latin, Greek and Hebrew, the forty-year-old President of St John's College, might well have noted and commented upon this undergraduate offering. His name was William Laud.

These compliments of academics, young and old, doubtless evoked admiration from those capable of appreciating their linguistic skills, but they lacked the breath of immortal life. We must turn to the fresh English verse of John Donne or Henry Wotton to capture the strange love affair of young Englishmen with their Princess, and the general rejoicing at her happy state. The elderly and celebrated William Shakespeare, then living in the country, struck perhaps a deeper note in his play *The Tempest*, traditionally written for the nuptial festivities. The golden voice of the poet's own generation, the age of Queen Elizabeth, gives the young couple both a blessing and a farewell: they must face their 'brave new world' alone. But history concerns real people, and Elizabeth was no Miranda, nor England the magic island of her father Prospero. At the most solemn moment in the wedding service, as the Archbishop of Canterbury pronounced them man and wife before a crowded congregation in the chapel of Whitehall, the sixteen-year-old girl succumbed to a fit of nerves and began to giggle uncontrollably.

In November 1613 Hampden became a member of the Inner Temple, and embarked upon two or three years of legal studies in London, a not uncommon practice for young landed gentlemen at that time. To be in London after those quiet years in Thame and Oxford must have been an exciting prospect to the nineteen-year-old John Hampden. Moreover, he had a temperament fitted to enjoy the people, sights and sounds of the capital city. Doubtless he saw the plays of Shakespeare at the Globe Theatre in Southwark and enjoyed the work of other dramatists in that golden age of the English theatre.

In 1613 London lay still in its springtime as a great city. Visscher's 'View of London', printed three years later, evokes the capital as no word-picture can: St Paul's Cathedral dwarfing its hundred rivals, the crowded tall houses of merchants and tradesman leaning against each other, the long waterfront with tall ships riding at anchor in the Thames, poor tenements at Southwark screening Shakespeare's Globe from the river. There are glimpses of windmill, field and hill beyond, the countryside which still reached almost to the medieval walls and gates of London proper, and made islands of such villages as Chelsea, Paddington, St Pancras and Islington. East of the Tower, and downstream from London Bridge, sprawled the wharves, warehouses, and whorehouses of one of the busiest seaports in Europe. On the other side of the city, through Lud Gate, lay the great houses of the nobility in the Strand, the Palace of Whitehall and the Palace of Westminster, close to the royal Abbey.

Bells, chiming clocks, the noise and din of shouting traders and angry customers, the clatter of horses and yelps of dogs: in our mind's ear we must fill the narrow streets and dark cool alleys with such sounds, and fill our lungs – if we can bear it – with the stench of that open sewer the Fleet River, or with the smell of decaying refuse and the overnight contents of chamberpots flung out on to the flagstones and cobbles of marketside or passageway. Above all, there was an endless procession of people in all their vanity and colour: sober-dressed merchants, courtiers in feathered felt hats with sword and walking-stick, maids of Court ladies bargaining in Cheapside, craftsmen and traders of every skill, burly watermen, vagabonds and beggars in rags, cripples, black-gowned clergymen, sallow-skinned Spaniards, blackamoors from Africa and the Indies – all drawn to London by the lure of money and the desire to be at the centre of England.

The Inner Temple shares with the Middle Temple the ground once occupied by the Knights Templar, who left behind their round church – modelled on the Moslem Dome of the Rock, which the Crusaders found standing on the site of Solomon's Temple in Jerusalem and then converted into a cathedral. The spacious hall and large garden by the river gave the Inner Temple the air of a large Oxford college. Here, in company with many other sons of the nobility and gentry, John Hampden applied himself to learning about the laws of England. Many of his fellow students enjoyed themselves in rioting and wantonness, or else contented themselves with a smattering of legal knowledge useful for their sole destinies as landowners. Term still ended in time for them to go home and help with the hay harvest, and the Long Vacation lasted until the corn had been cut and stored. But Hampden clearly possessed considerable intelligence and a good memory, and his studies bore fruit in his maturity. 'He had a great knowledge both in scholarship and in the law', wrote Sir Philip Warwick, who knew him in later years. 'He was very well read in history, and I remember that the first time I ever saw that of D'Avila of the civil wars in France it was lent me under the title of Mr Hampden's *Vade-Mecum*, and I believe that no copy was liker an original than that rebellion was like ours.' (A vade-mecum was a book carried constantly about with a person.)

Hampden probably stayed at the Inner Temple until he was twenty-one years old in 1615, perhaps two years in all. By the end of that time he would have made himself familiar not merely with the content of the law, but also with how it worked. We must imagine him walking two miles along the riverbank and wandering into the Palace of Westminster, where the law courts sat. It is difficult to visualize the vanished cluster of medieval and Tudor buildings which had grown up around the original wooden hall of Edward the Confessor. The long bed-chamber where Edward died in 1066 had been redecorated by Henry III with wall paintings of the Confessor's coronation and scenes from the Wars of the Maccabees. One mural depicted a crowned English monarch, holding in his left hand a shield emblazoned with the golden leopards of England, and a wooden club in his right, standing firmly on the back of a cringing subject. It was entitled 'The Triumph of Meekness over Anger'. From the fourteenth century onwards, and still more after Henry

VIII ended the tradition of royal residence in the Palace, this Painted Chamber had been used by the House of Commons on occasion, and in 1605 Guy Fawkes had placed his gunpowder barrels beneath this floor. But Anger had its victories. Hampden's first cousin Oliver Cromwell would sign the death warrant of Charles I in that very Painted Chamber.

The fact that the House of Commons could sit in the former royal bedroom underlines the origins of the Lower House as an extension of the king's advisers. Tribal Celtic and Saxon chiefs listened to the advice of wise old men and also to the powerful voices among the warriors. Transposed into medieval England the same relations prevailed: the king took council with the bishops and the nobles before enacting laws. Not without a struggle the Tudor monarchs had triumphantly re-established the dominance of the Crown against the possible pretensions of these traditional advisers. The Tudors had brought the nobility to heel, and then robbed and emasculated the Church in the name of Reformation. Yet they had done so with the help of the Commons, first summoned from the shires and boroughs in the thirteenth century to vote money and ratify laws. Gradually, the Commons evolved into an institution or House capable of retaining an identity, despite lengthy intervals between parliaments. Moreover, the Commons had long since discovered that the supply or withholding of taxes gave them a real influence over the content of those Bills which the king's ministers introduced into the House for their assent.

In 1398 Richard II reconstructed the New Hall, built by William Rufus three centuries earlier just north of the Painted Chamber. He increased the height of the walls, enlarged the windows and added the magnificent great hammer-beam roof of oak, adorned with painted angels and his own royal badge. Thus, Westminster Hall became one of the largest halls in Europe possessing a roof unsupported by pillars. Upon a platform at the south end stood the high marble table, known as the King's Bench, where monarchs presided over magnificent feasts and revels. Here the early monarchs sat with their judges to hear cases and give judgments.

By John Hampden's day the monarch no longer dispensed justice in person, but his appointed judges did so in his name. In Westminster Hall itself the Lord Chief Justice and three judges of the Court of King's Bench dealt with actions of the Crown against subjects, while the Lord Chief Justice and three judges of the Court of Common Pleas heard cases involving actions of subject against subject. The business conducted in the flat-roofed, two-storeyed Exchequer in New Palace Yard, between St Margaret's Church and Westminster Hall, gave rise to the Court of Exchequer, which concerned itself solely with taxation cases, and its four judges were known formidably as the Barons of the Exchequer. In the Court of Exchequer Chamber, named solely on account of its meeting place, judges from all three courts sitting together heard cases which awkwardly spanned their separate jurisdictions. It was this latter court which would sit in judgment on Hampden in his trial over the refusal to pay Ship-Money.

Students at the Inner Temple would stand behind the busy throng of plaintiffs, defendants and witnesses, listening to actual cases. In England justice was an open affair, and sight-seers or visitors to London crowded the courts, peering over the shoulder-high partitions at the various hearings. The crowds attracted shop-keepers, who did a brisk trade both inside the Hall and just outside its gates. Once a year the qualified students wanting to don the Serjeant's satin cap trimmed with white lace and the two-coloured robe of purple and tawny worn for the first year would process from the Inner Temple to Westminster Hall. Once inside the Hall they would see the four judges sitting at the King's Bench in their scarlet robes lined with fur. 'My Lord, I think I spy a Brother', the junior judge would announce in a loud voice. 'Yes', replied the Lord Chief Justice, 'send and bring him up.' Thus these fledgling attorneys had been literally 'called to the bar' of the Court of King's Bench.

These courts for administering the common law had established themselves as institutions over centuries, and they occupied a recognized place between the High Court of Parliament and the inferior courts of the Assizes, conducted by the Westminster judges on circuit in the shires, whose judgments they had the collective authority to alter. But other courts existed in the Palace for administering what was known as the royal prerogative. The special pre-eminence of the sovereign over all other subjects was held to include rights which lay outside the scope of the common law, and the exercise of them could not therefore be let or hindered. All men agreed that the royal prerogative existed, but wide differences had already begun to appear about its extent and nature. The king administered his privileges through several prerogative courts. The chief of them, dating back to the reign of Henry VII, met in the Star Chamber, which overlooked the river and the jetty swarming with ferry boats for hire. It was presided over by members of the inner Privy Council, the two Chief Justices and the Chancellor who summoned such lords, judges and bishops as he chose.

When John Hampden visited the Palace of Westminster as a student of the Inner Temple, King James I had reigned for ten years or more. Although not regal in appearance or behaviour, James manifested a sharp awareness of the dominance of the Crown in English affairs, both in practice and still more in theory by his devout adherence to the doctrine of the divine right of kings. In 1616 he dismissed Sir Edward Coke, Lord Chief Justice of the King's Bench, for leading the judges in the attack on the ecclesiastical Court of High Commission and the Court of Chancery, which had originally been set up to provide justice in cases where the other courts could only establish the technical right at common law. Francis Bacon, the King's advocate against the common law judges, had no doubts that Coke was wrong in his implicit claims for his own office and for the common law. 'Solomon's throne was supported by lions on both sides,' he wrote. 'Let the judges therefore be lions, but yet lions under the throne, being circumspect that they do not check or oppose any points of sovereignty.'

The early death of John Hampden's father had already brought him into the orbit of perhaps the most unpopular of all the royal courts, the Court of Wards. The right of the Crown to the wardship of tenants-in-chief who were minors was a profitable if archaic relic of the feudal system. The king could pocket the revenues from the lands of a minor or an idiot, and arrange the marriage of an heiress under age. In 1540 Henry VIII established the Court of Wards to administer his rights of wardship. Here the family of the minor might attempt to buy the wardship from the king, in order to prevent their estates from becoming an economic ruin or the ward married off to the young daughter of a spendthrift courtier. In 1610, under a proposal known as the 'Great Contract', both the king and the Commons explored the possibility of exchanging wardship and purveyance for a fixed annual income of £200,000 a year, but nothing came of it. The Commons wanted more concessions for their money; the Crown would not willingly relinquish a means of dominating the great families of the land. Moreover, in the opinion of the Chancellor of the Exchequer, Sir Julius Caesar, the abolition of feudal tenures would make easy 'a ready passage to a democracy, which is the deadliest enemy to a monarchy'.

After the death of her husband, Elizabeth Hampden had secured the wardship of her son by applying to Robert Cecil, son of the great Lord Burghley, who had obtained control over the Court of Wards. She wrote to him as follows:

> I understand through my good friend, Mr Maynard, that I shall have the wardship of the body and lands of my son for eight hundred pounds. The sum is very much more than my estate (without the help of my good friends) is able to perform, yet I will satisfy your Honour of the said sum.

The official fee payable to the Crown accounted for £153 of the £800, and the premium for the lease of the lands came to £90. After various smaller amounts there remained a substantial sum of £500, which doubtless found its way into Cecil's pocket. Four weeks after her first letter Elizabeth wrote again to Cecil. 'I would know to whom the five hundred pounds should be paid;' she inquired. The reply does not exist, but we can guess the answer with confidence. This element of corruption added to the unpopularity of the whole institution of wardship and of those associated with the exercise of it.

Elizabeth sent her younger son, Richard, to study abroad for three years in 1617. The Privy Council granted him a

licence to travel 'for his better experience' in November that
year, giving his place of residence as the Hampden manor of
Emmington in Oxfordshire. He was permitted to take with
him one servant, presumably a tutor, and some trunks of
apparel. While Richard journeyed on the Continent his
brother John settled down to marriage and his responsibilities as Lord of Hampden Manor.

On 24 June 1619 Hampden married Elizabeth, daughter of
Edward Symeon of Pyrton in Oxfordshire. By chance, the
long embroidered white kid gloves, edged with gold lace and
lined with salmon pink taffeta, that Elizabeth wore on that
day can still be seen in the county museum at Aylesbury.
Hampden took his bride back to the family house at Great
Hampden, which thenceforth became their home. Hampden
now applied himself to the management of his estates and
towards playing that part upon the stage of county and
national affairs for which his family background, wealth,
and education had equipped him.

Then, as now, the shire of Buckingham was shaped on the
map of England like an irregular foot-print some fifty-three
miles long and twenty-seven miles wide at the most. It is
linked across the instep from north-east to south-west by a
chalk escarpment some eight hundred and fifty feet high in
places. The northern half of the county is a low-lying clay
plain, veined with muddy brown streams meandering
through boggy fields. Quite different in character, the southern half spreads down from the Chiltern escarpment like a
tilted table top. Deep valleys and wooded ridges score the
slope until it levels out, at about three hundred and fifty feet,
beyond Beaconsfield, Chalfont St Giles and Rickmans-
worth. The upper reaches of the Chiltern Hills are mainly
dry, but small rivers – the Chess, Misbourne, Hamble, Wyle
and Colne – rise in these south-eastern foot-hills and find
their way eventually into the Thames. Possibly because of
this shortage of water, and also because of the effort needed
to clear some fields for their eight-oxen ploughs, the early
Saxons appear to have avoided the higher ground for their
settlements. Celtic communities survived there for a time,
giving way to scattered woodsmen, smallholders, exiles,

brigands and outlaws. An early medieval chronicler could call it *deserta Ciltine*, the wilderness of Chiltern. Later generations, including the Hampdens, in their manors, farmhouses and hamlets, added to the sparse population in the hills.

As one of the five counties which supplied food to London, Buckinghamshire possessed virtually no industry save some paper-making mills. For administrative purposes it was divided into eight hundreds: the five Vale Hundreds in the north and the three Chiltern Hundreds of Burnham, Desborough and Stoke in the south. About fifty-five thousand people lived in the county in 1600. Aylesbury was the only town of any size, followed by Wycombe and Amersham (which possessed only two hundred houses in 1769).

John Hampden's house, next door to the parish church, stood on a hill just over seven hundred feet high, not two miles from the lip of the main escarpment. There was no village in the parish; the population of perhaps forty families – about a hundred and fifty people – lived in farmhouses and cottages scattered across the two thousand acres encompassed by the parish boundary. A little less than half of the land within that seven-mile boundary carried the distinctive lofty beechwoods, carpeted with a soft brown bed of leaves. Oak, elm, maple, darker box and yew, lime and wild cherry trees mingled with the beeches in the hangers or copses, and the natural dryness of the soil often gave rich colours of yellow, gold and red to their autumn leaves. The woods abounded in game: deer and hares, pheasants and partridges.

The manor house, shaped like the letter E, faced south. The three-foot thick walls of the central wing mark it as the old medieval building and it stood a foot or two away in lofty detachment from the later Elizabethan backbone. Built in Tudor redbrick two storeys high, with an attic for the servants, the manor house as a whole looked more homely than grand. Stone mullion windows let in the sunlight, and fine stacks of brick chimneys with octagonal shafts let out the blue smoke of the log fires. Stables, barns and outhouses clustered behind the house. In one building the servants brewed the ale which owed its special flavour to the very pure and clear spring water, drawn up through chalk and sandstone, for the valley lacked even a brook. That splendid avenue of beech trees, hewn for Queen Elizabeth through the beechwoods, ran eastwards down the slope from the east wing.

The parish church of St Mary Magdalen, virtually unchanged since John Hampden's day, stands before the south front of the house. The ancient thirteenth-century porch and doorway bear the carved Tudor rose and the Hampden eagles of their coat-of-arms. Within the fourteenth-century nave there are fourteen Jacobean pews almost certainly ordered and paid for by Hampden. For at that time the Puritan gentry all over the county installed pews so that they could hear sermons in comfort. Many of them were high-sided and ugly box pews; others amounted to small rooms, with their own fireplaces and separate entrances, as at Langley Marrish on the south border of Buckinghamshire. Bells in the fifteenth-century tower summoned the scattered inhabitants of Great Hampden to worship. Since 28 March 1608 the Reverend Egeon Askew had served them as rector. He was a well-read man and a noted preacher, yet during his one- or two-hour sermons the gazes of the congregation doubtless strayed to the faded medieval paintings on the walls depicting some of the Seven Deadly Sins: Gluttony, Sloth, Anger, and Pride with a demon on her shoulder.

During the years of his minority a kinsman of John's called Sir Alexander Hampden, of Hartwell, near Aylesbury, had occupied the manor house of Great Hampden while John had presumably lived in London with his mother. Sir Alexander acted as guardian of the children of his dead brother Edmund Hampden of Wendover. Thus Hampden House belonged in a sense to the whole Hampden family: it served as their citadel.

What position did they occupy in county society? About two hundred families in Buckinghamshire – some of them very small – could claim the status of gentry at that time. In terms of size, wealth and political influence, thirty-two families stand out head-and-shoulders above the rest. In 1640, for example, thirty men from twenty-seven of these families possessed annual incomes of £1,000 or more; their combined revenue of £60,000 accounted for no less than one-third of the total for the county. With five other families not represented on the 1640 tax list they dominated the society and politics of Buckinghamshire at the time of John Hampden's early manhood.

Four of these county families had lived in Buckinghamshire for more than two centuries: the families of Hampden, Cheyne, Tyrringham and Verney. All of them had impressive records of public service in, and on behalf of, their county. Members of the Hampden family, by far the oldest of the four, had served seventeen times as High Sheriff of Buckinghamshire, and nine times as a county member in Parliament. The families of Dormer, Denton, Goodwin, Waller (of Beaconsfield), Bulstrode, Grenville, Proby and Croke formed a second group who established themselves in the county during Tudor times. More recent immigrants into Buckinghamshire since 1600, such as the families of Packington (who owned most of Aylesbury), Chester, Andrews, Borlase, Clarke, Barringer, Temple, Winwood, Whitelocke, Bennet, Pye and Ingoldsby, account for the remaining influential ones. An income of £1,000 in those days betokened very good estates, verging on the wealthy; an income of £1,500 put a man in the class of the very wealthy. John Hampden was among twenty-two other heads of Buckinghamshire families listed in 1640 as possessing an income of at least £1,500 a year; his more wealthy friend Arthur Goodwin, whose name is not on that list, may have received £2,000 a year. By comparison, the estates of the Earl of Caernarvon yielded an income of £7,000 a year.

Of course these Buckinghamshire families intermarried among themselves and with similar Puritan families in other counties, thus developing an intricate cobweb of kinship over the years. For example, the wife of Sir Alexander Denton was one of John Hampden's cousins. When the Civil War broke out Sir Alexander fortified his home at Hillesdon House and held it for the King, but most of the prominent Buckinghamshire families sided with Parliament. Thus the Buckinghamshire gentry seem to have been a close-knit society, bound together by ties of blood, religion and politics, and closely linked with other societies of the Puritan families in the south and east of England.

Despite these advantages of family name, connections and comparative wealth, Hampden did not enter the market for those honours which King James had begun to sell as a means of raising cash. In 1618, for example, the King created many new nobles, including four new earls. Two of them, Lord Cavendish and Lord Rich, merely exchanged their baronies for the earldoms of Devonshire and Warwick, each paying £10,000 for the privilege. At the lower end of the scale James had created the new rank of baronet in 1611. Hampden's position and wealth would certainly have secured him the title of baron or viscount, and his mother clearly thought that he should seize his opportunity. In 1620 she wrote to Anthony Knyvet:

> If ever my son will seek for his honour, tell him now to come, for here is multitudes of lords a making – Viscount Mandeville, Lord Treasurer; Viscount Dunbar, which was Sir Harry Constable; Viscount Falkland, which was Sir Harry Carew. These two last of Scotland, of Ireland divers: the Deputy, a Viscount; and one Mr Fitzwilliams a Baron of England; Mr Villiers, a Viscount; and Sir William Fielding a Baron . . . I am ambitious of my son's honour, which I wish were now conferred upon him, that he might not come after so many new creations.

We can but speculate on why John Hampden resisted this maternal pressure for his worldly advancement. Possibly he lacked that particular brand of ambition or baulked at the expense involved. Certainly at no time in his life did he evince a desire to be a great man at Court. As a person of considerable intelligence, he may have sensed that political power would shift to the House of Commons during his lifetime. He was destined to become a leader of the English gentry, and an elevation to the nobility to satisfy a family ambition would have disqualified him for that vocation. Within two years of his marriage he had secured his election to the House of Commons.

Thus John Hampden stood on the brink of a parliamentary career. What sort of person was he? He seems to have inherited a good nature, so that people found him easy and pleasant in conversation. He carried himself well in society and attracted people into friendship with him.

The young Puritans enjoyed the sports and pastimes of

country life, as well as the music, dancing and conversation which enlivened the evenings in their homes. Hampden was no exception, for Clarendon records that he was 'a gentleman of a good family in Buckinghamshire, and born to a fair fortune, and of a most civil and affable deportment. In his entrance into the world he indulged to himself all the licence in sports and exercises and company which was used by men of the most jolly conversation.'

Later in life Hampden's active disposition emerged again when he became a soldier in the Civil War. Like his cousin Oliver Cromwell, however, he showed no interest in gaining military experience in his youth. His natural bent lay more towards scholarship. Winning character and manners, an active fitness for sports, a keen and inquiring mind, the learning of a scholar and the knowledge of a lawyer, the possession of lands and position in his county's society: each of these gifts by itself may not have been remarkable, but the combination of them in one man struck even contemporaries as unusual. Together they marked out John Hampden as a man of great potential.

Chapter Two

APPRENTICE IN PARLIAMENT

Better laws and a happier constitution of government no nation ever enjoyed, it being a mixture of monarchy, aristocracy and democracy, with sufficient fences against the pest of every-one of these forms – tyranny, faction, and confusion.　　　LUCY HUTCHINSON

In 1621 Hampden took his seat as a member of the House of Commons for the borough of Grampound in Cornwall. Although the royal duchy had somewhat declined in prosperity and population, it still returned to Parliament two knights of the shire and forty-two borough members. The franchise in both East Looe (his father's former seat) and in Grampound was limited to the mayor, aldermen and less than a score of burgesses. As the Mayor of Grampound selected these freemen, his influence was decisive in choosing the two members for this small borough; out of goodwill, or perhaps for money, he returned John Hampden, aged twenty-seven years, to his first Parliament.

Like all new members in every century, Hampden entered the House of Commons at a particular point in the story of its evolution, not unlike a sailor embarking in a ship at one of its ports of call during a long voyage. Indeed Hampden may be compared to an apprentice navigator. One day men would look to him as the pilot who could take that ship of Parliament through stormy waters and between dangerous rocks. In 1621 the murmur of these angry seas lay far off. But Hampden's diligent reading of history may have given him a forewarning of things to come. In particular his studies at the Inner Temple would have equipped him with a high sense of the worth and dignity of Parliament.

The origins of Parliament, and of the House of Commons

in particular, lay in the early morning haze of English history even for men of Hampden's generation. Scholars can penetrate that mist of immemorial custom so far as to identify two major ingredients in the role of Parliament, but not to agree on their relative importance or order of emergence: the function of a supreme court and the function of a representative assembly. By tradition, however, the king actually governed the country, and had the necessary power to do so by virtue of being king. Government in this sense embraced then, as it does today, both more or less routine executive responsibilities, as for example the maintenance of law and order or the minting of coins, and also political leadership, such as making war or peace. How far Parliament as the chief representative assembly in the land had the right to influence the king in this latter field of policy-making remained an open issue.

A complex political and administrative system had evolved over the centuries to help the king to rule effectively. In London it included the offices of government, such as the Exchequer, and the law courts. The nobility and gentry governed the shires on behalf of the king with only infrequent interventions from Westminster, just as the bishops ruled the national Church in his name. The king exercised control mainly by his power of appointing at all levels officials whom he favoured and could count upon for support. With the exception of the bishops and clergy, he could also dismiss them at will.

The Privy Council stood next to the king at the top of the pyramid of local and central government. About twenty of the king's advisers, ministers of state and office-holders, comprised it. Rarely did all the privy councillors meet to confer together; for the most part, a small quorum of six or seven members carried out their common work. Under the early Stuarts membership of this powerful group came to be determined largely by the current royal favourite, a fact which caused jealousy and ultimately confusion. The Privy Council met in one or other of the rooms in the royal palace or wherever the sovereign happened to be, as its nominal successor does to this day. This proximity meant that the royal will could be made known and conveyed to the Privy

Council by councillors who were also courtiers, or through its secretary without the king having to submit himself to the tedium of the meetings. Leaving his servants to work their way through the long agenda of administrative work, such as granting passports to obscure gentlemen, he could chase the fallow deer through Windsor Forest with his bosom companions in the hot sunshine of an English summer.

The Privy councillors and royal servants of the Tudors played an important part in Parliament. Those who sat in the Commons initiated the bills which the Houses debated and enacted, so that they acted not unlike a modern government in that respect. Besides the opportunity of initiating legislation within the House through his servants who sat as members in it, the sovereign also held a wider initiative. The king could summon a parliament at will; he could also prorogue it if he wanted the sitting suspended for an interval. Most important of all, the monarch had the power to dissolve parliament whenever he wished, thereby causing all bills in passage through the stages of three readings in each House to be lost. Not until a bill received the royal assent did it become law. The king performed this act of transformation by touching the bill with the royal sceptre and uttering the time-honoured formula *Le Roi le veult*, thus infusing it with the power and authority of majesty.

The House of Commons had secured some important privileges designed to safeguard its function as a representative assembly. Besides protecting members from outside interference, these privileges served to secure the independence of the counsel offered to the Crown by Parliament. At the beginning of the first session of each parliament the Speaker sought royal confirmation of these privileges by presenting a petition. Freedom of access for the House to the royal presence on all matters of great importance; favourable interpretation of the Speaker's words when reporting the opinion of the House; freedom from arrest for members and their servants during the life of Parliament; and freedom of speech within their chamber: such were the fundamental privileges which the Commons regarded as essential.

The privilege of free speech within the House had engendered much conflict between the Commons and the sovereign. Queen Elizabeth had granted it before the first parliament of her reign on condition that the Commons kept in mind their 'duties, reverence, and obedience to their sovereign'. Did this proviso exempt from free debate such burning topics as the royal succession or the doctrine and practices of the Church of England? The Queen firmly believed so; the Commons did not. Mainly on account of such disagreements, Elizabeth allowed her ten parliaments to sit for no more than some thirty-five months in all during a reign of forty-four and a half years. Her Tudor policy of building up the direct revenues of the Crown and avoiding expensive military campaigns left her relatively self-sufficient in the early part of her reign. She did not have to summon Parliament and woo the Commons for money. Consequently these assemblies possessed little more than nuisance value: they could not make her change her mind. In her presence the Commons knelt down to hear what she had to say. She spoke to them like a stern and loving mistress of a great country house talking to the household servants and tenants.

When the flinty will of Elizabeth struck the steel of English character the sparks flew up, but there was no explosion. In 1575, when she employed the device of deliberately spreading rumours of royal displeasure at certain speeches in the Commons, a fiery Cornish member called Peter Wentworth stood up to declare:

> Free speech and conscience in this place are granted by a special law, as that without which the prince and state cannot be preserved or maintained . . . It is a dangerous thing in a prince to oppose or bend herself against her nobility and people . . . I beseech the same God to endue her majesty with his wisdom, whereby she may discern faithful advice from traitorous sugared speeches . . . For we are incorporated into this place to serve God and all England, and not to be time-servers, as humour-feeders, cancers that would pierce the bone, or as flatterers that would beguile all the world, and so worthy to be condemned both by God and man . . .

Shocked, the Commons stopped Wentworth in full flood, and committed him to the Tower of London.

John Hampden inherited the main convictions of Peter

Wentworth, and therefore it is worth pausing to underline them. Clearly Wentworth thought that only Parliament could be trusted to serve the common cause of God and England. By comparison, the other would-be advisers who jostled for position and influence at Court were in reality pursuing personal profit or family advantage. His words conveyed also a deep religious feeling that Christian men must first be servants of God if they are to serve truly their sovereign. Members such as Wentworth who had embraced the Puritan approach to life desired also the future reformation of the Church of England, which still retained in their view the 'dregs of Popery'. But the Queen proved adamant in maintaining the precarious *via media* of her Church with a heavy-handed impartiality.

After 1588 and the defeat of the Armada, an important change in the situation developed which would eventually alter the relations of the Crown and Parliament as sketched above. The extension of the maritime war with Spain, financial and military involvement in France and the Netherlands, and some large expeditions to curb the rebellion in Ireland, together proved too much for the ordinary revenues of the Crown. Therefore the Queen summoned the Parliaments of 1588, 1593, 1597 and 1601 with the intention of securing votes of subsidies to finance her many commitments. It may be recalled that John Hampden's father sat as member for a Cornish borough in the second one.

The turbulent Commons of the 1601 Parliament cavilled at the size of the subsidy made necessary by the Irish rebellion, but passed it under protest. Then they proceeded to attack the royal practice of granting monopolies for an ever-increasing list of goods and services, ranging from pilchards and vinegar to iron, lead and sea-coals. Francis Bacon pointed out that the granting of these monopolies lay well within the royal prerogative, yet the House did not heed his advice to leave the matter well alone. Sensing the strength of feeling against monopolies, the old Queen wisely promised a review of the practice, but her death intervened.

King James I received a warm welcome from his English subjects when he came south from Scotland to ascend the throne in 1603. After nineteen years of war, England concluded a peace with Spain in 1604. In Ireland the royal forces had put down the revolt. These events eased the burden on the Exchequer and enhanced the King's position in relation to Parliament. But he inherited a debt of £400,000 and would soon feel the need for parliamentary subsidies.

Parliament met in 1604, and almost immediately fell out with the King over a disputed election. Buckinghamshire had elected Sir Francis Goodwin, a declared outlaw, and his rival for the shire seat challenged the result. The King attempted to have the case decided in the Court of Chancery, but eventually he accepted that the Commons had the right, although not the exclusive right, to judge of returns. The Commons then proceeded to drag their feet over the King's proposals for a legal union between Scotland and England. Members also challenged the royal prerogative by asking questions about the lucrative medieval practices of purveyance and wardship. After expressing his displeasure in broad Scots tones, James abruptly ended the session.

In 1605 the attempt by Guy Fawkes and his fellow Catholic plotters to blow up the Painted Chamber, while the King was addressing Parliament, produced a much closer and warmer relationship between the sovereign and the House of Commons. In a speech which struck some jarring chords for finely-tuned Puritan ears, James assured the members that he would have infinitely preferred to have been blown up in their company than in, say, an ale-house or brothel.

Apart from the proposed union with Scotland, the main business in the sessions of 1605, 1606-7 and 1610 focussed upon the issue of impositions, as the customs duties imposed on imports were known. In 1605 a merchant called Bates refuesed to pay the increased impositions on some sacks of currants shipped into London from the Levant. At his trial the judges confirmed that the King certainly had the legal right to levy such impositions as part of the royal prerogative. The Commons were still returning to this unpopular financial practice in 1611 when James dissolved his first Parliament.

Before Parliament met again death had removed the

King's chief minister, Lord Burghley's son Robert Cecil. Into the power vacuum at Court moved some members of the Howard family who had prudently allied themselves to the King's favourite, a Scotsman called Robert Carr, created Earl of Somerset in 1613. Significantly, the Howard family stood for a pro-Spanish foreign policy, hardly a course which would be popular in the Protestant-minded House of Commons.

The 'Addled Parliament' of 1614, so called because it passed no Acts and granted no supplies, opened amid widespread allegations that Papists had tried to influence the elections in their own favour. In his speech from the throne, James asked the Commons to present him with separate petitions for the redress of grievance, not a joint one which would suggest much misgovernment and thus cause him unpopularity in the country. He added that the funeral expenses of his eldest son Prince Henry in 1612, and the cost of the sumptuous nuptials of Princess Elizabeth, meant that he must ask them for some subsidies. The Commons, however, went off at a tangent on to the old question of impositions, and spent some time in seeking without success to win round the House of Lords to their way of thinking. Without the prospect of any votes for subsidies James could see no point in prolonging the sitting, and he dissolved Parliament. It had sat for just nine weeks.

Seven years passed before the King summoned his third Parliament in 1621. At home the young and handsome son of a Leicestershire knight had supplanted Robert Carr and the Howards in the royal favour. The watery blue eyes of King James, always on the move like their nervous and restless owner, had alighted with a lasting pleasure upon the bearded face and elegant body of George Villiers. New titles marked his meteoric rise: knighted in 1616; enobled as an earl in 1617; advanced to marquess in 1618; and created Duke of Buckingham in 1623. During this intermission of seven years the government continued to levy impositions and grant monopolies, besides resorting to the imaginative expedient of asking each county to hand the King a gift of money according to a system of quotas. Predictably the shires sent him far less than the sum requested.

In a move which threatened to break the Catholic and Habsburg succession to the Imperial throne, the Elector Frederick accepted the Crown of Bohemia. This bold decision stands out prominently in the train of events which precipitated Europe into the Thirty Years War in 1618. For at one level the Austrian Habsburg family saw the ambitious step as a threat to their control over the German states. In a second perspective the Catholic powers could interpret the move by the Elector, who was a Calvinist, as evidence of a desire to further the Reformation in Europe. Lastly, by geographical accident the Palatinate lay astride the strategic corridor which joined the Low Countries with northern Italy, where the generals of Habsburg Spain recruited mercenaries for the continuing struggle against their revolted Dutch subjects. Thus Spain had a vested interest in denying the Palatinate to friends of the rebellious faction in the Netherlands, for the official peace between Spain and the United Provinces was due to expire in 1621.

Against the Catholic League – the alliance of Austria and Spain – the Elector Palatine could expect immediate support from at least some of the minor German Protestant states. The Dutch would be too preoccupied with their struggle against Spain to lend him aid. The Protestant powers of Northern Europe – Denmark and Sweden – would help on religious grounds, but they lay far away beyond the protective barriers of Catholic lands. It would take time for them to fight their way through Europe to the succour of Frederick and his two domains, and the Catholic League intended to stamp out the lighted fuse in their citadel before the Danes or Swedes could even raise their armies. France might be expected to oppose the conversion of all Europe into a Habsburg empire, fearing for her own long-term security. But France was a mainly Catholic country and her attitude towards Frederick as the champion of the Protestant Reformation could only be ambivalent at the best. Could France be trusted? Not really. There remained England, a Protestant land ruled by Frederick's own father-in-law. Perhaps on the advice of his wife, Frederick doubtless gambled on the support of England when he agreed to become the King of Bohemia.

Frederick's decision placed King James upon the horns of a dilemma. His streak of canny wisdom, developed over many years as King of Scotland, convinced him that peace was the best policy, that foreign wars would only breed domestic trouble. As a person he was the least martial incumbent of the throne of England since Henry VI. On the other hand, he sensed the predicament of the Protestants in Europe and shared the concern of his subjects that the Palatinate should not be lost to the Catholic powers. Moreover, as a father he could not but feel a growing anxiety for his young daughter's safety as the weeks passed and the political skies darkened.

Elizabeth had already won the hearts of the English gentry. She was attractive, gracious and youthfully gay. Perhaps of all the Stuarts she alone possessed their virtues without their vices. By 1618 she was universally popular. Among the vast congregation of Protestant England who worshipped her, the young Puritans who had been at Oxford and Cambridge when she married the Prince Palatine formed an ardent sect. When the defeat of a Protestant-paid mercenary army under Count Mansfeld's command at Sablat in June 1619 opened the road for a Catholic invasion of Bohemia, King James agreed to send an expeditionary force under Sir Horace Vere to safeguard his daughter. Many young Protestant nobles and gentlemen flocked to his colours. For example, Robert Devereux, Earl of Essex, the twenty-nine-year-old son of Queen Elizabeth's beheaded favourite, made haste to join the expedition at Gravesend.

Sir Horace Vere dispatched a troop of horse composed of these young volunteer gentlemen across Europe to serve as the Queen's Life-guard. It included twenty-three-year-old Ralph Hopton from Somerset, who would one day become a Royalist general of distinction in the Civil War. During this adventure he formed a firm and life-long friendship with a twenty-one-year-old scion of an old Kent family, William Waller, who held the hereditary title of Chief Butler of England. Both the Hampdens and the Kent Wallers were cousins of the Wallers at Beaconsfield.

The army of the Catholic League's general, Count Tilly, shattered the Bohemians who fought for their new king at the battle of the White Mountain, just outside Prague, in November 1620. While the Cossack mercenaries of Catholic Europe scoured the countryside, the Queen's Life-guard of sixty horsemen escorted her through the dark winter landscape towards safety at Frankfurt-on-the-Oder. When deep snow drifts halted the carriages, the twenty-four-year-old Queen, pregnant with her fourth son, Prince Maurice, mounted behind Ralph Hopton on his horse for several miles. Thirty years later when the Civil War was over and he had seen Elizabeth again in exile in Holland, William Waller could still write of her as 'that queen of women, the Queen of Bohemia, whom I had the honour to serve at Prague in the first breaking out of the German war'.

Two days before the disaster outside Prague, King James issued writs summoning the third Parliament of his reign to meet on 16 January 1621. John Hampden, again like his cousin Oliver Cromwell, did not volunteer for military service on the Continent, but he shared the general desire that England should act to preserve the now-threatened Palatinate. The undergraduate who had written graceful Latin verses on the marriage of Elizabeth and Frederick could not have been indifferent to their fate in the inferno of Continental politics.

Parliament duly assembled on 30 January 1621. On that day Hampden took his seat for the first time in the chamber of the House of Commons, the Chapel of St Stephen. This high narrow building in the English Perpendicular style, with soaring pinnacles and flying buttresses, stood near the river at a right angle to Westminster Hall. Originally Edward III had erected the magnificent building in order to rival the French royal chapel, the Sainte Chapelle in Paris. In 1348, much to the annoyance of the monks of Westminster Abbey, he made it a collegiate foundation, appointing a dean and chapter with vicars choral and choristers. Fire swept away most of the attendant buildings in 1512, but the last dean had completed the new fan-vaulted cloisters (still in use today as office space for M.P.s) before the foundation was dissolved under the Second Chantries Act of 1547. The King then assigned St Stephen's Chapel to the House of Commons for their permanent use (an arrangement which lasted until 1833 when fire destroyed the building except for the vaulted lower chapel of St Mary Undercroft and the cloisters).

Once within the chamber, the young Hampden could have seen plenty of signs of its origin as a royal chapel. Statues of royal saints adorned the stone piers between the windows and occupied niches in the walls. Somewhat faded painting covered the walls in the arcades just below the edges of the wooden barrel-vault roof and spread down the marble columns. Beneath the arched window at the east end five tiers of benches rose up behind the Speaker's solid oak chair, which bore the royal coat-of-arms on its canopy. Steep rows of wooden benches lined both the long sides, with tables in the centre for the clerks and the Speaker's mace, and a gallery for spectators at the west end, still reached by a ladder in 1621.

King James, now fifty-four years old, rode down from Whitehall to open the Parliament, waving and calling out 'God bless ye, God bless ye' to the crowds who gathered to see him. In his speech, which Hampden heard at the bar of the House of Lords, the King assured Parliament that he would not allow the proposed marriage between his only surviving son, Prince Charles, and the Infanta of Spain to endanger the national religion. On the more popular subject of the fortunes of his daughter, the Queen of Bohemia, he announced his intention of raising an army that summer to preserve the Palatinate. For that venture he would want money.

Back in their own chamber the members of the Commons, sitting with their hats on and their swords by their sides, addressed themselves to their own business. The large group of privy councillors and courtiers who had managed the Lower House so effectively in the interests of the King's policies in the past had now lost their position of leadership. Thus the House responded to their official appeal for money with a rather perfunctory grant of two subsidies, reserving their major financial support until their grievances had been met.

As usual in the early days of a parliament some disputed elections were brought before the House. One concerned Sir

Thomas Wentworth, one of the two members for Yorkshire. It was alleged that he had demanded from the constables a list of those electors who intended to vote for his rival and then prevented them from doing so on polling day. By a narrow majority the Commons found in favour of the proud young baronet, but the constables who supplied him with the list received a public reprimand from the Speaker, which they heard kneeling at the bar of the House.

Depressed trade, inflation, and unemployment throughout the country, brought in their train an angry mood in the Lower House. Although they could not identify or tackle the deeper causes the members saw that monopolies reduced competition and pushed up prices, and that the heavy profits they produced went into the pockets of the undeserving monopolists. Such tangible abuses and those who made profits from them should be attacked. The House responded with fury to the extortions of Sir Francis Mitchell and Sir Giles Mompesson, who held the monopoly for licensing new ale-houses. Summoned to the bar, Mitchell was condemned without a hearing. But did the Commons have the right to punish offences which had nothing to do with their privileges? Once this question had been raised, and a search for precedents proved inconclusive, the King intervened with a vague speech to the Lords recommending the impeachment method, whereby the Upper House sat as judge and jury while the Lower House acted as prosecutor. Both Mitchell and Mompesson eventually stood condemned by the House of Lords.

During some parliamentary investigations into the workings of the courts of law, evidence came to light that Francis Bacon, Viscount St Albans and Lord Chancellor of England, had accepted bribes to hasten the course of justice in the Court of Chancery. On 25 March, in a letter to the King, Bacon acknowledged the substantial truth of the charges and offered the unimpressive excuse that everybody else was doing it. 'My Lords, it is my act, my hand, and my heart', he declared to the commission receiving his confession. 'I beseech your Lordships to be merciful to a broken reed.' Mercy there was, and Bacon lived in retirement until his death five years later.

The mood of the Commons concerning the turn of events upon the Continent can be gauged by their reaction to a Catholic barrister who had expressed pleasure that the King and Queen of Bohemia had been 'turned out of doors'. Members rose on the benches to specify the kind of punishment which they thought appropriate to the offence. As the government pointed out, however, the case did not lie within their jurisdiction and the barrister escaped the sentence one of them proposed, namely to ride from Westminster to the Tower wearing a placard inscribed 'A Popish wretch that hath maliciously scandalized His Majesty's children', but he was branded with a hot iron.

Meanwhile feeling against the proposed Spanish marriage steadily mounted. One April morning a London apprentice in Fenchurch Street had caught sight of the Spanish ambassador Gondomar being carried inside his litter (for coaches were not allowed in the City). 'There goes the Devil in a dung-cart,' he yelled, and knocked down an over-excited Spanish servant of the angry ambassador who got in his way. The magistrates sentenced the apprentice to be whipped through the City at a cart's tail. Three hundred of his fellow-apprentices decided otherwise, and staged a dramatic rescue of him while the brutal sentence was being carried out. Gondomar complained about the rescue to the Lord Mayor, and then to the King himself. James came down to the Guildhall, threatening to confiscate the City's charter and to throw soldiers into the Guildhall if justice was not done. The lad subsequently died under the lash.

After the King adjourned Parliament at Whitsuntide it did not meet again until the autumn. James spent the summer at Newmarket. He asked the Commons 'to avoid all long harangues, malicious and cunning diversions'. Although, in the early stages of the new session, the Lower House obediently voted a supply for the maintenance of the English expeditionary force in Europe, it proceeded to draw up a petition setting forth the causes of the unhappy state of the nation. It is significant that the members did not draw a distinction between the successes of militant Catholicism on the Continent and the increase of Popery in England. In order to understand the underlying causes of the Civil War it is vital to grasp this particular fusion of ideas.

As an answer to the hydra-headed challenge of Popery, the Commons recommended a war against the Catholic alliance and the marriage of Prince Charles to a Protestant. Hearing of this petition in the making King James wrote to the Speaker prohibiting the 'fiery and popular spirits' from meddling with his government or prerogative. The King declared himself 'very free and able to punish any man's misdemeanours in Parliament, as well during their sitting as after, which we mean not to spare hereafter upon any occasion of any man's insolent behaviour there'. Brushing aside the petition and the accompanying explanation presented to him by the Commons, the King then found himself confronted with the famous Protestation of 18 December 1621, in which the House denied his assertion that their privileges came to them by royal grace and permission alone, for their liberties were 'the ancient and undoubted birthright and inheritance of the subjects of England'. Informed that twelve members had been appointed to bear the petition to him, the King called out, 'Chairs! Chairs! – a God's name, here be twelve kings a coming.' The petitioners reiterated yet again their right to debate and give counsel on any matter of policy touching the State or Church, and also asserted their freedom of speech and immunity from arrest while doing so.

King James acted on his beliefs. Having dissolved the Parliament, he issued a warrant committing to prison the leaders of the Commons: Sir Edward Coke, Sir Robert Phelips, John Selden, John Pym and five others, although four of the latter were subsequently assigned to a commission to Ireland. To emphasize his displeasure, the King had the Journal of the House of Commons brought to him and he tore out the Protestation with his own hand.

John Hampden had been more than a spectator in his first Parliament. The House appointed him to serve on a committee to discuss a Bill 'against certain troublesome persons, relators, informers and promoters', and to manage a conference with the House of Lords concerning it. The object of the Bill was to ensure that offences against the penal statutes were tried in the first instance at local level in the counties rather than in Westminster Hall. On 28 November the Bill came back from the committee to the House with thirteen amendments, and passed its third reading. Thus Hampden had served his apprenticeship. He had taken part in the system of passing Bills through Parliament, entailing three readings in each House and detailed discussion – often in conference with the peers – on the implications of each sentence or clause of the proposed Act. Above all, he had sensed the remarkable common mind, the corporate personality of the House, and how individuals such as Sir Edward Coke and John Pym could sway it. Doubtless he reflected that the more talkative speakers did not always command respect or even attention. For some men, who spoke little but with a depth of knowledge of their subject and an accurate sense of the underlying mood of the House, could magically still the chatter, shuffling feet and scraping of sword scabbards on the high wooden benches.

On the eve of the dissolution of this Parliament the Spanish ambassador Gondomar dined in a happy mood with King James in the royal bedroom. As he stood in front of a blazing log fire, waiting while the King dressed for a court masque, he could contemplate the favourable turn of events. For he informed the Spanish king:

> It is certain that the King will never summon another parliament as long as he lives, or at least not another composed as this one was. It is the best thing that has happened in the interests of Spain and the Catholic religion since Luther began to preach heresy a hundred years ago.
>
> The King will no longer be able to succour his son-in-law or to hinder the advance of the Catholics. It is true that the wretched people are desperately offended against him, but they are without union among themselves and have neither leaders nor strong places to lean upon. Besides, they are rich and live comfortably in their houses; so that it is not likely that there will be any disturbance.

Perhaps because they now felt more confident of England's impotence, the Spanish showed less interest in the proposed marriage of Prince Charles with the Infanta. As alliance with Spain formed the cornerstone of Buckingham's foreign policy, the signs of this change of policy caused the young Duke much agitation. In order to bring matters to a head he and

Prince Charles, who had been captivated by his great charm, badgered the King into allowing them to travel to Spain incognito with only two attendants. Eventually the pair of gallants reached Madrid, where the Spanish allowed them to gaze upon the sallow Habsburg features of the Infanta; but not to talk with her alone. Prince Charles once scrambled over a garden wall in the hope of meeting her, but Spanish protocol proved to be as impenetrable as a Toledo suit of armour. Bullfights in the listless heat and stuffy Court functions between the interminable political discussions about the proposed marriage treaty proved too much for Buckingham and his manners steadily grew worse. Observing him in action, some of the Spaniards were heard to say that 'they would rather put the Infanta headlong down a well than into his hands'.

Meanwhile, back in England, the King alternated between fits of fatherly pride at the romatic adventure of his 'boys', as he called them, and gusts of anxiety for their safety. Buckingham's letters to his 'dear Dad and Gossip', in which he signed himself as 'your humble slave and dog', reassured the King about their safety, but his anxiety about the whole undertaking persisted. Like King Lear, James heard the plain truth through the privileged mouth of the Court fool. One day Archie, his jester, told the King that he had come to change hats with him.

'Why?' demanded James.

'Because,' replied Archie, 'you have sent the Prince into Spain, from whence he is never likely to return.'

'But,' answered the monarch, 'what will you say when you see him coming back again?'

'Marry,' exclaimed the jester, 'I will take off the fool's cap which I now put upon thy head for sending him there, and put it on the King of Spain's for letting him return.'

To which James could make no answer.

After seven months away, Buckingham and Prince Charles returned home in October 1623 with nothing to show for their journey except that the latter had grown a pointed beard. Indeed Buckingham's unpopular foreign policy was virtually in ruins, for discussions on the marriage treaty had completely broken down. The Spanish refused to offer guarantees that the Palatinate would not be invaded by the forces of the Catholic League. For their part, the English could not satisfy the Spaniards that the Catholic religion would be tolerated. By accident rather than design the returning adventurers found themselves in tune with the popular will and they came home to an enthusiastic reception. At Cambridge, for example, the church bells rang all day, while bonfires blazed at every street corner. Sermons and orations in Great St Mary's were followed by celebrations far into the night, with drums sounding, fireworks crackling and cannon booming in the meadows around the town. The undergraduates in that Puritan university sat down to dinner that evening with an extra course. In London, the poet Ben Jonson composed a special masque to hail the Prince's return which he called 'Neptune's Triumph'. Debtors were set free, and convicted thieves escaped the gallows at Tyburn. Whenever the crowds sighted the Prince's coach they surged about it, roaring their approval.

The Duke of Buckingham took his cue from the popular mood: he gave a vast banquet for the King and Prince at which three thousand meat dishes alone were served. Smarting from wounded vanity and pride at the treatment he had received in Spain, the Duke now stepped forward as the champion of England against her traditional foe. At his suggestion King James summoned Parliament to meet in February 1624 in order to prepare for a war of vengeance against Spain.

Parliament opened with an unusual display of public accord. On 27 February 1624 Prince Charles and Buckingham attended a conference of both Houses and found themselves applauded. For the government had now resolved upon a resumption of the sea-war against Spain and the raising of an army to save the Palatinate. Despite the popularity of the cause against Catholicism, the costs of setting forth a full-scale Protestant crusade from English shores proved daunting, and Parliament voted three subsidies totalling about £300,000 to that end, which was to be expended under the direction of their own commissioners. In June the King signed a treaty with the Dutch, agreeing to pay six thousand soldiers in their struggle against Spain, and during that summer the mercenary general

Count Mansfeld began assembling a force of twelve thousand volunteers at Dover to recover the Palatinate.

Hampden did not sit in this Parliament during its first weeks. Before it was summoned he had already withdrawn from his Cornish seat at Grampound and promoted a scheme to secure the restoration of the rights of three Buckinghamshire boroughs to elect members to Parliament. He paid the fees of Hakewill, an eminent lawyer, who carried out the necessary legal work to prepare and submit a petition to the House of Commons on behalf of the boroughs of Wendover, Amersham and Marlow, claiming that 'they were ancient parliamentary boroughs by prescription, and ought thereby and of right to send burgesses to Parliament'. The House appointed the lawyers Noy and Selden to investigate the archives, and they reported back in favour of the petitioners.

According to Sergeant Glanville, chairman of the committee of privileges, the King opposed the move, 'declaring he was troubled with too great a number already, and commanded his then solicitor, Sir Robert Heath, being of the House of Commons, to oppose it what he might; and most of the courtiers then of the House, understanding the King's inclinations, did their utmost endeavours to cross it'. Yet the House stood firm and the Speaker sent a warrant to the clerk of the Crown in the Court of Chancery for the issuing of the necessary election writs. Thereupon Amersham elected Hakewill himself and a wealthy Northamptonshire lawyer named John Crew, who had taken his degree at Magdalen Hall, Oxford, in 1618. Marlow chose a Mr Cotton and a member of the well-established and wealthy neighbouring family of Borlase, who owned no less than ten manors in Buckinghamshire and Oxfordshire. Wendover returned John Hampden and Sir Alexander Denton, who was married to his cousin Mary Hampden of Hartwell, near Aylesbury.

During this Parliament the Duke of Buckingham, with the active connivance of Prince Charles, instituted impeachment proceedings against a powerful adversary, Lionel Cranfield, Earl of Middlesex, who as Lord High Treasurer had done more than any other man to put the royal finances in good shape. Apparently the King besought the Duke and the Prince to stop this prosecution. In an angry outburst at Buckingham he shouted: 'By God, Steeny, you are a fool, and will shortly repent this folly, and will find that, in this fit of popularity you are making a rod with which you will be scourged yourself.' Turning to the Prince he muttered, 'You will live to have a belly full of Parliament impeachments, and when I shall be dead, you will have too much cause to remember how much you have contributed to the weakening of the Crown.'

Middlesex possessed only a few influential friends and none of these was prepared to speak for him in public save one peer. Middlesex had certainly given and taken bribes, but who had not? A fat gratuity for lifting an imposition of £3 a barrel on French wines found its incriminating way into his own pocket. Voted guilty by a unanimous verdict in the House of Lords, Middlesex received a fine of £50,000 and lifelong banishment from Court. Another victim on Buckingham's list was the Earl of Bristol, who had served as English ambassador in Spain during the Prince's visit. Buckingham cast him in the role of scagpegoat-in-chief, but Bristol would have none of that. He hastened home from Madrid and entered the Upper House 'his hat stuffed full of papers' which contained his damning counter-charges against Buckingham. After a brief spell in the Tower he was set at liberty and suffered no more than a censure.

The King had prorogued two Parliaments without assenting to any Bills, except one for subsidies in 1621. He gave the royal assent to several statutes in 1624, perhaps the most important being an Act abolishing the practice of granting monopolies for the sale of goods or the practice of trades. It declared that such monopolies had always been contrary to the ancient and fundamental laws of the realm. The King gave his assent graciously, but shortly afterwards he dissolved the Parliament in spite of a list of outstanding grievances which the Commons presented to him.

A sense of diminished national pride, caused by England standing aloof from the struggle against the Catholic League, darkened the closing months of the reign of King James. 'Tom Tell-Troath', author of a London broadsheet, assured the King that all companies – even gamblers and dicers – made jests of his name. His subjects drank ten healths to the Elector Palatine before one to him. 'They make a mock of your word *Great*

Britain', wrote Tom, 'and offer to prove that it is a great deal less than little England was wont to be, less in reputation, less in strength, less in riches, less in all manner of virtue.'

On 27 March 1625 King James died at the age of fifty-eight. Followed by nine thousand mourners dressed in black, a draped hearse designed by Inigo Jones carried the coffin to Westminster Abbey. Many eyes watched the young King Charles. During his two-hour funeral sermon Bishop Williams of Lincoln made a reference to the stammer of Moses, which some onlookers thought that the new King seemed to take amiss, for he was painfully conscious of his own impediment. It remained to be seen whether or not Charles would prove to be that Protestant Moses whom the Puritans in particular longed to see.

Chapter Three

THE SPARKS OF DISCONTENT

It is not possible for man to devise such just and excellent bounds, as will keep in wild ambition, when prince's flatterers encourage that beast to break his fence.   LUCY HUTCHINSON

At the time of his accession, King Charles was betrothed to Henrietta Maria, third daughter of King Henry IV of France, who had been born in November 1609, just six months before the assassination of her father. The young couple were married by proxy in Notre Dame in May 1625, and some days later the Duke of Buckingham – the bridegroom's best friend – arrived in Paris to escort Henrietta to her strange new home beyond the narrow sea.

The Duke travelled in grand style. One of his attendants wrote that:

> His Grace hath for his body twenty-seven rich suits, embroidered and laced with silk and silver plushes, besides one rich white satin uncut velvet suit, set all over both suit and cloak with diamonds, the value thereof is thought to be worth fourscore thousand pounds, besides a feather made with great diamonds; with sword, girdle, hat-band, and spurs with diamonds, which suit his Grace intends to enter Paris with. Another suit is of purple satin, embroidered all over with rich orient pearls; the cloak made after the Spanish fashion, with all things suitable, the value whereof will be £20,000.

With a sparkling company of nobles and knights at the head of a train of over seven hundred persons, Buckingham made a brave sight as he entered Paris. Like many Englishmen, however, the Duke no sooner found himself in a foreign country than his restraining standards of behaviour gradually deserted him. Unchecked by his superficial morals his latent contempt for foreigners, who began then as now at Calais, erupted first in boorish behaviour and then in an outrageous flirtation in public with the French Queen Anne of Austria. Meanwhile King Charles played the part of an impatient lover, although anxiety may have coloured his emotions more than passion for he had yet to set eyes upon his bride. He made his headquarters at Canterbury and made excursions to Dover for the purpose of superintending the preparations for receiving his Queen. He watched as workmen erected a splendid tented pavilion on the beach at Dover, where Henrietta and her ladies could rest after their voyage.

After a passage through stormy seas, Henrietta's ship made its landfall under the white cliffs of Dover at seven o'clock on the evening of Sunday 12 June. When she met Charles next morning the pent-up emotions of the fifteen-year-old girl proved too much for her and she burst into tears, but he comforted her as best as he could. At a banquet in the open air later that day, the King gallantly acted as carver to his bride, slicing for her some pieces of pheasant. During the dinner one of her French Roman Catholic chaplains stood like a black crow behind her chair, continually exhorting her to remember that it was the eve of the Nativity of St John the Baptist – a fast day – and that she should therefore eat no meat. The tossing of the ship and her uncertain emotional future may have robbed Henrietta temporarily of her appetite for a day or two, but it was now happily restored, and she ate her plate of pheasant with relish. To a perhaps too-inquisitive English courtier who asked her if she could abide a Hugnenot, she replied pertinently: 'Why not? Was not my father one?'

After the consummation of the marriage at Canterbury, the royal couple set out for London. At Gravesend they embarked upon the state barge and were rowed up the river. Fifty good ships, including many tall men o'war of the royal fleet, which Charles pointed out proudly to his wife, fired over fifteen hundred rounds of welcome as the gaily-painted line of barges dipped by towards the capital. From the batteries under the grey-silver walls of the Tower more white smoke and bangs bellowed forth as the heavy pieces fired in unison their mighty salute. People on the bank and London Bridge caught glimpses of the King and Queen, both dressed in green, through the barge-windows which had been left open despite a heavy rain shower which ruffled and pitted the river. The petite and vivacious Queen waved happily to the crowds through the window before the barge came to rest at the steps of Somerset House, her new home. Bells from a hundred towers and steeples, and bonfires in the streets added to the crescendo of noise and excitement.

Rain on the river; rain over the Kingdom. Behind the high storeyed houses fronting the river, in the narrow filthy lanes, the plague killed about five thousand Londoners that week and a grimly exact total of 35,417 people that year. But England feared a more insidious plague. On the Continent the Catholic powers had now overrun the Palatinate and most of central Germany. The Protestant princes of the northern German states realized that they stood next in the path of Catholic conquest. King Christian of Denmark was preparing an army to march to their aid, but Gustavus Adolphus of Sweden still remained preoccupied with Poland. Somewhere in the flat marshes of Flanders lay camped a small English army under the mercenary general Count Mansfeld, which had finally embarked in January 1625. The government, however, planned a much larger contribution to the struggle against Spain and Austria: a naval war in conjunction with the Dutch against the fleets and ports of the common enemy. For this enterprise, however, England needed at least the implicit support of the other great power in the Channel – France.

Besides the marriage of Henrietta Maria to the King of England there were other reasons for supposing that France would prove co-operative. Cardinal Richelieu, the chief minister of King Louis XIII since May 1624, had already enlisted the help of Venice and Savoy in his successful bid to occupy the Valtelline, thus cutting the road between Spanish-held lands and Austria. Doubtless he would have done more had not the French Huguenots chosen this hour to launch a revolt. In January 1625, under their leader Soubise, the Huguenots raised their flag over the harbour town and fortress of La Rochelle and demanded their liberty from Catholic dominance.

The English government now found itself in a quandary. On the one hand, King Charles and his ministers desperately needed the political, economic and military support of France in order to restore the balance of power in Europe and to recover the Palatinate. On the other hand, the Huguenots in La Rochelle naturally looked across the water to England for succour, and the government could not stand by idle through another St Bartholomew's Massacre.

Under the sway of Buckingham as his adviser, the King met this daunting situation with a series of compromises which involved a certain amount of straightforward English duplicity. In order to win credit in France the English government announced a stay in prosecutions of recusants, while quietly postponing the implementation of the measure on the grounds that it would have caused an uproar in the impending Parliament of 1625. A squadron of ships, which in a rash moment James had promised to lend to France, was eventually dispatched, but Admiral Pennington received secret orders to withdraw it from any operations directed against La Rochelle. Meanwhile the English government had offered its services as a mediator between Richelieu and the Huguenots. Yet during his visit to Paris in order to fetch Henrietta Maria, the Duke of Buckingham had failed to get negotiations under way. Moreover, the Cardinal refused to send reinforcements to Count Mansfeld's motley army or to pour gold into the war chest of King Christian of Denmark.

These difficulties in foreign policy formed the backcloth when the first Parliament of the new King's reign assembled at Westminster on 18 June 1625. In the Low Countries at the end of May the Spanish army had captured Breda. Mansfeld's diseased and hungry soldiers took their infrequent English pay, but had yet to cross the Rhine and engage in the fighting. An air of doubt and uncertainty about the real situation pervaded the conversation of the Members of Parliament as they spoke in clusters in Westminster Hall or walked together. Yes, the French marriage had taken place, but where was the French treaty? No one knew.

The Commons speedily addressed itself to the one contribution it could make, namely to check the spread of Catholicism in England. Forming itself into one large Committee of Religion and Supply, the Lower House drew up a petition beseeching the King to execute the penal laws of the land against Catholics, laws which had not been rigorously enforced in some areas since the scare of the Armada faded in the English mind. Significantly the Commons also asked Charles to purge from the Church of which he was 'Supreme Head and Governor under Christ' all practices and beliefs that savoured of Rome. As a High Church or Arminian group of clergy had emerged in the Church of England, who wished to emphasize the more Catholic doctrines and attitudes, with all their outward manifestations of dress, furniture and rubric, there was bound to be a conflict.

At first the privy councillors and courtiers who managed the King's business in the House of Commons met with some opposition when they asked for money to prosecute a war which had been undertaken without their counsel. 'We know of no war', retorted Phelips, 'nor of any enemy.' This was nonsense in view of what the Commons had promised in 1624. Before granting more money some opposition members thought that the House should discover how the last lot of taxes had been spent – or misspent. At length the Commons sitting in committee recommended a vote of two subsidies of about £140,000 which came nowhere near the million pounds which the King had in mind. Moreover, instead of voting the customs duties known as tonnage and poundage to the new monarch for life, as their predecessors had always done, this House voted them for only one year. As the House of Lords would not concur with that somewhat distrustful tactic, the Bill failed to pass Parliament.

In July a committee of the House of Commons made its report on the case of Richard Montague, a clergyman of the Church of England who had published a tract in 1624 entitled *A New Gag for an Old Goose* wherein he advocated for his fellow-countryman a midway position between Rome and Geneva on such vital doctrines as predestination. In 1625 he penned a second pamphlet called *Appello Caesarem* in which he appealed to the King to lend royal support to his views. 'Defend thou me with the sword', he wrote, 'and I will defend thee with the pen.' The Commons committee charged Montague with disturbing the civil and ecclesiastical peace and setting Parliament at defiance, and they issued orders for him to be placed in custody. At Hampton Court the King heard the petition moving him to hound the Papists and purify the Church with outward civility. But he revealed the direction of his own thoughts by appointing Montague as one of his royal chaplains. The Commons could hardly fail to interpret the action correctly.

To escape the plague, which still raged in London, the Commons met in the great hall of Christ Church at Oxford for the second session of that Parliament. By then Richelieu had begun negotiations with the Huguenots. After much confusion over the meaning of his orders, Admiral Pennington had also handed over the *Vanguard* and six other ships of his squadron to the French. With considerable self-confidence Buckingham defended his policies in a speech to the Commons in a bold attempt to remove their grave doubt about his competence. He did not succeed. 'Let us lay the fault where it is', muttered a member called Seymour, still not daring to name the favourite as the culprit responsible for England's condition. On 2 August the King cut short any further move towards naming names by dissolving Parliament.

The late winter of 1626 saw London in a festive mood again for the coronation. Religious scruples prevented Henrietta from participating in the ceremony on 2 February in Westminster Abbey; at the last moment she even declined to occupy the gallery especially prepared so that she could watch the proceedings. Thus the Queen did not see her short dignified husband vested in a white surplice, nor hear Archbishop Abbot's sermon on the text 'Be thou faithful unto death and I will give thee a Crown of Life.' That Charles heeded these words in the depths of his mind and soul is one facet of his complex character, caught in an immortal way by the eye and brush of Van Dyck. Later, when he was desperate for money in 1642, he would try to pawn in the markets of Amsterdam the Crown Jewels he received that day, the sacred instruments of royalty.

As the two subsidies voted by the 1625 Parliament fell so

far short of his expectations, the King issued privy seals for each county to make him a loan. The share expected from Buckinghamshire amounted to £3,052. Hampden's assessment for £13.6s. 8d. may seem small, but it seemed excessive at the time. Sir William Borlase, writing to Sir Thomas Denton, could comment: 'I do think Mr John Hampden to be £13.6s.8d and his mother £10 a harder rate than I find upon any other.' Hampden disputed the assessment, and it was reduced to £10.

Had the nation's taxes bought victories against Spain, the Puritan members of the second Parliament of the reign, which assembled at Westminster on 6 February 1626, might not have complained. But the English fleet had suffered a humiliating disaster. On 8 October the navy had set sail from Plymouth, bound for Cadiz. It was poorly prepared for a raid on the Spanish coast. The patched and threadbare sails of the *St George* had formerly billowed on the masts of the *Triumph* during the glorious rout of the Armada nearly forty years before. One report described the shrouds and ropes of the veteran vessel, the *Garland*, as 'all stark rotten'. The fleet's beer leaked from faulty kegs and came up from the bilges in the ship's pumps. Consequently the sailors were given as a substitute the coarse West Country cider 'that stinks worse than carrion'.

The English fleet arrived to find that the Spanish had strengthened their garrison at Cadiz. After a week of ineffectual skirmishing around the defences the weather-battered ships stood out to sea. A convoy from Mexico laden with silver and gold then slipped into Cadiz roads under the bowsprits of the English ships. With nothing to show for their pains, the ships limped back to Plymouth. The Vice-Admiral of Devon, who owed his appointment to the favour of Buckingham, stood on the quayside and watched the crews throwing overboard the canvas-clothed corpses of sailors and soldiers dead from sickness. He saw seven sailors from the ships collapse and die from their ailments publicly in the streets of the town. His name was Sir John Eliot.

In order to rid himself of the turbulent presence in Parliament of Coke, Wentworth, Seymour and Phelips, the King had pricked holes by their names in the list of possible sheriffs. Sir John Eliot, already a member of the House of Commons, assumed the mantle of leadership among those bitterly critical of the government. In his first speech that February, Eliot summed up the national feeling in terse and telling phrases: 'Our honour is ruined, our ships are sunk, our men perished; not by the sword, not by the enemy, not by chance, but . . . by those we trust.' Eliot began to collect evidence against Buckingham, and at about this time he asked John Hampden to list the possible charges. Among Eliot's papers at Port Eliot there exists a document in Hampden's handwriting entitled 'The Causes'. Ten heads for discussion are listed:

1. The increase of Papists and the countenancing of them.
2. The narrow seas and the coasts have not been guarded since the breach of the treaties with Spain.
3. The plurality of offices in any one man's hand.
4. The intercepting, the unnecessary exhausting and misemploying the King's revenue.
5. The sales of honour in general.
6. The conferring of honour upon such whom the King's revenue doth maintain.
7. Buying of places of judicature in the commonwealth.
8. The delivery of our ships into the hands of the French which were employed against Rochelle.
9. Impositions upon commodities in general both native and foreign without assent of Parliament.
10. The misemployment of the money given by the Act of Parliament and not employing the money according to the four ends expressed in the act.

Hampden added 'A cause of stop of trade', but on reflection crossed out these words.

On 15 March King Charles summoned the Commons to Whitehall and lectured them severely. 'I would not have the House to question my servants. much less one that is so near to me,' he declared. Eliot and his companions would not be thus gagged. Two weeks later the King threatened the Commons with dissolution. Another speech in person by

Buckingham to the Commons, this time to explain why he had 'proceeded with art', as he put it, over the squadron surrendered to Cardinal Richelieu, only served to make things worse, for it revealed his political incompetence. On 8 May the Commons faced the real issue and impeached the great favourite at the bar of the House of Lords.

Now Buckingham enjoyed the complete confidence of the King. He had committed neither treason nor crime; he had not accepted or given bribes. Yet, apart from the judicial process of impeachment, there was no way by which Parliament could call the King's chief minister to account and get rid of him. But such a design challenged the King's ancient right to rule through ministers accountable to him. An attack upon the favourite could only be interpreted by the King as an onslaught upon the very citadel of royal authority.

To give the colour of an impeachable offence to their case, Sir John Eliot and Sir Dudley Digges both alluded to the slanderous rumours circulating that Buckingham had administered poison to hasten the end of King James. Summoned to the doors of the chamber, the two opposition leaders found the King's guards waiting to arrest them. News of their seizure rippled through the Commons – 'Rise! Rise,' the members chanted. The House abandoned the sitting. Small groups of members gathered that afternoon in Westminster Hall, hotly debating the affair. Next morning, when the Speaker rose to start the business of the day, he found himself greeted with shouts of 'Sit down!' and 'No business until we are righted in our liberties!' The King set free Eliot and Digges, but he dissolved Parliament on 15 June. 'Thus,' says Whitelock, 'this great, warm, and ruffling Parliament had its period.'

Shorn of parliamentary grants, the royal government now experienced a real shortage of money. Ministers considered and rejected some possible financial expedients, such as imposing a subsidy directly on freeholders. They began to debase the coinage, but fortunately stopped before too much damage was done. Instead, they sold off a large amount of gold plate and appealed for another benevolence from the country. By September it had become clear that forcing subjects to give money would prove ineffectual. When royal officials announced the benevolence in Westminster Hall, their voices were drowned by cries of 'A Parliament! A Parliament!' London and the maritime counties did bow to tradition and to royal pressure so far as to contribute money for some ships to recruit the fleet at Portsmouth.

In September 1626 the Privy Council hit upon the expedient of raising a great sum, equivalent to five subsidies, by means of a forced loan. But the royal tax collectors found it difficult to gather the money, especially when the judges in London refused to endorse the lawfulness of the forced loan. King Charles promptly dismissed Sir Randal Crew, his Lord Chief Justice, and appointed the more pliant Nicholas Hyde in his place, yet the moral effect of the judgment could not lightly be undone. Fifteen or sixteen peers, headed by the Earls of Essex and Warwick and Lord Saye, flatly refused to contribute. The privy councillors and other appointed commissioners did their best to ensure obedience to the royal writs by going into the shires in January 1627 in order to interview and reprimand those who would not pay.

John Hampden was among those who refused to pay the forced loan. Having been bound by a sum of £500 to appear before the Privy Council when called, he eventually received a summons to appear at their table on 27 January. According to a later printed report, Hampden – like others on the same charge – answered the privy councillors as follows: 'I could be content to lend as well as others, but I fear to draw upon myself that curse in Magna Carta which is to be read twice a year against those who infringe it.' The Privy Council committed him forthwith to prison in the Gatehouse.

The Dean and Chapter of Westminster Abbey leased two medieval gates for use as the Gatehouse gaol. One gate, built in the time of Edward III, facing Tothill Street, just in front of the west door of the Abbey as an entrance to Great Dean's Yard, served as a receptacle for felons; while the other accommodated clerks in holy orders committed to it by the Bishop of London. Hampden and his fellow prisoners occupied the former tower. Sir Walter Raleigh had spent the last night of his life there in 1618, composing the immortal poem 'E'en such is Time' in his stone cell after his wife had bid him farewell. Paradoxically it was a Royalist prisoner in

1642, Colonel Richard Lovelace, who wrote in the Gatehouse his poem 'To Althea from Prison', who may best have captured Hampden's feelings in 1627 as he moved into his vaulted room, a Puritan captive:

> *Stone walls do not a prison make,*
> *Nor iron bars a cage;*
> *Minds innocent and quiet take*
> *That for an hermitage.*

He shared this prison with his cousin, Sir Edmund Hampden, and Sir John Eliot. Gradually London's prisons began to fill with other opponents of the forced loan, such as the Earl of Lincoln at the Tower and Sir Thomas Wentworth in the Marshalsea. After seventeen days of imprisonment, John Hampden and his cousin, with two Northamptonshire knights – Sir John Pickering and Sir Erasmus Dryden – petitioned unsuccessfully for freedom from the Gatehouse.

Hampden remained a prisoner in the Gatehouse throughout 1627, although his warder probably allowed him considerable liberty in London and possibly a vacation at Great Hampden. Hampden probably spent some of his time in his mother's house, which occupied much of the present site of Downing Street. In 1581 Queen Elizabeth had granted to her Keeper of the Palace, Sir Thomas Knyvet, some old premises occupied by a goldsmith on the edge of Whitehall Palace near the great Tennis Court, an area bounded by the Peacock Inn and two unused passages – one leading to Pheasant Court and another leading to the Privy Garden. In 1622 Sir Thomas died, leaving the house he had fashioned there to his wife, who also died that year bequeathing the lease to her 'welbeloved Neece, Elizabeth Hampden, Widdowe'. Elizabeth lived in Hampden House, as it was now called, until her death in 1665, paying a rent of £90 a year.

With the help of a report from a parliamentary commission in 1650 it is possible to reconstruct Hampden House in the imagination. The commission described it as:

> built part with brick and part with timber and Flemish wall and covered with tile, consisting of a large and spacious hall, wainscotted round, well lighted and paved with brick pavements, two parlours whereof one is wainscotted round from ceiling to the

floor, one buttery, one cellar, one large kitchen well paved with stone and well fitted and jointed and well fitted with dresser boards. Also one large pastry room paved and jointed as aforesaid. And above stairs in the first storey one large and spacious dining room . . . fitted with a fair chimney with a foot pace of painted tile in the same.

Six more rooms and three closets occupied the same floor, with four garrets for the servants on the second floor. The whole house resembled a miniature Oxford college, with ranges of old buildings standing around an open cobbled or paved courtyard. A passage from the court led into

one large garden containing 252 feet of assize in length and 100 feet in breadth, the said large garden being fitted with variety of wall fruit and divers fruit trees, plants, roots and flowers, very pleasant to the eye and profitable for use. Also several handsome delightful gravelly walks, seats and arbours . . .

It is not impossible to imagine Hampden whiling away the time of his imprisonment by reading, strolling and talking in this garden.

The course of public events gave Hampden and his fellow captives much to discuss. At a desperate time for the Protestant cause in the war, when north Germany lay at the mercy of the Catholic League, Charles and Buckingham had allowed England to drift into war with France. Part of the trouble sprang from the King's growing dislike for the French courtiers who had invaded his court. In July of the previous year he had dismissed the Queen's attendants, not without scenes of domestic discord. Astonished yeomen-of-the-guard witnessed Henrietta Maria smashing a window with her clenched fist so that she could bawl out her protests, and the King dragging her away from the window by force, her hands bleeding. Both England and France had also seized each other's ships and merchandise in the Channel, acts of aggression which tilted the balance in favour of war. Early in 1627 the two nations had acknowledged that they stood at war. The English government made ready the fleet in the south coast ports to go to the aid of beleaguered La Rochelle.

On 11 June Charles dined with Buckingham in the great

cabin of the admiral's ship at Portsmouth, and talked with excitement about the prospect of the forthcoming expedition to assist the Rochellese. But the venture proved as dismal a failure as Cadiz. On the Isle of Ré, just off La Rochelle in the Bay of Biscay, Buckingham attempted to storm the fortified town of St Martin, but the French defenders held it. By November the fleet carried the army – looking distinctly the worse for wear – back to England. Of the 6,884 soldiers mustered outside St Martin, only 2,989 haggard survivors landed at Portsmouth and Plymouth.

This military disaster strengthened the continuing resistance to the forced loan. Five imprisoned knights, including Sir Edmund Hampden, appealed in November to the Court of King's Bench for a writ of *Habeas Corpus* to secure their release. For the second time the judges addressed themselves to the questions of how far and by what means the royal prerogative could be employed to extract money from unwilling subjects. The judges wriggled uncomfortably in their seats and evaded the issue by refusing to grant bail on the grounds that the commitment must be presumed to be a matter of State. Yet they also avoided any judgment that the Crown possessed the right to imprison subjects indefinitely.

On 2 January 1628 the King released from his gaols John Hampden and seventy-five other prisoners who refused to pay the forced loan. Possibly he did so to create a better atmosphere for more arbitrary taxation to finance a further attempt to relieve La Rochelle from Richelieu's besiegers. On 11 February the Privy Council issued writs for the collection of Ship-Money from all shires, not just the ports and sea-board counties. Compared to such expedients as the granting of new pensions or the revival of medieval forest laws, the extension of Ship-Money to the whole country was an altogether bigger matter: if it could be collected regularly the King would have thereby secured a permanent and adequate source of income independent of Parliament. Hence Ship-Money possessed a crucial significance for the constitutional development of England. If Charles could secure his right to this tax it would serve him, as Clarendon stated, 'for a spring and magazine that should have no bottom, and for an everlasting supply on all occasions'.

The Ship-Money writs proclaimed the reasons why the ships and crews were urgently needed: the distress of the King of Denmark's army; the ruin of English trade in the Baltic; the danger to La Rochelle, and the possibility of a French and Spanish invasion of England. Therefore the English fleet must put to sea by 1 March, the writ declared. If £176,000 had been received by that date the King undertook to summon Parliament. Meanwhile the government explored other sources of revenue. On 15 February the clergy of the Church of England received a direction to donate their 'Supreme Head and Governor' a free gift of £20,000 forthwith. Various sales, grants and fines brought some £170,000 to the Exchequer. But the King needed the large sum of approximately £200,000 a year just to pay the wages of his 4,000 seamen and 7,557 soldiers. He required another £110,000 to meet the bills for repairs, victuals and military stores necessary to make ready fifty ships.

No government of England at that time, or at any other, could work without a certain minimum of consent. In 1628 a substantial number of the Lords Lieutenants (the peers appointed in each shire by the King to be responsible for matters of military defence) began to jib at collecting a tax so unpopular with the gentry. Sensing that the time was not yet ripe for a trial of strength, the King's ministers rather tamely withdrew the writs for Ship-Money. Thus in mid-March the fleet still rode at anchor in English harbours. Six hundred men had yet to be found and paid. Bread, beer and cheese stored in the holds of the ships slowly went rotten as high tides ebbed and flowed. On shore the soldiers had been billeted in the towns and villages, and idleness turned them into ill-disciplined drunkards and thieves.

The third Parliament of the reign assembled on 17 March 1628, hearing first a sermon from Bishop Laud on the text 'Endeavour to keep the unity of the Spirit in the bond of peace'. The King hardly heeded that injunction when, in his opening speech, he hinted heavily that the Commons must vote money or expect a short sitting. This remark was no threat, he added tactlessly, for he scorned to threaten anyone but equals. Yet neither priestly sermon nor arrogant threat could restrain the pent-up venom of the leaders of the resistance movement in the House of Commons. They mounted a relentless attack upon arbitrary taxation, illegal imprisonment and other abuses of power. Whereas Sir Thomas Wentworth contented himself with criticizing those who 'extended the prerogative beyond its just symmetry', making no mention of its abuse in the sphere of religion, Sir John Eliot boldly linked all the obnoxious financial measures, infringements of rights, privileges and liberties, with the idea of some form of Popish conspiracy to undermine England. Thus he spoke out against the growth of those doctrines and practices which would be associated with the name of William Laud, for they were as Popish mines sapping under the walls of the Church of England. If the royal prerogative worked to bring down these bulwarks by persisting to favour the fellow-travellers of Rome among the clergy, then it must be called into question.

John Hampden had lived with Eliot for almost eleven months in the Gatehouse, and his natural genius for friendship had drawn the two men closely together. They entertained a deep respect and affection for each other which survived the tests of time. As Eliot assumed a leading position in the third Parliament he may have been responsible for the more active part which his friend from Buckinghamshire now played. On 21 March Hampden served with Sir Edward Coke and Sir Dudley Digges on a committee to draw up a Bill 'to restrain the sending away of persons to be Popishly bred beyond the seas'. Religion in one way or another occupied no less than eight of the fifteen committees on which Hampden sat. Clearly his contemporaries saw him at this stage as a man primarily concerned with the Puritan renewal of the Church of England in order to preserve and enhance its scriptural character. With John Pym and others he enquired into 'the better continuance of peace and unity in the church and commonwealth'. Another committee considered possible measures against scandalous and unworthy ministers. Yet another met specifically to hear the petitions of two preachers who claimed to have been persecuted by the Bishop of Durham. Two other committees dealt with the treatment of Papist recusants. On a more practical note, Hampden also looked into the appropriation of vicarages.

His membership of a committee 'for redressing the neglect of preaching and catechizing' again underlines Hampden's known interest in religion and Church affairs.

The financial and military troubles in the realm provided the topics for the remaining six committees upon which Hampden sat in the afternoons. With Sir Thomas Wentworth and others he met 'to examine the warrants for billeting soldiers or levying money in Surrey'. This mild purpose disguised a serious matter, for a hundred or so soldiers had gone on the rampage in that county, terrorizing the inhabitants and threatening to burn their cottages if their demands were not met. In April, with Sir John Eliot himself, Hampden sought 'to relegate the pressing of men as ambassadors, or on other foreign service, so as to promise the good of the people as well as the service of the state'. He also investigated charges concerning the procuring of judicial appointments for money. Yet another committee considered the case of the merchants trading with Turkey whose goods had been detained because they would not pay the tonnage and poundage now being levied. With others he sat in committee 'to take the certificate of the Trinity House merchants for the loss of ships'. Preparations for a more sustained political opposition might be read into the purpose of his last committee, which was put vaguely as 'to search for records and precedents'.

Some parliamentarians excel as orators, others in committee. There can be no doubt that Hampden won his reputation in these committees of the 1628 Parliament. His fellow members came to appreciate his quick and subtle mind, his ability to listen, his knack of guiding the discussion, and above all the deep knowledge and learning which informed his interventions. Many saw him as a modest, able and pleasant man; a few perceived in him an unusual character, a potential for greatness at some future time.

Despite efforts by the King to stave off the storm of criticism by promises to observe Magna Carta and other statutes in future, the House of Commons moved inexorably towards drawing up the Petition of Right. On 8 May the House discussed four grievances: forced loans, arbitrary imprisonment, compulsory billeting and the increasing use of martial law. The House of Lords attempted to blunt the axe aimed at some of the branches of the royal prerogative by inserting clauses safeguarding the King's rights, but the Commons would have none of them. On 28 May the Lords gave way and the Petition of Right passed both Houses.

Meanwhile the second English expedition to raise the siege of La Rochelle had ended in failure. On 1 May the royal fleet of sixty-six ships under the Earl of Denbigh had dropped anchor in sight of the town. Under the eye of Richelieu, however, the French army had narrowed the mouth of the harbour by building two moles, leaving only a narrow gap defended by iron chains and gun boats. Denbigh prepared some fireships to clear the passage, but the direction of winds proved contrary. Then it occurred to him that these very winds might encourage the French to send fireships among his densely-packed fleet. He gave orders for the fleet to stand out to sea. Wanting inspiration, Denbigh and his captains could think of nothing better to do than to return home. It was an extraordinary display of lack of enthusiasm in a nation which had harried Spain with such relish and inventiveness. 'If the ships had been lost, I had timber enough to build more', declared the angry King when he heard the news later that month.

Now Charles looked for some evidence that he would not surrender any part of his prerogative if he assented to the Petition of Right. He consulted the judges, who rather obscurely replied that his royal prerogative to imprison on occasion would not be affected. On 2 June the King tried to by-pass the Petition by promising to both Houses that right would be done according to the laws and customs of the realm. The Commons did not rest content with this verbal affirmation and they resolved upon yet another remonstrance setting forth their grievances.

Eliot struck the keynote of the debate by reminding them that they met as the Great Council of the King. Then he began to criticize the war against France. A privy councillor named Sir Humphrey May rose to interrupt him, but shouts of 'Go on! Go on!' resounded through the chamber. 'If he goes on,' retorted May, 'I hope that I may myself go out,' and sat down to howls of 'Begone! Begone!' Eliot continued his damning review of the state of the nation. 'What perfect English heart is not almost dissolved into sorrow for the truth?' he asked the now silent rows of members.

Behind the proposed remonstrance lay the fear that the King would abruptly dissolve Parliament before Eliot and his colleagues had time to make what he called 'a perfect inquisition' into the causes of England's sorry condition. Despite a message from the King asking them to vote him money and trouble themselves no more with grievances, the Commons went into committee on the remonstrance. The debate drifted back to the subject of Buckingham. On 5 June the King intervened again, prohibiting any business which might lay any scandal or aspersion upon 'the State, Government or ministers thereof.'

Cautiously Eliot began to explore the possibility that there had been a misunderstanding: 'I am confident no minister, how dear soever, can ——' The Speaker stopped him short by rising to his feet and, weeping profusely, informed the House that by royal command he could permit no hint of an attack on the King's ministers. Digges raised the issue of free speech, and the House paused in silence. The House of Lords, however, came to the rescue, and proposed a joint deputation to the King for a clear reply to the Petition of Right. Aware of the strength of feeling in both Houses, the King gave it his assent on 7 June. Shouts and applause greeted his words; bells rang and bonfires burned in the City that evening. More to the King's pleasure, the subsidy Bill now passed both Houses.

Yet Charles had won for himself only a brief respite. Four days later the Commons voted a remonstrance with clauses against the Popish corruption of the Church and for the full execution of laws against the recusants. Moreover, it asked for the removal of Buckingham from the royal counsels. On 17 June Buckingham on his knees besought the King's permission to reply, but Charles would not allow it, and significantly gave him his hand to be kissed. The Commons then received from the King a haughty message bidding them to abstain from any more interference with his sovereign powers.

Popular feeling against Buckingham mounted that summer in London, bearing upon its hot wind the seeds of his destruction. Someone nailed to a post in Coleman Street this squib:

> *Who rules the kingdom?*
> *The King.*
> *Who rules the King?*
> *The Duke.*
> *Who rules the Duke?*
> *The devil.*
> *Let the Duke look to it.*

On 13 June an astrologer and doctor called Lambe, whom Buckingham had consulted on occasion, came out of the Fortune Theatre and found himself recognized by a mob of apprentices. 'There goes Buckingham's devil,' the crowd chanted. With some presence of mind, Lambe hired a bodyguard of burly sailors to escort him to a tavern in Moorgate Street, where he ate a leisurely supper. When he opened the inn door, however, he saw an even larger and angrier crowd waiting for him, and he foolishly shouted a threat to the effect that 'he would make them all dance naked at the rope's end'. He made his way with difficulty to the Windmill Tavern, and attempted to move on from there in disguise. But the apprentices caught up with him and beat him to the ground. The night watch hauled him more dead than alive to the Compter prison for security. Lambe died next morning.

In order to prevent yet another remonstrance, this time against the gathering of tonnage and poundage, the King suspended the sitting of Parliament on 26 June: it did not meet again for its second session until 20 January 1629. In the intervening six months Charles demonstrated his contempt for broadly Puritan opinions of the majority in the Commons by pardoning a clergyman called Manwaring, who had been impeached, fined £1,000 and barred from all office by the House for preaching that the clergy had an independent existence apart from the community and that the King possessed a divine right of obedience apart from the laws. Manwaring received a fat Crown living. Bishop Montaigne, who had licensed Manwaring's sermons for publication when the more Protestant-minded Archbishop Abbot had suffered house confinement rather than do so, now received his reward: he was translated from his see of London to the archbishopric of York. This unsavoury prelate symbolized all that the Puritans disliked about episcopacy. John Milton once speculated that the bishops of his day would not find the life of a bishop in the early Church very satisfying: 'What a plural endowment to the many-beneficed-gaping mouth of a prelate, what a relish it would give to his canary-sucking and swan-eating palate, let old Bishop Montaigne judge for me.'

Laud took Montaigne's place as Bishop of London, thereby consolidating his position as the King's chief adviser on religious and ecclesiastical matters. At this juncture Laud's friend, the Yorkshire baronet Sir Thomas Wentworth, quitted both the House of Commons and the popular cause. The new Lord Treasurer, Weston, introduced him into the Court where, despite his blunt voice, and northern roughness of manner, the sheer drive and efficiency of the man won him recognition. Charles made him a peer and promised him the presidency of the Council of the North.

Early in August an unbalanced young man bought a tenpenny knife in a London cutler's shop, and set out for Portsmouth, hitching lifts on wagons where he could. The clear country air did not dispel the sinister intention which had formed in his troubled mind. He had heard the sermons and ballads portraying Buckingham as the enemy of the kingdom and read the remonstrance calling for his removal. A personal grudge sharpened his sense of mission. For John Felton had served as lieutenant in a company of foot in the first expedition to La Rochelle, but Buckingham had not promoted him into the captain's place when his commander was killed in action. At Portsmouth he watched and waited. On 24 August Buckingham came from breakfast, and paused in a dark crowded corridor to listen to a senior officer who had something to whisper in his ear. Felton leapt forward and plunged his dagger into Buckingham's heart. 'The villain hath killed me,' gasped the Duke as he wrenched out the knife. Calmly the assassin gave himself up in the court-yard outside the house. He was brought to London and conveyed past a silent and respectful crowd into the Tower for a remorseless interrogation. But torture was not used, and the young man eventually paid for his crime at Tyburn at the end of the hangman's noose.

Charles heard the news of Buckingham's death while he was at prayers, and maintained his composure until after the service. Then he flung himself on a bed and wept. David had lost his Jonathan. Yet no tears flowed in the nation for the Duke. That summer an undergraduate called Alexander Gill, son of the High Master of St Paul's School, babbled happily to a friend in Oxford college hall that 'the King is fitter to stand in a Cheapside shop, with an apron before him, and say "What lack ye?" than to govern a kingdom.' He proposed Felton's health and speculated on what King James and Buckingham would be talking about in hell. A don of the college, an Arminian theologian named Dr William Chillingworth, reported the conversation to Bishop Laud who had the lad brought before the Court of Star Chamber. Only the good standing of his father with Laud secured a pardon for young Master Gill.

In September the English fleet returned to La Rochelle and landed soldiers for a half-hearted military operation to relieve the beleaguered town. Meanwhile Richelieu had promised the Huguenots religious toleration if they would surrender La Rochelle first. King Charles opposed these terms but to no avail. On 30 October King Louis XIII made a triumphal entry into the Huguenot stronghold. With the immediate reason for their presence thus removed, the English fleet turned homewards across the storm-tossed Bay of Biscay.

At home the government's efforts to extort tonnage and poundage and other impositions met stiff resistance. 'Merchants are in no part of the world so screwed and wrung as in England,' remarked one of them named Richard Chambers. 'In Turkey they have more encouragement!' The Privy Council called him to their table to account for these words, and then committed him to the Marshalsea Prison. Royal customs officers seized the goods of thirty other merchants who owed dues, including some merchandise valued at £5,000 from the warehouse of John Rolle, a member of the

House of Commons.

More trouble for the country brewed and fermented in the vats of the Church of England, sending up bubbles of discontent. The Arminians objected to the usual position of the Communion table in the nave of the church. Visitations by archdeacons revealed that the congregation tended to festoon it with felt hats, cloaks and walking-sticks. Moreover, many of the gentry brought their dogs to church . . . . Efforts by the clergy to restore it to the traditional altar position in the chancel and to fence it with altar rails, a kind of priestly enclosure act, met with violent opposition. The parishioners of Grantham in Lincolnshire settled the matter by a riot in the nave of the church, as men tugged the table this way and that while their fellow Christians belaboured them with walking-sticks and hurled prayerbooks at each other.

In December 1628 the King issued a declaration to be read by all incumbents in which he asserted the right of Convocation under his own headship to decide all disputed matters of doctrine and ceremonial. But the tension in the soul of the Church of England could not be stilled by a declaration, nor could the Puritans entrust their souls and those of their children to a Church ruled by a king so inclined, as they believed, towards Popery.

The second session of the third Parliament of the reign, which assembled in January 1629, devoted a fortnight to these religious matters. Under Eliot's leadership the Lower House passed a resolution condemning the interpretations placed upon the Thirty-nine Articles by 'Jesuits and Arminians' and bringing forward the more Calvinist 'Lambeth Articles' of 1595 as the true expression of the English doctrinal position. Hampden played a part in these discussions, for he served as a member of the committee appointed to consider 'the differences in the several impressions of the Thirty-nine Articles'..By 24 February the House had begun to contemplate resolutions which would have laid penalties upon Papists and Arminians alike.

In February the Privy Council summoned John Rolle, with the other merchants who refused to pay impositions, to attend the Star Chamber Court to answer charges. This raised acutely the question of parliamentary privilege. Eliot resolved to launch a counter-attack against the customs officers involved. As the customs farmers paid a fixed sum to the Exchequer in return for the right to collect taxes, technically the goods seized in the warehouses went to them, not to the King. Two of the offending officials, Abraham Dawes and Richard Carmarthen, were summoned to the bar for examination, but their employer had so far not been questioned. On the morning of Friday 20 February Hampden, who served on two committees relating to the matter, made his first recorded speech to the whole House when he moved, 'That Sir John Wolstenholme, the Customer, might also be called in, being in the same case with Dawes and Carmarthen, so that they might proceed with all alike.'

Wolstenholme declared that he had seized the goods for the non-payment of tonnage and poundage. His lease and royal warrant were read aloud in the House, and some lawyers fastened on the phrase which allowed the tax farmers to 'receive, levy and collect'. There being no addition of the word 'seize', they concluded, the officers had no right to confiscate the merchandise of John Rolle. Yet on Monday morning the secretary of the Privy Council rose to inform the House that the King 'could not sever the act of the officers from his own act, neither could his officers suffer from it without high dishonour to his Majesty.'

The House adjourned for two days to consider this difficult situation, and when they reassembled on Wednesday the Speaker announced another adjournment for a week. Discerning that the King would probably dissolve Parliament when they met again on Monday 2 March, Eliot and his coterie of friends and associates, almost certainly now including Hampden, decided upon a protest. There was danger in the air. Sir Dudley Digges, who had made his peace with the King and received promises of an office, sent a hastily scribbled note to his former prison-fellow Eliot early that Monday morning: 'Let me pray you to preserve yourself clear, a looker-on; which, credit me – if my weakness be worth your crediting – will both advantage you and much content me.'

'No! No!' shouted the Commons when Speaker Finch announced the royal command that they should adjourn again until 10 March. Eliot stood up from his seat on the top bench at the back of the House, paper in hand, but the Speaker checked him with a refusal to allow any speeches. As he rose from his chair Denzil Holles (who, as a peer's son, sat on the benches behind the Speaker) rushed forward and forced Finch back into his seat. An angry knot of privy councillors and their opponents gathered around the chair, and above the uproar Holles could be heard bellowing, 'God's wounds! You shall sit till we please to rise!'

Eliot hurled his paper down, but neither the Speaker nor the Clerk of the House would read it. At last Eliot spoke, his clear voice outlining the substance of his written protestation against those who made Popish or Arminian innovations a religion on the one hand, and against those who advised the taking or paying of tonnage and poundage illegally: such men should be accounted traitors, 'capital enemies of the State, and whensoever we sit again, if I be here (as I think I shall) I shall proceed against the person of that man.' As Eliot's paper had drifted – or been thrown – into the great log fire that warmed the Chapel of St Stephen, and word came that the King had sent for guards to disperse the sitting, Holles volunteered to repeat the clauses from memory and the House passed them by acclaiming shouts of 'Ay! Ay!' The doors opened and the members pushed their way past the King's guards. Eleven years would pass before they entered those doors again.

Chapter Four

THE DEATH OF SIR JOHN ELIOT

Give me the man that with a quaking arm
Walks with a steadfast mind through greatest harm;
And, though his flesh doth tremble, makes it stand
To execute what reason doth command.   GEORGE WITHER, 1628

Within days of that tumult at the end of the 1629 Parliament
the Privy Council summoned nine members of the House of
Commons to appear before it and to answer for their part in
those proceedings. The defiant mood had not evaporated.
Denzil Holles asked the privy councillors if he might be
subject to the King's mercy rather than his power. 'Than of
his justice, you mean,' the Lord Treasurer Weston intervened. 'I say of his majesty's power, my lord,' replied Holles.
Nor would Sir John Eliot retract his statement that he would
answer to none except Parliament for the words he had
spoken there as a public man, and 'being now but a private
man, he would not trouble himself to remember what he had
either said or done in that place as a public man.' But private
men had no defence against the King's wrath. That day the
Privy Council committed the nine members to prison to
await his majesty's pleasure.

Sir Allen Apsley, Lieutenant of the Tower, carefully carried out his orders to keep his seven members in close custody. He would not allow them books, or even pen and paper
upon which to write letters. Friends, clergymen and fellow
countrymen from their shires, who sought permission to talk
to the prisoners, met with polite refusals. Some of the visitors
wandered about inside the Tower trying to find the whereabouts of the prisoners by shouting up at the windows, until
the warders apprehended them and escorted the offenders

out of the fortress. Two friends of Eliot, Sir Oliver Luke and a companion, who had requested in vain for the opportunity to see him, did actually catch sight of Denzil Holles across a green lawn. With nothing to read, Holles had whiled away the long hours by exercising with dumb-bells and whirling a top. He held them up for Luke to see, and made 'antick signs and devoted salutations at their parting'.

The more scholarly prisoners, such as John Selden and Eliot himself, found their deprivation from books, writing materials and intelligent conversation especially irksome. 'Let me not wholly lose my hours,' pleaded Selden in a petition to the Lieutenant. In the summer the Lieutenant received authority from the King to keep them in safe custody, which meant that, unlike the close custody prisoners, they could receive books, write letters and entertain visitors. On the other hand the safe custody prisoners paid for their own food and laundry expenses, thus saving the Exchequer about £400 a year.

According to Apsley's daughter, Lucy, who later married Colonel Hutchinson, the Parliamentarian Governor of Nottingham, and wrote her celebrated *Memoirs* of her husband's life, Sir Allen 'was a father to all his prisoners, sweetening with much compassionate kindness their restraint, that the affliction of a prison was not felt in his days'. Her mother spent some of her annual allowance of £300 encouraging Sir Walter Raleigh, who became addicted to chemistry during his time as a prisoner in the Tower, to make his rare experiments. She made broths and medicines for the sick, and visited them. As a constant frequenter of week-day lectures and a great patron of good ministers, Lady Apsley was clearly a Puritan. Eliot must have often seen the ten-year-old Lucy at play in the Tower.

Between 25 June 1629 and 29 March 1632 Eliot wrote one hundred and twenty-nine letters that have survived, and received some thirty-three. Fifteen of his letters addressed to Hampden, and nine of Hampden's letters to him, are extant. Among the first of Eliot's correspondents was Richard Knightley of Fawsley, a member of the House of Commons for Northamptonshire, whose son later married one of Hampden's daughters. He made the initial contact with

Eliot by sending his servant with a letter and some gifts. Eliot replied at considerable length, apologizing for the fact that 'having begun again to write, I forget to make an end'.

Eliot spent much of his time in close confinement reflecting on the future of his five motherless children. He decided to send the two elder boys, John and Richard, who were seventeen and fifteen years old respectively, and both at school in Tiverton, to complete their education at Oxford University. Under Eliot's general direction, his father-in-law made the necessary arrangements with a cousin of Richard Knightley, who happened to be a tutor at Lincoln College.

On 29 October the Tower warders took Eliot and some of the prisoners by river up to the prison of the Court of King's Bench, where the preliminaries to their trial had already begun. As Eliot jovially put it in a letter to a friend, they had left 'their Palace in the Tower and betaken themselves to their Country House in Southwark'. Here they found another of the nine members, named Walter Long, who had been held in another London prison. While Attorney-General Heath continued his efforts to assemble a credible case, the prisoners made their home in the dank rooms of the Marshalsea Prison in Southwark. Hampden had already written several letters to Eliot, but the first extant one dates from this period and it is a request for the loan of a paper possessed by his friend, containing some general observations on a colony in New England:

> NOBLE SIR – I hope this letter is conveyed to you by so safe a hand that yours will be the first that shall open it. Or, if not, yet, since you enjoy, as much as without contradiction you may, the liberty of a prison, it shall be no offence to wish you to make the best use of it; and that God may find you as much his, now you enjoy the benefit of secondary helps, as you found him yours while, by deprivation of all others, you were cast upon his immediate support.
>
> This is all I have, or am willing to say; but that the paper of considerations concerning the Plantation might be very safely conveyed to me by this hand, and, after transcribing, should be as safely returned, if you vouchsafe to send it me.
>
> I beseech you present my service to Mr Valentine, and Mr Long my countryman, if with you, and let me be honoured with

the style of
> Your faithful friend and servant,
>
> JOHN HAMPDEN

Hampden, December 8th [1629]

Two days later Eliot replied in a warm vein. He expressed
his appreciation by saying that Hampden's letters possessed
a great virtue; besides signifying health and love, they
'imparted such variety of happiness in his counsels and
example that it made a degree of liberty to have them.'
Hampden's merits placed so great an obligation on him, he
wrote, that no command or opportunity to serve him should
be neglected or refused. Apologizing for the haste in which
the paper had been copied, Eliot sent it to him, twelve folio
pages long under the title of 'The Grounds for Settling a
Plantation in New England: Objections and Replies there-
to'. Doubtless Hampden wanted it in connection with the
Massachusetts Bay Company, which came into being that
year. 'In the meantime,' concluded Eliot, 'having nothing
else of which I dare communicate, my affections being
wholly yours by a former disposition, kissing your hands, I
rest your most faithful friend.'

Three weeks later Hampden returned the papers, and his
accompanying letter reveals that Eliot's two sons had spent
their first Christmas vacation from Oxford enjoying the
'rough-hewn entertainment' of Hampden House. Eliot must
have been delighted and encouraged by Hampden's good
opinion of their potential abilities:

> SIR– If my affections could be so dull as to give way to a sleepy
> excuse of a letter, yet this bearer, our common friend, had power
> to awaken them and command it: to the public experience of
> whose worth in doing, I can now add my private of his patience
> in suffering the injuries of a rough-hewn entertainment: to be
> tolerated by the addition of your sons' company, of whom, if
> ever you live to see a fruit answerable to the promise of the
> present blossoms, it will be a blessing of that weight as will turn
> the scale against all wordly afflictions and denominate your life
> happy.
>
> I return your papers with many thanks: which I have trans-
> cribed, not read. The discourse, therefore, upon the subject
> must be reserved for another season when I may with better
> opportunity and freedom communicate my thoughts to you, my

friend.

Till then, with my salutations of all your society, and prayers for your health, I rest

Your ever assured friend and servant,

JOHN HAMPDEN

Hampden, January 4th [1630]

Eliot had spent a less comfortable Christmas in the Marshalsea. The keeper of the prison allowed him to attend a morning sermon at the church of St Mary Overy. He shared a food parcel with Valentine and Long. Strode and Selden joined them from the Tower in time for Christmas, and they could at least keep themselves warm. For Sir Oliver Luke had sent up a cart-load of logs from Bedfordshire, with a note expressing his concern for Eliot's 'little thin carcass', in the winter months.

In late January and early February the prisoners stood trial in Westminster Hall before the Court of King's Bench. Having resolved that they had jurisdiction in such a case, the judges found the defendants guilty of unlawful disorder and assaulting the Speaker, and sentenced them to imprisonment during the King's pleasure. They could secure their release by giving security for good behaviour, making a submission to the King, acknowledging their offences, and paying the fines which the judges laid upon them.

Eliot could not accept such conditions. As for his fine of £2,000 – by far the largest – he declared that if the King's servants could pick that much from his assets of two cloaks, two suits, two pairs of boots, wooden goloshes or slippers and a few books, the best of luck to them. Meanwhile he asked the Lieutenant of the Tower to choose a 'convenient lodging' for him and to allow his upholsterer to come and furnish it. Eliot laughed heartily when word reached him from the royal judges complaining about the conduct of the pages and servants of the Marshalsea prisoners. The lads had amused themselves by tossing up dogs and cats in a blanket in the streets of Southwark. When justly reprimanded, they retorted, 'We are the judges of these creatures, and why should we not·take our pleasure upon them as those other judges have done upon our masters.' On 27 February 1630 the keeper of the Marshalsea handed over Eliot to Sir Allen Apsley at the Tower Gatehouse in a little ceremony, saying: 'Mr Lieutenant, I have brought you this worthy knight whom I borrowed of you some months ago, and do now repay him again.'

By the end of 1630 all other prisoners except Eliot had secured their release by various means, some making submission and some successfully pleading reasons of a compassionate nature. Alone, the stubborn Eliot lingered in the Tower, sustained only by the visits and letters of such loyal friends as Richard Knightley, Sir Bevil Grenville, Sir Oliver Luke and John Hampden.

Meanwhile young Richard Eliot spent most of his time at Oxford with dubious company in the town rather than at his books in college. In a fatherly letter Eliot asked him to remember that his enemies would make political capital out of Richard's misbehaviour if they could 'to extract some scandal or disadvantage against me'. He begged the boy not 'in the sea of vanity to make shipwreck of all my hopes' and urged him to recover his 'gravity and composure'. Eliot's humanist philosophy, child of both the Renaissance and the Reformation, shines forth from the letter. Beasts have affections, wrote Eliot, but man alone has reason. Therefore 'propound goodness not pleasure for your object. Lose not yourself for liberty, or rather make not liberty a vice.' By the messenger he wrote to Thomas Knightley, the tutor of his two sons, asking him to correct the boy's faults and explaining what provision he had made for their expenses.

'After your pleasure in the Country', wrote Eliot to Hampden on 30 July, 'it may be some entertainment to your leisures to hear from your poor friend in the Tower.' Not that Eliot had much news, except the current talk in the Tower that a Scottish soldier called Sir William Balfour might succeed the deceased Apsley as Lieutenant. Without any intellectual company Eliot amused himself by observing the sight-seers who poured into the massive whitewashed keep to view some additions to the Crown Jewels, such as the silver basin in which the King's son had been christened. Eliot thought that they looked like doves flocking into a white dovecote. The spectacle of a blind clergyman being led into the presence of these earthly baubles promoted a vein of religious meditation in his letter to Hampden describing these parochial events, but he broke off to assure his friend that he had not forgotten the papers.

Bess Eliot, his eldest daughter, lived with Sir Oliver and Lady Luke in Bedfordshire. In August 1630 Eliot replied to a query from them by agreeing that she should have music lessons, and expressing his willingness to pay for the tuition and instruments. The Lukes had decided not to send back the fourteen-year-old girl to her boarding-school in Stepney, but to educate her with their own children. Hampden stayed with the Lukes at Woodend House that summer, and clearly shared their views for he wrote as follows:

> SIR – I write indeed rather to let you know that you are frequent in my thoughts than for any business which at the moment requires it; and if those thoughts can contrive anything that might conduce to my friend's service, I should entertain them with much affection.
>
> This last week I visited Sir Oliver and with him your virtuous daughter, who meets with much happiness by her entertainment in that place, for he is not for a man (to whom you will give suffrages) more complete than his Lady is for a woman friend.
>
> She gives an excellent testimony of your daughter, both in regard to the fruits of former breeding and present tractability; but, if I mistake not, she'll not give consent to her return to the common mistress. Not for any particular blame she can lay upon her, but that in such a mixture of dispositions and humours as must needs be met with in a multitude, there will be much of that which is bad; and that is infectious, where good is not so easily diffusive.
>
> And, in my judgment, there is much more danger in such a nursery than in a school of boys, for, though an ill tincture be dangerous in either, yet it is perfectly recoverable in these, hardly or never in the other.
>
> I have not yet sent for my academic friends by reason of my own employments and absence; but this week I intend it. And when I shall thus again have before me your own picture to the life, I shall the oftener be put in mind to recommend your health and happiness to him only that can give it.
>
> Your faithful friend ever,
>
> JOHN HAMPDEN

Hampden, August 18 [1630]
   Present my love to Wat Long.

This letter reveals Hampden as an exemplar of a most attractive characteristic in the early Puritan tradition, namely a loving care for the spiritual and intellectual life of young girls. Too little notice has been paid by historians to the cultural development of the English middle class, under the influence first of the Renaissance, and then of the Protestant religion. From these two sources there developed a new attitude towards the education of women, and to the relationship between husbands and wives, quite distinct from the traditional beliefs of earlier centuries. Shakespeare's women characters reflect the light and laughter of these new Puritan girls. Where did the well-bred heroine like Juliet or Desdemona – or for that matter Anne Page – find the spirit to defy their fathers over the choice of their husbands? Where did ladies-in-waiting such as Nerissa or Maria learn their easy manners and readiness for a lark? It is possibly the very Puritans exemplified by Hampden, the generation before those narrow, dogmatic and kill-joy enemies of the theatre known today as the Puritans, who provided the educated audiences during the golden age of playwrights between 1590 and 1630; they would both understand Shakespeare's girls of spirit and perhaps recognize in them their own daughters and nieces.

Hampden had clearly given the matter of girls' education some thought, for his own Elizabeth had already reached eight years of age, while Anne was five years old, and below them came Ruth, now two, and the new baby born that year, Mary. Boarding-schools for girls were a comparatively recent innovation: the first of which there is any record being the Ladies Hall at Deptford, which opened at about the time of Shakespeare's death in 1616. Some of the grammar schools re-established or founded in the second half of the previous century had admitted some girls. At Uffington in Berkshire, for example, there is a note in the records for 1637 that girls should not attend the school. For, though it was a 'common and usual course', their presence was 'by many conceived very uncomely and not decent'.

Most wealthy Puritan parents preferred private tuition for their daughters. Lucy Apsley, who was ten years old in 1630 and lived within a bowshot of Sir John Eliot in the Lieutenant's house, could read perfectly at four, and when she was seven years of age she had at one time eight tutors in such subjects as languages, music, dancing, writing and needle-work. She proved to be so apt at Latin that she outstripped her brothers who were at school. By this time she regarded her tutor, her father's chaplain, as 'a pitiful dull fellow'. She turned out to be a book-worm: 'As for music and dancing, I profited very little in them, and would never practise my lute or harpsichord but when my masters were with me; and for my needle I absolutely hated it.'

Eliot replied to Hampden's letter of 18 August two days later, professing yet again his admiration for Hampden's virtues and character. How welcome such correspondence must have been to him we can deduce from his letter five days later to Luke, in which he wrote that 'the deadness of this place prevents all occasion of intelligence, and we are so unactive ourselves, as we are hardly capable of the knowl-edge of what is done by others.'

'My academic friends', as Hampden pleasantly called John and Dick Eliot, had spent their summer vacation at Hampden House, but for some reason they did not come for Christmas; which caused him to wonder. Eliot wrote a letter to Hampden hinting at the reasons why he had not allowed it, but he could only ask his friend to trust him for he could not set down an explanation on paper.

When Hampden wrote again in April, it is clear that both boys had fallen foul of the university authorities. They prob-ably carried a letter by Hampden about their conduct with them to London, for they visited their father that month. In this accompanying letter Eliot found also his friend's criti-cism of the manuscript he had sent him, the first part of 'The Monarchy of Man'. Eliot had made over four hundred quo-tations from close on fifty classical authors, compared with hardly thirty references from the Bible. Although he lapsed occasionally into long-winded pedantry, Eliot wrote primar-ily as an orator, and there are some moving and illuminating passages in praise of Man (to be read by those who today believe that Puritans were essentially anti-humanist). Strangely for one thus imprisoned, Eliot argued that monar-chy is the ideal form of government, best suited to man, but monarchy must be guided by wisdom and virtue. It was a relatively simple though enormously important message, and Hampden clearly thought that it could stand on its own feet. For in a graceful and subtle way, Hampden pointed out to the author the fault of excessive reliance on classical authorities. His gentleness and tact as revealed so plainly in this letter remained prominent characteristics throughout his life:

Sir – I hope you will receive your sons both safe, and that God will direct you to dispose of them as they may be trained up for His service and to your comfort. Some words I have had with your younger son, and given him a taste of those apprehensions he is like to find with you – which, I tell him, future obedience to your pleasure rather than justification of past passages must remove.

He professeth faith, and the ingenuousness of his nature doth it without words; but you know virtuous actions flow not infallibly from the flexiblest dispositions: there's only a fit subject for admonition and government to work on, especially that which is paternal.

I confess my shallowness to resolve, and therefore unwillingness to say, anything concerning his course; yet will I not give over the consideration because I much desire to see that spirit rightly managed.

But, as for your elder, I think you may with security return him in convenient time; for certainly there is nothing to administer from a plot, and, in another action that concerned himself which he'll tell you of, he received good satisfaction of the Vice Chancellor's fair carriage towards him.

I searched my study this morning for a book to send you of a like subject to that of the papers I had of you, but find it not. As soon as I recover it, I'll recommend it to your view.

When you have finished the other part, I pray think me as worthy of the sight of it as the former; and in both together I'll betray my weakness to my friend by declaring my sense of them. That I did see is an exquisite nosegay, composed of curious flowers, bound together with as fine a thread. But I must in the end expect honey from my friend – somewhat out of these flowers digested, made his own, and giving a true taste of his own sweetness: though for that I shall await a fitter time and place.

The Lord sanctify unto you the sourness of your present estate and the comforts of your posterity.

Yours ever the same assured friend,

John Hampden

April 4th, 1631

After long discourses with Richard, his father concluded that he was 'more apt, I think, for action than study', and he sent him off to the Lowlands to become a soldier under Sir Edward Harwood. Not wishing to fall a step behind his younger brother, John Eliot now expressed a reluctance to return to Oxford. Eliot decided to allow him to continue his education in Paris, and within a week the two boys had taken ship for the Continent, leaving their father to explain matters to Lincoln College. Their tutor Thomas Knightley accepted the decision to remove Dick from Oxford as 'most welcome', although he thought that the ending of John's studies at the university should have been 'less speedy'. The tutor enclosed their account, which included fourpence for mending stockings and a bookbinder's bill for their 'introductions to astronomy' which the lads had ordered but not paid for.

Eliot's precipitate action in ending the university careers of both boys evoked the longest of all the letters from Hampden's pen. Although he did not agree with Bishop Hall of Exeter, who had recently written a book against the practice of educating young men on the Continent, Hampden made it clear that he would have rather seen John sent to Cambridge. Nor was Hampden entirely satisfied with the plan for Richard for he had a 'crotchet' (a musical term for a whim,) which might have involved him. What Hampden had in mind we do not know, but it may have been some sort of educational experiment.

> SIR – I am so perfectly acquainted with your clear insight into the dispositions of men and ability to fit them with courses suitable, that, had you bestowed sons of mine as you have done your own, my judgment durst hardly have called it into question: especially when, in laying the design, you have prevented the objections to be made against it. For if Mr Richard Eliot will, in the intermissions of action, add study to practice, and adorn that lively spirit with flowers of contemplation, he'll raise our expectations of another Sir Edward Vere, that had this character: 'All summer in the field, all winter in the study'; in whose fall fame makes this kingdom a great loser. And, having taken this resolution from counsel with the Highest Wisdom (which I doubt not you have) I hope and pray the same Power will crown it with a blessing answerable to our wish.
>
> The way you take with my other friend declares you to be

none of the Bishop of Exeter's converts, of whose mind neither am I superstitiously; but had my opinion been asked, I should (as vulgar conceits use to do) have showed my power rather to raise objections than to answer them. A temper between France and Oxford might have taken away his scruple, with more advantage to his years: to visit Cambridge as a free man for variety and delight, and there entertained himself till the next spring, when University studies and peace had been better settled than I learn it is.

For, although he be one of those that, if his age were looked for in no other book but that of the mind, would be found no ward if you should die tomorrow, yet 'tis a great hazard, methinks, to see so sweet a disposition guarded with no more amongst a people whereof many make it their religion to be superstitious in impiety, and their behaviour to be affected in ill manners. But God, who only knows the periods of life and opportunities to come, hath designed him (I hope) for His own service betime, and stirred up your providence to husband him so early for great affairs. Then shall he be sure to find Him in France that Abraham did in Gerar and Joseph in Egypt, under whose wing alone is perfect safety.

Concerning that Lord [the Earl of Castlehaven, imprisoned in the Tower for incest] who is now reported to be as deep in repentance as he was profound in sin, the papers, et cetera, I shall take leave from your favour and my strait of time to be silent till the next week, when I hope for happiness to kiss your hands, and present you with my most humble thanks for your letters, which confirm the observation I have made in the progress of affections: that it is easier much to win upon ingenious natures than to merit it. This, they tell me I have done of yours: and I account it a noble purchase which to improve, with the best services you can command and I perform, shall be the care of

Your affectionate friend and servant,

JOHN HAMPDEN

Hampden, May 11, 1631

Present my services to Mr Long, Mr Valentine, etc.

Do not think by what I say that I am fully satisfied of your younger son's course intended, for I have a crotchet out of the ordinary way which I had acquainted you with if I had spoken with you before he had gone, but am almost ashamed to communicate.

Eliot wrote to Hampden later that month 'from my summer house i'th Tower' to recommend to his friend one Thomas

Wyan, a solicitor who had served him well when he was
Vice-Admiral of Devon but now wanted employment.
Hampden assured him that he had not trespassed beyond
the bounds of friendship by this request to help Mr Wyan in
what ways he could:

> SIR, – I received your commands by the hands of Mr Wyan and
> was glad to know by them that another's word had power to
> command your faith in my readiness to obey you, which mine, it
> seems, had not. If you yet lack an experience, I wish you had put
> me upon the test of a work more difficult and important, that
> your opinion might be changed into belief.
>
> That man you wrote for, I will unfeignedly receive into my
> good opinion, and declare it really when he shall have occasion
> to put me to the proof.
>
> I cannot trouble you with many words this time. Make good
> use of the book you shall receive from me, and of your time. Be
> sure you shall render a strict account of both to
>
> > Your ever assured friend and servant,
> >
> > JOHN HAMPDEN
>
> Hampden, June 8th, 1631
>
> Present my service to Mr Long. I would fain hear of his health.

By the end of June Hampden had finished reading 'The
Monarchy of Man', and he returned the manuscript with a
letter to the author. Clearly Eliot had not heeded his earlier
suggestion that the writer should speak more for himself and
reduce the lengthy quotations and allusions to antiquity. Yet
Hampden again pointed out these faults with a rare sensitivity and a gentleness of touch:

> SIR – You shall receive the book I promised by this bearer's
> immediate hand; for the other papers I presume to take a little –
> and but a little – respite. I have looked upon that rare piece only
> with a superficial view; as at first sight to take the aspect and
> proportion in the whole; after, with a more accurate eye, to take
> out the lineaments of every part. 'Twere rashness in me, there-
> fore, to discover any judgment before I have ground to make
> one.
>
> This I discern, that 'tis as complete an image of the pattern as
> can be drawn by lines; a lively character of a large mind; the
> subject, method and expressions, excellent and homogenial,
> and, to say truth (sweet heart) somewhat exceeding my com-
> mendations. My words cannot render them to the life, yet (to
> show my ingenuousness rather than wit) would not a less model

have given a full representation of that subject? – not by diminu-
tion, but by contradiction, of parts. I desire to learn; I dare not
say. The variations upon each particular seem many; all, I
confess, excellent.

The fountain was full, the channel narrow – that may be the
cause. Or that the author imitated Virgil, who made more
verses by many than he intended to write. To extract a just
number, had I seen all his, I could easily have bid him make
fewer; but, if he had bidden me tell which he should have
spared, I had been a-posed.

So I say of these expressions; and that to satisfy you, not
myself, but that, by obeying you in a command so contrary to
my own disposition, you may measure how large a power you
have over

JOHN HAMPDEN

Hampden, June 29th 1631

Recommend my service to Mr Long and, if Sir Oliver Luke be
in Town, express my affection to him in these words; the first
part of the papers you had by the hands of B. Valentine long
since. If you hear of your sons, or can send to them, let me know.

These letters are important not least because they reveal
some clues to Hampden's later effectiveness as a politician.
He praised before he criticized. He stressed his own limita-
tions. He guided by asking questions. Through them all
breathes the warm, generous and disciplined spirit of a
deeply Christian and civilized man. Writing on 19 July in
tortuous prose and at some length, Eliot thanked Hampden
for his letter. He defended his extensive use of quotations in
'The Monarchy of Man' on the grounds that politics lend
themselves to such treatment and that all writers cite
authorities in this fashion. Moreover, Eliot added, he had
discarded quite a number of citations already and he wanted
Hampden to be more specific in his criticism of the remainder. He had received news from his son John in France but
'the Souldier I have not heard of'. Could Hampden return
the rest of his manuscript?

Dear Sir – I received a letter from you last week, for which I
owe you ten, to countervail those lines by excess in number that
I cannot equal in weight. But time is not mine now, nor hath
been since that came to my hands. In your favour, therefore,
hold me excused.

The bearer is appointed to present you with a buck out of my paddock, which must be a small one to hold proportion with the place and soil it was bred in.

Shortly I hope (if I do well to hope) to see you; yet durst I not prolong the expectation of your papers. You have concerning them laid commands upon me beyond my ability to give you satisfaction in; but, if my apology will not serve when we meet, I will not decline the service to the betraying of my own ignorance, which yet I hope your love will cover.

Your ever assured friend and servant,

JOHN HAMPDEN

Hampden, July 28, 1631

I am heartily glad to learn my friend is well in France. Captain Waller hath been in these parts, whom I have seen, but could not entertain; to my shame and sorrow I speak it.

During 1631 news of the campaigns of Gustavus Adolphus of Sweden against Count Tilly, supreme commander of the forces of the Catholic League, reached England and encouraged every Protestant heart. Tilly had stormed Magdeburg and massacred the garrison in May but in the Battle of Breitenfeld on 17 September his army, 34,000 strong, suffered defeat at the hands of the combined Swedish and Saxon armies with a loss of between 7,000 and 12,000 men. Besides elevating Gustavus Adolphus to the heights of fame as 'the lion of the North', this important battle paved the way for a Swedish offensive against the stronghold of Catholic power in Europe. Also it occasioned much diplomatic activity, not least by the English government mindful of the interests of the dispossessed ex-Elector Palatine. 'I interrupt your quiet in the country', wrote Eliot to Hampden on 23 September, in a letter sending news of these events. 'If at once', he wrote, 'the whole world be not deluded, fortune and hope are met.' The Tower buzzed with the news that the Lieutenant, Sir William Balfour, had been named as an emissary to Brussels. Some days later Hampden replied in a good humour:

SIR – In the end of my travails I meet the messengers of your love, which bring me a most grateful welcome. Your intentions outfly mine, that thought to have prevented yours, and convince me of my disability to keep pace with you or the times.

My employment of late in interrogatory with like affairs hath deprived me of leisure to compliment, and the frame of depositions is able to jostle the style of a letter!

You were far enough above my emulation before; but, breathing now the same air with an ambassador, you are out of all aim. I believe well of his negotiation for the large testimony you have given of his parts; and I believe the King of Sweden's sword will be the best of his topics to persuade a peace. 'Tis a powerful one now, if I hear aright; fame giving Tilly a late defeat in Saxony with 20,000 loss; the truth whereof will facilitate our work – the Spaniard's courtesy being known to be no less than willingly to render that which he cannot hold.

The notion of these effects interrupts not our quiet, though the reasons by which they are governed do transcend our pitch. Your apprehensions, that ascend a region above those clouds which shadow us, are fit to pierce such heights; and others to receive such notions as descend from thence; which while you are pleased to impart, you make the demonstrations of your favour to become the rich possession of

Your ever faithful friend and servant,

JOHN HAMPDEN

Hampden, October 3rd, 1631

God, I thank Him hath made me father of another son.

The autumn leaves fell once more, and cold grey mists arose on the bosom of the river and invaded the Tower. As the weather grew colder the Tower authorities – acting on orders emanating from Court – assigned another room to Eliot and placed restrictions upon certain of his visitors. In a letter asking for a word or two from Hampden about those translations in 'The Monarchy of Man' which he had 'excepted at', Eliot informed him of these changes:

My lodgings are removed and I am now where candlelight may be suffered but scarce fire . . . . None but my servants, hardly my sons, may have admittance to me. My friends I must desire, for their own sakes, to forbear coming to the Tower. You amongst them are chief, and have the first place in this intelligence.

In March 1632 Eliot fell sick. On the 15th he wrote to Richard Knightley a brief account of his ailment:

It comes originally from my cold, with which the cough, having been long upon me, causes such ill effects to follow it that the symptoms are more dangerous than the grief. It has weakened much both the appetite and concoction, and the outward strength. By that, some doubt there is of a consumption; but we endeavour to prevent it by application of the means, and as the Great Physician seek the blessings from the Lord. He only knows the state of soul and body, and in his wisdom orders all things for his children as it is best for both. Our duty is submission to the cross which he lays on us, who in his mercy likewise will give us strength to bear it.

Hampden may have heard about Eliot's indisposition, although their correspondence lapsed until March 1632. He renewed it with a suitably penitential letter, which hints at his busy life at Hampden House. His postscript, referring to the presence of Dick with his father, suggests that news of Eliot had reached him, probably from the Lukes:

> NOBLE SIR – 'Tis well for me that letters cannot blush, else you would easily read me guilty. I am ashamed of so long a silence and know not how to excuse it, for as nothing but business can speak for me, of which kind I have many advocates, so can I not tell how to call any business greater than holding an affectionate correspondence with so excellent a friend.
>
> My only confidence is I plead at a bar of love, where absolutions are much more frequent than censures. Sure I am that conscience of neglect doth not accuse me, though evidence of fact doth. I would add more, but the entertainment of a stranger-friend calls upon me, and one other inevitable occasion. Hold me excused, therefore, dear friend, and if you vouchsafe me a letter, let me beg of you to teach me some thrift of time, that I may employ more in your service, who will ever be
> Your faithful servant and affectionate friend,
> JOHN HAMPDEN
> Commend my service to the soldier, if not gone to his colours.
> Hampden, March 21, 1632

Eliot in his reply, dated the following day, urged Hampden to return his papers: 'quit you in this as speedily as you can', he chided with humour, 'for without it you are faulty'. He understood, however, the reasons for Hampden's silence:

> I know your many entertainments and small leisure, and myself unworthy to interrupt the least particular of your thoughts. It satisfies me to have the assurance of your friendship and, when it was allowable, that I had the fruition of yourself.

But Eliot could not shake off the wasting disease of consumption. On 29 March he wrote to Hampden saying that he had been out of his bed for three days, for the physicians could only recommend fresh air and exercise. But each time he returned to his chamber he 'brought in new impressions of the cold'. His appetite and strength improved but 'heat and tenderness by close keeping my chamber has increased my weakness'. This letter, the last to survive from the pen of Eliot, contained a long paeon of praise of 'our Master' Christ and a stout profession of the author's Christian faith. Disease could not waste such a master-spirit:

> This, dear friend, must be the comfort of his children; this is the physic we must use in all our sickness and extremities; this is the strengthening of the weak, the enriching of the poor, the liberty of the captive, the health of the diseased, the life of those that die, the death of that wretched life of sin! And this happiness have his saints. The contemplation of this happiness has led me almost beyond the compass of a letter; but the haste I use unto my friends, and the affection that does move it, will I hope excuse me.
>
> Friends should communicate their joys; this, as the greatest therefore, I could not but impart unto my friend, being herein moved by the present speculation of your letters, which always have the grace of much intelligence, and are a happiness to him that is truly yours,
>
> J.E.

Not content with this literary testimony, Eliot commissioned a remarkable portrait of himself. The artist painted him in the Tower, dressed in his laced nightgown as if he were standing up beside his sickbed. He holds a tortoiseshell comb in one hand, while the other hand rests defiantly on his hip. The hair certainly needed combing. Eliot's black eyes gaze steadily at the beholder from his sallow, tired face. More than 'The Monarchy of Man' or even his letters, this painting portrays the essential spirit of the leader whom Hampden loved.

The King refused a petition from Eliot asking him 'to set me at liberty, that, for the recovery of my health, I may take some fresh air'. For Eliot offered no submission: he intended to return to the Tower as soon as he had recovered his health, 'there to undergo such punishment as God has allotted to me'. In a vindictive mood, the King would grant no mercy. On 27 November 1632 Eliot died in his smoky dark cell in the Tower of London. When his son John petitioned for the right to bury the corpse of his father at the family home of Port Eliot, King Charles himself wrote on the document: 'Let Sir John Eliot's body be buried in the Church of that parish where he died.'

Chapter Five

AT HAMPDEN HOUSE

God has blessed me with a competent fortune, and given me a mind (it is his gift) fitted to enjoy that blessing. In that retired way I enjoyed myself freely . . . in the kingdom of mine own mind, without other thoughts than such as might arise from quiet seas, looking upon public affairs as men use to look upon pictures, at a distance.

SIR WILLIAM WALLER

During the years after 1629 the large rambling house on the hill at Great Hampden, besieged by farm buildings and outhouses, was occupied by a young garrison of John Hampden's children and their friends. Perhaps like many Puritan couples, John and Elizabeth Hampden may have heard sung the words of the 128th Psalm at their wedding on Midsummer Day 1619: 'Thy wife shall be as the fruitful vine: upon the walls of thine house; thy children like the olive-branches: round about thy table.' Certainly in their case the promise was fulfilled. Elizabeth bore her husband nine 'hopeful' children. John, the firstborn, would serve as a soldier in the Civil War, dying at a tragically young age in the spring of 1643. His brothers, Richard and William, born respectively in 1631 and 1633, both survived into maturity. According to the Royalist newspaper *Mercurius Aulicus* in 1643 one of these two sons 'is said to be a Cripple, and the other a Lunatick', but there is no other evidence to support either assertion.

His beloved eldest daughter, born in 1622, who married Richard Knightley of Fawsley in Northamptonshire (a cousin of Eliot's friend of the same name), would also die young in 1643. Anne, her younger sister by three years, eventually married Sir Robert Pye, while Ruth, born in 1628, one day married a Sussex gentleman called Sir John Trevor. Mary, born in 1630 during these years of Hampden's quiet life in Buckinghamshire, married first Colonel Robert Hammond (later Governor of Carisbrooke Castle and jailer of King Charles), and then Sir John Hobart of Blickling in Norfolk. There were two other daughters who both died unmarried, one of them certainly before 1643, whose names are not known. Both Richard Knightley and Sir Robert Pye sat as members of the Long Parliament, and Richard one day would help George Monck to restore the Stuarts to the English throne.

From papers and correspondence of the Verney family, who inhabited Claydon House some sixteen miles as the crow flies to the north-west of Great Hampden, the world of the Hampden household can in our imaginations be reconstructed. How was the house furnished? Sir Edmund Verney lived at Claydon with his twelve children. His heir, Sir Ralph, ordered an inventory soon after his father's death. Writing from exile in France to his brother, he mentions:

> the odd things in the room my mother kept herself, the iron closet, the little room between her beds head and the backstairs, the little and great fripperies [i.e. hanging closets for gowns], your own green wrought velvet furniture, the red velvet furniture, the looking-glasses (there should be at least four), leather carpets for the dining and drawing rooms, the stools with nails gilt, the great cabinet like yours, the tapestry, the great branch candlestick, all such wrought work as my mother had from London and was not finished, the book of martyrs and other books in the with-drawing room, the preserving room, the spicery with furnaces and brewing vessels, plate left for the children's use, all the locks that are loose in the closet . . .

A household community such as those at Claydon or Hampden lived a self-sufficient life. Their members churned milk and ground meal, baked bread and brewed beer. They bred, fed and slew their beeves and sheep, and reared poultry and pigeons at their own doors. Their planks were sawn at home, their horses shod and their rough ironwork was forged and mended. The slaughter-house, the blacksmith's, carpenter's and painter's workshops, the malting and brewhouse, the

John Hampden

Views of London in 1616 drawn by C.J. Visscher

Hampden's daughter, Ruth, with her husband, Sir John Trevor, and family

The trial of Strafford, 1641, from an engraving by Wenceslas Hollar

The House of Commons, from an engraving by John Glover

THE TRVE MANER OF TH
...les of Parliament, upon the trye...

A. The Kings Mai.ᵗⁱᵉ
B His feate of ſtate.
C the Queenes Mai.ᵗⁱᵉ
D the Prince his highnes.
E. Thomas Earle of Arundell,
    Lord high Steward of England

F. the Lord Keeper.
G the Lord Marques of
H the Lord high Cham
    of England,
I the Lord Chamberl
    his Mai.ᵗ houſhold,

TING OF THE LORDS & COMMONS OF BOTH HOW
nas Earle of Stratford, Lord Lieutenant of Ireland, 1641

the Lord cheefe Iustice of the Kings bench,	O. the Mrs of the Chancery.	T. the Clarkes
2 Pryui Councellers,	P. the Earles,	V. the Earle of Stratford.
the Mr of the rolls.	Q. the Vicecounts,	W. the Lieutenant of the Tower.
the Iudges and Barons of the Exchequer.	R. the Barons.	X. the Plaintiues.
ldest Sonnes of some of the Nobility.	S. the Knights, Cittizens, & burgeses of the howse of Commons,	Y. the Deputis councell & officers
		Z. the Countes of Arundell.

SIR JOHN ELIOT
Painted a few days before
his Death in the Tower
A. D. 1632.

Sir John Eliot, dressed in his nightshirt. This portrait was painted
shortly before his death

wood-yard stacked with timber, the sawpit with logs cut for
burning, the laundry, the dairy with a large churn turned by
a horse, the stables, stalls and barns, the apple and root
outhouses: all of them served the needs of the Hampden
family and household.

The difficulty of keeping cattle and sheep alive in the
winter on the scanty stores of hay meant that the practice of
killing and salting down most of the herd and flock continued
until about the middle of the century, when improved farm-
ing methods made a shy appearance. Thus fresh meat was
eaten mainly during the summer months up to about Mar-
tinmas. Among the Verney letters there is frequent mention
of skin diseases – caused by the salt diet, unrelieved by
vegetables for many months – especially among the women
and children. Thus any fish or game must have been most
welcome during the winter months. The only note we have
on John Hampden's appearance mentions such a skin disease. Sir Philip Warwick, who saw him often in the House of
Commons, says that 'his blood in its temper was acrimonious, as the scurf on his face showed'.

Within doors the activity of the family and household was
as busy as the work in the pastures and beechwoods, workshops and outhouses. The spinning of wool and flax (so
common that an unmarried woman of any rank became
known as 'a spinster'), embroidering and plying the bone
needle, cooking, curing meats, preserving fruit and distilling
essences went on incessantly. Lace-making had been introduced into Buckinghamshire by Katherine of Aragon, and
possibly one of the maids or daughters of the house would
learn that craft. In the still-room the womenfolk worked
making fruit syrups and jellies, vinegar and pickles. The
home-made wines – currant, cowslip and elder – were
important drinks at a time when tea, coffee, and chocolate
were unknown. No doubt Elizabeth Hampden kept a large
chest for herbs and medicines full of 'decoctions, infusions,
and essences' she had prepared herself in the copper pans
and vats of the distillery.

Gardens occupied much attention at this time. The
Hampdens would have grown many vegetables, such as the
potato which Sir Walter Raleigh had introduced into the

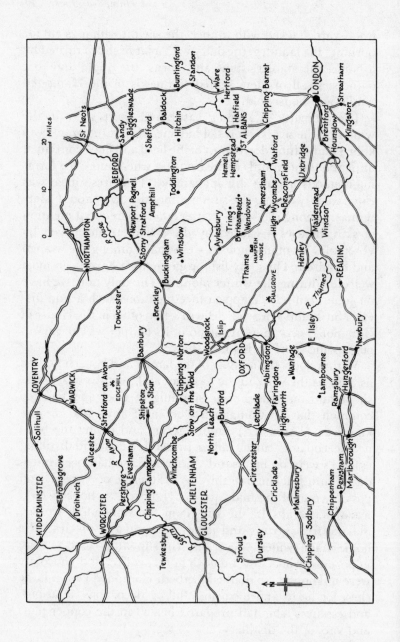

South Midlands

country. Travellers on the Continent sent or brought home seeds and roots of all kinds. Vines and fig trees stood beside the walls of the garden, with a profusion of flowers in the beds, including perhaps some of the 'Persian tulips and ranoncules' from Holland which certainly grew at Claydon House alongside pinks, gilliflowers, melon seeds and pear-grafts. At Hampden House the gardens, set with boxhedges and yew trees, stood under the cool shade of lofty elms, the breeze perpetually whispering in their branches.

This growing interest in gardens illustrates the more general cultivation by the Puritan gentry of the private and domestic life, where they thought that true joys were to be found. They would contrast the secluded peace and beauty of their gardens with the public parks of London, where women paraded in a never-ending Vanity Fair of the fading world. Andrew Marvell, who was tutor to the daughter of General Fairfax, has left us a vivid picture of that godly man, retired from office as Lord General of the New Model Army, quietly at work in his garden at Nunappleton House in Yorkshire. In his poem 'A Garden, Written after the Civil Wars', composed at Nunappleton where 'the arching boughs unite between the columns of the temple green', Marvell captured that deep feeling of longing which must have besieged the hearts of the Puritan commanders-in-arms as they sighed for the day:

> When gardens only had their towers,
> And all the garrisons were flowers;
> When roses only arms might bear,
> And men did rosy garlands wear.

The deep interest in God as more important than earthly concerns bore other active fruits in the lives of the Puritans. Their purity of life and respect for women made them truly chivalrous to ladies in need or distress. In the Civil War this particular virtue was exemplified by Sir William Waller, who treated the Cavalier ladies who fell into his power with a singularly graceful courtesy and kindness. John Milton's *Comus*, a masque written for performance at Ludlow Castle in 1634, reveals the spiritual value which the Puritans saw in chastity as well as temperance. Their attitude owed nothing to a prudish dislike of sex. Chastity is 'a hidden strength' which comes to those who look to Heaven for all gifts and graces:

> *Mortals, that would follow me,*
> *Love Virtue; she alone is free.*
> *She can teach you how to climb*
> *Higher than the sphery chime;*
> *Or, if Virtue feeble were,*
> *Heaven itself would stoop to her.*

The Puritan husband and wife saw the hand of Providence in the prosaic events which brought them together. As they had received each other from God, so they looked to him to sustain them in a spiritual relationship with each other. In marriage they came to a deeper knowledge of their partners. Lucy Hutchinson wrote a glowing testimony to her husband's noble Christian character. Clearly she admired and loved him deeply. But the book is also a revelation of herself, and we can glimpse there something of the joy that young Puritan gentlemen certainly found in marriage to such daughters of their faith. More than bed-and-board fellows, they were companions in spirit. Thus they experienced a deep sense of unity which nothing could shake. As William Penn wrote home to his wife from New England: 'Those who are united beyond the world cannot be separated by it.'

These large Puritan families valued the unreproved joys of country life. At meal times the conversation was spiced with humour and wit. Some fathers, like Cromwell, enjoyed fooling around with their children. Hunting, hawking, fencing, bowling, dancing, making music and playing chess balanced all that hard bookwork at school or with the tutor. John Hampden had immersed himself in such activities during his youth and there is no reason to suppose that he denied them to his children. He had certainly become a more grave man, but not out of any natural or sudden ill-humour. Meditation and prayer, historical study and perhaps reflection upon his own life and times induced this certain gravity of mind. Yet he retained the serenity of countenance of a man who has cause for contentment and knows it. His children probably saw still in him – his friends certainly did – that true lightness of heart which had characterized his early years.

Between 1632 and 1638 Milton lived in the south Buckinghamshire village of Horton, not twenty miles from Great Hampden, and he wrote *L'Allegro* during his time there. The poem evokes the countryside of Buckinghamshire, and the high spirits of those large young Puritan families who enjoyed it to the full. Milton saw Mirth as a carefree delight in all the cheerful sights and sounds of nature and natural social conversation. He includes the plays of Shakespeare and Ben Jonson in this large sphere of unreproved pleasure. It is attractive to think that Milton may have visited Hampden House, and have seen the flocks of sheep nibbling on the Chiltern slopes. Certainly he journeyed to Ashridge House, just over the border of the county some thirteen miles to the north-east of Great Hampden, where the Earl of Bridgewater's eight daughters lived before moving with their father to Ludlow.

> *Haste thee nymph and join with thee*
> *Jest and youthful jollity . . .*
> *Sport that wrinkled care derides,*
> *And Laughter holding both his sides.*
> *Come, and trip it as ye go*
> *On the light fantastick toe . . .*
> *Oft list'ning how the hounds and horn*
> *Cheerly rouse the slumbring morn . . .*
> *While the plowman near at hand,*
> *Whistles o'er the furrowed land,*
> *And the milkmaid singeth blithe,*
> *And the mower whets his scythe,*
> *And every shepherd tells his tale*
> *Under the hawthorn in the dale.*

Besides drawing women up towards equality through the partnership of 'holy matrimony', the Puritan gentry also paved the way for wider social changes. In 1642 Thomas Fuller, a divine who served as chaplain in the Royalist Army, wrote of the yeoman of the day as 'a gentleman in ore, whom the next age may see refined'. The Puritan gentry certainly saw in many yeoman the makings of true Christians. This knowledge was connected with the steady development of

Puritan 'good works', such as the foundation of schools and alms-houses, and the countless local acts of Samaritan kindness. Colonel Hutchinson, for example, 'had a loving and sweet courtesy to the poorest'. When a great storm blew down a shed on Sir Edmund Verney's estate, he could write: 'I am glad my hovel fell on no Christian creature.' In his anxiety to make sure that neither man nor beast had suffered injury, Verney quite omits to raise any questions in that letter about the financial cost of the damage. Letters asking for help of various kinds – jobs for relatives or brides for sons – fill portfolio after portfolio in the Verney correspondence. Had John Hampden's own papers survived, they would probably have told the same tale.

The development of a living Puritan faith and way of life among common folk such as John Bunyan paved the way for the social revolution of our own time. Oliver Cromwell, who both sensed and harnessed this new source of spiritual energy in the land, had an advantage in that he stood closer in the social order to the yeomen farmers and tradesmen than John Hampden, a man of considerable wealth and property. But Hampden probably shared his emphasis upon the value of character and spirit above social rank and status. One story of the rise of a common man involved them both. Thomas Shelbourne, who worked for Hampden as a shepherd 'in which capacity he served him for many years', received a commission in the Buckinghamshire militia. During the Civil War he rose to be Lieutenant-Colonel in Cromwell's double regiment of 'Ironsides'; and when the regiment was divided, he commanded one part with the rank of Colonel until his death in Ireland in 1651.

In August 1634 John Hampden suffered a severe blow in the loss of his wife Elizabeth, probably in childbirth. Hampden received the death of Elizabeth with characteristic humble faith in God, although he measured for us his loss in the graceful epitaph which he composed for her. He bore his affliction like a Christian, and it prepared him for the next uphill leagues of the pilgrimage he had shared with her. In composing her epitaph Hampden expressed perfectly the spirit of their marriage:

TO THE ETERNAL MEMORY
OF THE TRULY VIRTUOUS AND PIOUS
ELIZABETH HAMPDEN,
WIFE OF JOHN HAMPDEN, OF GREAT HAMPDEN,
ESQUIRE.
SOLE DAUGHTER AND HEIRE OF EDMUND SYMEON
OF PYRTON, IN THE COUNTY OF OXON, ESQUIRE.
THE TENDER MOTHER OF A HAPPY OFFSPRING
IN 9 HOPEFUL CHILDREN

In her pilgrimage,
The staie and comfort of her neighbours,
The love and glory of a well-ordered family,
The delight and happiness of tender parents—
But a crown of Blessings to a husband.
In a wife, to all an eternall paterne of goodness
And cause of love, while she was
In her dissolution
A losse invaluable to each,
Yet herselfe blest, and they fully recompenced
In her translation, from a Tabernacle of Claye
And Fellowship with Mortalls, to a celestiall Mansion
And communion with a Deity.

20 DAY OF AUGUST 1634,
JOHN HAMPDEN, HER SORROWFUL HUSBAND,
IN PERPETUALL TESTIMONY OF HIS CONIUGAL
LOVE,
HATH DEDICATED THIS MONUMENT.

The loss undoubtedly served to purify and strengthen his spirit. Beneath Hampden's familiar pleasant smile, unfailing courtesy and easy charm, contemporaries sensed a firmer commitment to the public good. Perhaps he needed the fire and heat of personal tragedy to temper the many layers of his personality opposite qualities of strength and flexibility.

In a letter to Sir Henry Vane the elder, written on 26 August 1634, Hampden gave his 'sad affliction' as a reason for not replying sooner about a business discussion he had held with a Mr House and a Mr Chadbourne, probably about the sale of some property. Their demands (the lowest being above eight years purchase) seemed so high, Hampden explained, that he made them no certain offer at that time. Hampden's contact with Vane illustrates the width of his circle of acquaintances. A courtier and royal official of long experience, Vane did not lightly miss opportunities to increase his estate. By 1640 he had acquired lands worth £3,000 a year. Later he became Treasurer of the Household and Secretary of State, although he and his son, also named Henry, ultimately sided with Parliament against the King.

In 1634 Vane attended the proceedings against a Puritan barrister called William Prynne and acquiesced in the decisions about the brutal penalties. Thus he was no friend of Hampden, who disliked the ecclesiastical policies of William Laud. The year before Elizabeth Hampden's death Laud had become Archbishop of Canterbury. Thereupon he intensified his campaign to defend the Church of England and its bishops from Puritan sedition. He had already chosen to make an example of a Scottish minister called Alexander Leighton, who in a tract entitled *Sion's Plea against the Prelacy* had exhorted the people to kill all bishops by smiting them under the fifth rib, and for good measure denounced the Queen as a Romish idolatress, a present-day Canaanite. After sentence by the Court of Star Chamber, the sixty-year-old divine was committed to the Fleet Prison, but made his escape to Bedfordshire. Recaptured and brought back to London, Leighton endured the full wrath of Laud. He was severely whipped before being stood at the pillory in Cheapside, where he had one of his ears cut off, one side of his nose slit and was branded on one cheek with a red-hot iron with the letters S.S. signifying a 'Stirrer up of Sedition'. After a week the other side of his face was mutilated in like fashion. William Prynne, John Bastwick, Henry Burton and John Lilburne also learned the hard way that agitators against the now firmly-entrenched ecclesiastical order could expect no mercy from Archbishop Laud.

Laud did play the part of an overbearing prelate, but in his way he sought the same end as the Puritans, namely the purification of the Church of England into a more holy and Christian institution. His failure lay in a lack of understanding of the laity and their theological nature. His changes could be interpreted as an attempt to restore the position and status of the priesthood and thus to make the Church of England more priestly and Catholic while remaining outside the allegiance of Rome. A majority of the articulate English laity, however, soon became Puritans and as such they stood considerably closer to the Reformation than did the Laudian clergy. The Elizabethan settlement of the Church was intended to be a compromise between the Catholic tradition and the new Reformation theology, but it left the door open for further conflict.

In 1634 Laud ordered a general visitation in order to begin the work of tightening up the ecclesiastical discipline of clergy and laity alike. In October 1634 Sir Nicholas Brent, the Vicar-General, reported that John Hampden had been reprimanded for holding a muster in the churchyard at Beaconsfield. With Sir Edmund Verney and the other deputy lieutenants responsible for the military readiness of the county Hampden had summoned the trained bands of the militia for inspection and possibly some drill at Beaconsfield. The Laudians disliked such a profane use of consecrated ground, and attempted to stamp out the practice. But the informer who denounced Hampden to the Church authorities himself suffered the spleen of the gentry.

Both Sir Edmund Verney and John Hampden had also fallen short in the matter of attendance at their parish churches. Possibly the vicar of Great Hampden who replaced Egeon Askew in 1630 had lost his fervour, or could not satisfy the deeper spiritual needs of an intellectual Puritan such as John Hampden. Yet Sir Nicholas Brent reported in October 1634 that Hampden had given so much satisfaction about this charge of 'going sometimes from his own parish church', and so much assurance of his willing obedience in the future to the laws of the Church, that he decided to proceed no further with the case. A contemporary clergyman records, however, that the injunctions of the Vicar-General were kept for a day or two in Buckinghamshire – and then forgotten. In 1638 Hampden, as patron, appointed to the parish church of Great Hampden an eminent Puritan divine, named William Spurstow, who subsequently served as chaplain to his regiment in the Civil War.

On 28 June 1636 Hampden drew up his will. He wished to be buried under one plain gravestone of marble, with engraved portraits of himself, his wife and their children and the inscription *In Christo mortuus, Christum resurrecturus, cum Christo regnaturus*. In the event this wish was not carried out and in order to see what John Hampden had in mind it is necessary to visit Penn Church, about six miles south-east of Great Hampden, where there are brasses set in gravestones commemorating William Penn, his wife and children. These brass portraits, laid down in 1639, probably came from the hand of the craftsmen who would have made the plates for John Hampden. But in 1643 all the brass available went to the cannon foundries.

The will includes an arrangement whereby Hampden conveyed lands and tenements to some relatives and friends as trustees in order to pay his executors – his mother and his father-in-law – a sum of £14,000, sufficient for them to give his younger children small annuities. These trustees included Sir Gilbert Gerrard of Harrow in Middlesex, Richard Knightley of Preston in Northamptonshire, Richard Hampden of Emmington in Oxfordshire, and Edmund Waller the younger of Beaconsfield. Hampden's man-servant received £50 and his 'loving neighbour' Thomas Stile of Little Missenden £10. On 30 June 1642, following the marriage of Elizabeth to Richard Knightley junior and Anne to Sir Robert Pye, Hampden added a codicil to the will to allow for the fact that he had paid out two dowries of £2,500 and £2,000 respectively.

During the two decades before the Civil War, Hampden served as a justice of the peace in Buckinghamshire. No doubt he saw this unpaid work as a part of his Christian vocation to serve his neighbour, and he seems to have applied himself diligently to it. He was never a justice of the 'quorum': those justices, usually of special qualifications, whose presence was necessary to constitute a bench. Nor did he confine himself to one area. In 1634, for example, he was a justice in Aylesbury Hundred, while in 1636 he served in the Wycombe division.

Justices possessed both judicial and administrative functions. Pairs of magistrates meeting in their own parishes
might deal with such minor offences as petty larceny. More
serious misdemeanours such as grand larceny and rioting
were reserved for the Quarter Sessions, held four times a
year in the chief county towns. The justices of the Quarter
Sessions in their turn reserved cases involving treason, mur-
der, and rape for trial at the Assizes conducted by the king's
judges. On the more administrative side, the justices super-
vised the operation of the poor laws, the statutes of labour-
ers, the bastardy laws and many others. William Lambarde,
the author of a handbook for justices published in 1581,
could wonder how many magistrates would be needed 'to
bear so many, not loads, but stacks of statutes' laid upon
them since the reign of Henry VII. Licensing alehouses,
fixing wages and prices, introducing measures to safeguard
public health, enrolling land sales, apprenticing boys to
trades, relieving the sick, encouraging lawful sports: all these
responsibilities and many more constituted their daily and
unpaid burden.

Fragments of Hampden's work as a justice have survived
in the public records, and they illustrate the manifold tasks
of local government which fell on the shoulders of the pre-
dominantly Puritan gentry. For example, the justices saw to
the maintenance of the highways and roads in the country.
The roads through the wooded hills of the Chilterns ran deep
with water, mud and snow in the winter, and they could
prove treacherous, if not impassable, to the coaches and
wagons of the day, necessitating much uncoupling of horses
and man-handling of vehicles. When the Privy Council
directed them to consider how to contribute towards the
carriage of a third part of a thousand loads of timber from
Shotover and Stow-on-the-Wold to London, Hampden and
his fellow justices replied in April 1632 by asking for a delay
until the summer, for 'the ways are at present altogether
impassable, or at least so foul that loads which should be
carried must be very small – to the great increase of carriages
and price.'

The upkeep of bridges posed the magistrates with many
problems. For example, a notorious stone bridge stood in the

parish of Sherington, a Buckinghamshire hamlet with the distinction of possessing the only church in England dedicated to St Laud (a sixth-century French Bishop). As this bridge carried a highway over the River Ouse, the matter came before the Assizes in 1630. Hampden became involved both as a magistrate and also because he owned some land in one of the parishes divided by the stream. In 1630 he wrote to Sir William Andrews about the bridge:

> NOBLE SIR – I have acquainted Sir William Fleetwood with your advertisement concerning the track about Sherington bridge. He intendeth to be himself at the Assizes to follow the business. Whether I shall appear in it or be at the Assizes I am not yet resolved in regard of a particular occasion befallen, with which at our next meeting I will at full acquaint you.
>
> In the meantime 'tis Sir William's desire that you will procure somebody, though yourself appear not, to warn the witnesses and to learn of William Arpen and George Hewlett what they can say that is material. Of the jury no doubt is made but by your care they shall be honest and indifferent.
>
> This issue must be left to God. The witnesses must be solicited to appear. I beseech you let me hear as soon as conveniently you may whether this letter be come into your hands and what you think farther fit to be done.
>
> With leave of my humble service to my Lady, I rest
>
> > Your very assured friend,
> > JOHN HAMPDEN

A second letter on the same subject to Andrewes, dated from Aylesbury on 21 March 1634, reveals that the dispute had dragged on for more than four years:

> SIR – At this meeting I had some conference with Sir Thomas Tyrringham in presence of Mr Chubnall and the two High Constables of Newport Hundreds, but no way could be thought upon for the repair of the bridge. Then I went to the Clerk of the Assizes to see how things stood there and found that the bridge was indicted the last Assizes and that now issues would go out against the town of Sherington if they did not appear of the indictment or take some other course to prevent it – with which I acquainted Sir Thomas.
>
> He (upon the bench next day) moves Mr Justice Berkeley, that then sat, for the stay of issues; whereupon an order was made for four justices to view the bridge Q.C. with relation to the statute, of which number I was nominated to be one. But-

upon that reason, that in regard one end of the bridge was in a parish wherein I had some land, and so might be held unindifferent, I was put out and two others put in my room: the copy of which order I have sent you here enclosed; the time of meeting thereupon is appointed to be upon Wednesday in Easter week, about twelve o'clock, where I doubt not but to meet you, to whom, with my Lady, I present my service and rest

Your assured friend,

JOHN HAMPDEN

As a supplier of food to the capital, Buckinghamshire enjoyed something of a special relationship with London, an economic tie which would have political implications for Hampden later in his life. As a justice he played his part in regulating the sale of corn and other commodities in the county's market towns of Aylesbury, Wycombe, and Chesham, which vied with Uxbridge, Brentford, and Staines in importance for the populous capital. In November 1630 the Privy Council directed Hampden and the Buckinghamshire magistrates to check the 'strange practice' of certain millers of mixing in barley flour with wheaten meal to deceive their customers. In December that year Hampden and two other justices attended the market at Chipping Wycombe to ensure that the mayor Thomas Locke saw to it that the badgers – the middlemen who bought corn – licensed by the Lord Mayor of London could buy grain at the price fixed by the Privy Council. The low yield of harvest in the Vale of Aylesbury that year meant that the farmers lost money by having to sell at the authorized price, and the badgers for their part declined to make any allowances for the poor faced with the winter months ahead.

As his first letter to Sir John Eliot in the Tower reveals, Hampden had shown interest from the beginning in a project of establishing a Puritan colony in New England. In 1629 the Massachusetts Bay Company received a royal charter with this end in view, although the first settlers had already set sail the previous year. Of course they were not the first Europeans to land in Massachusetts Bay. A congregation of English Puritans, who had separated themselves at Leyden from the Church of England under a minister called

Robinson, sailed in August 1620 for Virginia and were carried by the winds northwards to the Bay, where they dropped anchor at a place they called Plymouth after their last port of call on the other side of the Atlantic.

In contrast to these 'Pilgrim Fathers', as Robinson's congregation is known to history (although perhaps that phrase should be applied to all the twenty thousand Puritans in New England in 1640), the Massachusetts Bay Company envisaged a different kind of Puritan commonwealth. Instead of the narrow and theocratic model of Geneva which the Leyden brethren imported into the New World, the adventurers contemplated something along the lines of a truly spiritual and intellectually invigorated Church of England, with a proper distinction between the spiritual and temporal authorities. Before sailing the new emigrants – the true Pilgrim Fathers – issued this noble declaration:

> We are not of those that dream of perfection in this world, yet we desire you would be pleased to take notice of the principals and body of our company as those who esteem it our honour to call the Church of England, from whence we rise, our dear Mother, and cannot part from our native country, where she especially resides, without much sadness of heart and many tears in our eyes, ever acknowledging that such hope and part as we have obtained in the common salvation, we have received in her bosom and sucked it from her breasts. We leave it not, therefore, as loathing the milk wherewith we were nourished there, but, blessing God for the parentage and education, as members of the same body shall always rejoice in her good and unfeignedly grieve for any sorrow that shall ever betide her: and while we have breath sincerely desire and endeavour the continuance and abundance of her welfare, with the enlargement of her bounds in the Kingdom of Jesus Christ.

The Puritan emphasis upon the value of an educated mind in ministers and laity alike bore early fruit in the new colony. At Boston in 1638 the settlers established a college which one of their number – John Harvard, a graduate of Emmanuel College, Cambridge, a centre of Puritan learning – generously endowed with £700 and four hundred books. He intended the college to form the nucleus of a university, a second Cambridge on the Charles river. Here the sons of the New England gentry could study not only the Bible and the

works of the great Reformation divines, but also the authors
of the ancient world and the literature of the Renaissance.
Here they would tread in the steps of Copernicus and Galileo
(then a prisoner of the Inquisition) on the new pilgrimage of
science which would one day take man into the heavens.

On 19 March 1632 the Earl of Warwick, in his capacity as
president of the government's Council for New England,
re-granted the land south of the Massachusetts Bay Company's colony to a company of eleven members, including
John Hampden. Their shares entitled them to possess the
land for a distance of forty leagues from the Narragansett
river. The Indians who inhabited this tract of forest called it
Quonoktacut, 'The Land of the Long River', hence the name
Connecticut. In 1635 a small vessel with twenty pioneers,
under the leadership of John Winthrop and the young son of
Sir Henry Vane, sailed south from the Charles river; and,
landing on the coast of the new territory, they built a fort and
houses of 'a spungie kind of timber called read oack'. They
named the little settlement Saybrook in honour of the company's two leading shareholders. Both these men, Lord Saye
and Lord Brooke, themselves seriously considered emigrat-
ing to the New World. Although Hampden probably owned
some land in Connecticut, there is no evidence that he
contemplated a similar step.

Besides Lord Saye, Lord Brooke, and Hampden, the other
patentees were Lord Rich (the Earl of Warwick's heir),
Charles Fiennes, Sir Nathaniel Rich, Sir Richard Saltons-
tall, Richard Knightley, John Pym, John Humphry, and
Herbert Pelham, all of them men of proven interest in the
Puritan migration to Massachusetts. Six of them had shares
also in the newly-formed Providence Company, which
aimed at founding another Puritan settlement on the island
of Santa Catalina (renamed Providence) in the Caribbean,
as well as making a good return on capital invested from
produce and trade. Hampden did not have shares in the
Providence Company, but he maintained close links with the
governing body of patentees. Two of them are named in
Hampden's will: Richard Knightley and Sir Gilbert Gerrard. Some of the trustees named in Hampden's will are also
appointed in Pym's will of 1637. Thus it is clear that the

colonial enterprises of these years formed the matrix for the friendships which would have considerable political significance in the coming constitutional crisis.

In August 1635 the Privy Council issued more writs for the collection of Ship-Money, this time summoning the inland counties to contribute. Henceforth Hampden's opposition to this arbitrary tax absorbed most of his time, leaving him little leisure for the affairs of the Puritan colony at the mouth of the Connecticut river. Eventually, during the Civil War, the promoters sold their Saybrook settlement to the other towns in Connecticut – Hartfield, Wethersfield and Windsor. Meanwhile the intellectually limited and fanatical brand of Puritanism made headway in the main community in Massachusetts. Many Puritans of wider mental and spiritual horizons moved to Rhode Island; others contemplated a further emigration southwards to the islands of the Providence Company in the Caribbean.

The management of the Providence Company fell largely upon the willing shoulders of its treasurer, John Pym. His efforts to achieve the first aim of adventurers – the establishment of a Puritan colony on Providence Island as a bridgehead for a much larger settlement on the mainland of South America – ran into persistent difficulties. The spiritual state of the first settlers did not inspire their ministers, nor did the pastoral competence of the general run of ministers please the shareholders of the Providence Company. Besides hearing of cases of drunkenness and insolence against the Governor, Captain Philip Bell, the Puritan gentlemen learned that some of their settlers had sent to London for cards, dice and tables.

One minister called Ditloff returned to England in disgrace during May 1634 and appeared before the board of the Company. Pym asked him if it was true that he and others used to sing profane songs on Sunday. Ditloff replied that another minister who had died of a fever on the island within a few months of landing had 'taught him songs, called *catches*, the meaning of which word he understood not, the matter of which was the motion of creatures as the nightingale and the like.' The other two ministers sang these catches with him, but never on the Lord's Day. Ditloff then informed Pym that many of the planters who had sailed out with the deceased minister thought him insufficient 'not being able to pray extemporary and would soldier-like beat his men' and thus he judged him to be 'fitter for a buff-coat than a cassock'.

The second aim, which was to achieve for the shareholders a return on the capital they had invested, proved equally out of reach. To the production and sale of timber, indigo, tobacco, cotton, salt, fruit, sarsaparilla and sugar cane, the colonists added a trade in negroes with the West Indies and Massachusetts, a traffic to which one or two of the more sensitive Puritan ministers on Providence – to their everlasting credit – protested with moral vigour. Some shipbuilding developed on the larger, low-lying and heavily wooded island of Henrietta, which lies some sixty miles south-west of Providence and had formed part of the original grant to the Company.

In 1635 the Spanish seized the island of Tortuga, which lies off the coast of Hispaniola or Haiti. The Providence Company had owned that island – known as Association – since 1631, and its loss gave them the necessary grounds for securing as a monopoly the right to make armed retaliation against Spain in the Caribbean. The hilly island of Providence, some six miles long by four miles wide, possessed a fine natural harbour protected by shoals and rocks. Moreover, it stood slap in the middle of the main Spanish sea routes between Porto Bello and Cartagena in the south and Mexico and Havana to the north.

Thus the Puritan nobles and gentlemen of the Providence Company began to commission privateers to wage their private war against Spain in the spirit of Drake and Raleigh. After the capture of Providence by the enraged Spanish in 1641, the company virtually foundered, its decks awash with debt. In the wake of these Puritan pirates came the privateers and buccaneers of all nations. They flocked to Tortuga to continue the endless quest for Spanish yellow gold and gems, establishing there a. godless fraternity far removed from the Puritan commonwealth once envisaged by John Pym and his colleagues.

Hampden's many friends in the Providence Company kept him fully informed of these chances and changes in the

southern adventure. In 1637 the Company chose him as
their arbitrator in a dispute with the former Governor of
Providence, Captain Bell, whom they replaced after the loss
of Association with a more experienced soldier. Three years
earlier the Company had occasion to reprimand him for
grounding his authority on the island 'upon a supposed
privilege, which you call *Prerogative*, annexed to your place'.
The shareholders had pointed out 'that we know no such
thing as the Governor's Prerogative, being such that you
cannot find in our Instruction, neither do we like the use of
that horrid word . . .' Subsequently Bell had fallen foul of
both the planters and the ministers, a fate he could hardly
have avoided. In London in 1637 Bell named his brother as
his arbitrator in the dispute over what money the Company
owed him, but as neither party would bind themselves in
advance to accept the award of the two independent asses-
sors, nothing came from this attempt at arbitration.

As lord of the manor of Great Hampden and master of
Hampden House, and as a justice of the peace and a deputy
lieutenant in Buckinghamshire, John Hampden led a busy
and full life during these eleven years when King Charles
ruled without Parliament. His general interest in Puritan
emigration to the New World, and his particular involvement with the Saybrook colony, led him deeper into the
counsels of Lord Saye, Lord Brooke, John Pym and their
associates. But in these respects he was no different from a
dozen other Puritan gentlemen, such as Sir William Waller
or Sir Arthur Heselrige – both members of the Providence
Company. His true quality only manifested itself in the
Ship-Money affair. In choosing to prosecute John Hampden
for the non-payment of that tax, rather than Lord Saye or the
merchant Richard Chambers, King Charles may have
thought that he had hit upon a weak link in the chain, a
relatively insignificant man who could be trounced in the
law courts. But the King had mistaken Hampden, or his
advisers had served him ill. Death had pruned the private
garden of Hampden's affections, but it also freed him to
spend himself and his fortune on behalf of the people of
England, their property, laws, and freedom.

Chapter Six

THE SHIP-MONEY
TRIAL

Twixt kings and subjects there's this mighty odds,
Subjects are taught by men; kings by the gods.

ROBERT HERRICK

John Hampden's refusal to pay Ship-Money in 1635 took his name into every household and made it a byword for patriotism. Before that historic stand, wrote Clarendon, 'he was rather of reputation in his own country than of public discourse or fame in the kingdom, but then he grew the argument of all tongues, every man inquiring who and what he was that durst at his own charge support the liberty and property of the kingdom, and rescue his country from being made a prey to the court.' Why did this wealthy man resist the demand for a mere twenty shillings assessed on his land in Stoke Mandeville? What principles underlay his opposition to Ship-Money?

Beneath the apparent success of the monarchy in governing without Parliament since 1629 there lay the ever-imminent danger of financial crisis. Without the authority of Parliament and despite much grumbling and some resistance from the merchants concerned, the government collected the important tonnage and poundage customs duties. Yet they could not suffice for all the demands on the public purse nor support the stately splendour of the Court at Whitehall. Nor could such expedients as levying large fines on those who had inadvertently broken the ancient forest laws make up the balance, although Lord Treasurer Weston showed considerable ingenuity in exploiting these opportunities from the feudal past. The brilliant idea of resurrecting the Ship-Money tax, however, is attributed to William

Noy, who became Attorney-General in 1631 and remained in that office until his death three years later.

One contemporary described lawyer Noy as 'a most indefatigable plodder and searcher of ancient records' and 'clownish but knowing'. In other words, he was a learned man of unpolished behaviour. Clarendon also commented tartly on his lack of courtly manners and suggested that Noy's susceptibility to flattery allowed 'the great persons who steered the public affairs' to use him as an instrument: they led him to believe 'he could not give a clearer testimony that his knowledge in the law was greater than all other men's, than by making that law which all other men believed not to be so.' Noy may have possessed much legal knowledge, but he certainly lacked political sensitivity and human understanding. 'In a word', concluded Clarendon, 'he was an unanswerable instance how necessary a good education and knowledge of men is to make a wise man, at least a man fit for business.'

Noy's shortcomings had first become evident in the 'odious and crying project of soap'. Acting on his advice in 1631, the King had granted the monopoly of making a supposedly superior brand of soap from vegetable oil to a small group of entrepreneurs for fourteen years in return for a levy of £4 a ton on the 5,000 tons they promised to make each year. Although the existing Bristol soap-makers opposed this monopoly and mounted a public demonstration to prove that their brand washed whiter than white, the King ordered the shutting down of seven out of the eleven soap factories in that city. Furthermore, the monopolists secured a prohibition against their London and Bristol rivals using fish oil in the manufacture of soap, and even enlisted the Star Chamber Court in their vain attempt to suppress competition by these unfair means. In 1637 the King revoked the monopoly by buying them out for £40,000. The London soap-makers contributed a half of this sum, and secured thereby the freedom to continue in open business upon payment of £8 a ton to the Crown.

In essence Ship-Money was a traditional means of financing the construction of a royal fleet. Each county bordering the sea, and the inland ports such as London, contributed one or more ships fully equipped and manned – or money in lieu of them – according to a quota based upon an assessment of the county's wealth. Then each sheriff broke down the assessment into smaller portions payable by the boroughs and individual property owners in the shire in proportion to their wealth or lands. As the inland counties benefited from the protection of the warships it might seem but a logical step to extend to them the financial burden of Ship-Money. Yet an attempt to do so in 1628 had proved so unpopular that the government had wisely abandoned it.

For what purpose in 1634 did the King require a battle fleet? Six years earlier England had stood at war with France, but now the King could not point to declared enemies at sea other than Dunkirk privateers in the Channel and pirate ships from Tunis and Algiers at its western approaches. Under the protection of Spain the Dunkirkers raided the sea-lanes, snatching up English merchantmen homeward bound with cargoes from every part of the known world. The Barbary corsairs had landed on the coast of Cornwall, carrying off Christians to the slavery of the galleys. Certainly the King's admirals must deal with such menaces, but it was by no means clear that a 'Navy Royal' of the size envisaged by the Ship-Money writs was needed to scatter the sea-rovers. Hence the suspicion that the King intended to use Ship-Money as his principal means of securing a permanent independence from Parliament.

In October 1634 the first writs for Ship-Money were sent to the sheriffs of the coastal counties and seaports. The City of London protested at once that tonnage and poundage money should be used for guarding the seas. The Privy Council summoned the Lord Mayor and cunningly explained to him that as tonnage and poundage had not been granted by Parliament, being collected by prerogative powers, that argument could not be advanced. Despite such dubious reasoning, rather than because of it, London capitulated to the imposition. In all, the Crown raised about £104,000 on this first writ, and spent perhaps £40,000 on the Navy.

The Earl of Portland, as Lord Treasurer Weston became, died in March 1635, and the King entrusted the Treasury to a commission with Archbishop Laud at the head of it. By granting patents the commissioners squeezed money from the manufacturers of salt and starch, brewers, vintners and brickmakers. A new Book of Rates pushed up the customs duties, but still revenue fell short of expenditure. Thus in August 1635 the Privy Council issued writs for extending the collection of Ship-Money to all counties irrespective of their geographical position. At the close of the Midsummer term in Star Chamber, the Lord Keeper Coventry asked the judges to urge prompt payment during their progress on circuit. In a plain-speaking and persuasive manner Coventry justified to them the writ for Ship-Money on the predictable grounds that as the whole nation stood to gain by the defence of England's trade so all the shires should pay for warships. 'The wooden walls are the best walls of this kingdom,' he concluded.

Thus, in company with every other sheriff in England, young Sir Peter Temple, Sheriff of Buckinghamshire, received the royal writ informing him that 'certain thieves, pirates and sea-robbers, as well as Turks and others, confederated together' had interrupted English trade. By 1 March 1636 the King required the county of Buckinghamshire to provide for him at Portsmouth a 450-ton ship complete 'with men as well skilful officers as able and experienced mariners, a hundred and fourscore at least; as also with a sufficient quantity of cannon, muskets, gunpowder, pikes and spears and other arms necessary for war.' If the county preferred to pay cash instead of the ship and its victuals for twenty-six weeks, then it should send £4,500 to the Treasurer of the Navy.

Peers as well as commoners opposed this precedent of extending Ship-Money to the inland shires. Lord Danby, for instance, wrote a letter to the King imploring him to call a Parliament to vote the money rather than to raise it in this manner. When the King read the protest it is said that he grew pale and silent, and paced up and down the room deep in thought. He summoned the Earl of Warwick to Court and asked him whether or not it was true that he opposed the tax in the county of Essex. Warwick openly admitted the fact, adding that Parliament would grant all the money necessary for a war against the Catholic powers. The King smiled and ignored the advice, merely commanding Warwick to give a good example to his tenants and countrymen by obeying the writ.

To strengthen his hand in the teeth of growing opposition, the King sought the opinion of his judges on the legality of Ship-Money in order to defend the kingdom in time of danger. With his question phrased in that way, ten out of the twelve judges agreed that the King possessed such a right, and moreover was the 'sole judge both of the danger, and when and how far the same is to be prevented and avoided.' Also the King endeavoured to influence public opinion by cunningly reprinting John Selden's book *Mare Clausum*, which argued persuasively for England's sovereignty over the Channel. The potential Dutch threat to English fleets, coupled with the danger of pirates, added substance to these legal and judicial opinions, and the King now felt that he possessed a case for the imposition of Ship-Money on the whole realm.

Opposition to the tax faltered but did not fade away. The redoubtable Richard Chambers appealed to the Court of King's Bench but could not gain a hearing. Thomas Cartwright, the squire of Aynhoe in Northamptonshire, resisted with force the sheriff's constables who came to collect his share of the county's £6,000 assessment. A correspondent of the Earl of Strafford summed up the general feeling when he declared: 'I had rather give and pay ten subsidies in Parliament, than ten shillings this new-old way.'

After the appointment of new sheriffs, doubtless chosen for their known willingness to collect Ship-Money, the Privy Council wrote on 25 January 1636 to Sir Peter Temple and his successor Heneage Proby commanding the former to send up all money received and the latter 'to apply your best endeavours and diligence in the execution of his Majesty's writs'. Yet by the end of that January the Treasurer of the Navy had received only £119,000 of the expected £208,000, and the government brought more pressure to bear on the sheriffs. Temple received a summons 'to give your attendance upon the Board' at Oatlands on 3 July. At first he successfully pleaded ill-health, but wrote to his mother from

Stowe on 8 July: 'I am to attend the King at Theobalds on the 17th day of July, to give an account to him what I have done in the service, and, as he likes my proceedings, I am to continue in the messenger's hand, or be released, or worse. My life is nothing but toil and has been for many years, to the Commonwealth and now to the King . . .' Ground between the millstones of local unpopularity on the one hand and the royal displeasure on the other, the lot of such sheriffs was not a happy one.

On 6 October 1636 the King issued a third writ for Ship-Money. Realizing that his authority to levy the tax might be publicly questioned in the courts, he sought to deter such a challenge by demonstrating that the verdict would be in his favour. Therefore once again he submitted the matter to the judges, setting out his reasons for so doing in a lengthy sentence of preamble:

> Finding that some few, haply out of ignorance what the laws and customs of this our realm are, or out of a desire to be eased and freed in their particulars, how general soever the charge ought to be, have not paid and contributed the several rates and assessments that were set upon them; and foreseeing in our princely wisdom, that from hence divers suits and actions are not unlikely to be commenced and prosecuted in our several courts at Westminster, we, desirous to avoid such inconveniences, and out of our princely love and affection to all our people, being willing to prevent such errors as any of our loving subjects may happen to run into, have thought fit in a case of this nature, to advise with you our judges.

This time all the judges agreed that the King had the right to command his subjects to provide ships in time of national danger, and that he was the sole judge 'both of the danger and when and how the same is to be prevented and avoided'. Sir George Croke and Sir Richard Hutton, however, only signed this counsel on the assurance that thereby they did not bind themselves into giving such a judgment in any particular case.

After the judges had delivered this corporate opinion in February 1637, Lord Wentworth, now Lord Deputy of Ireland, described it in a letter to the King as 'the greatest service that profession has done the Crown in my lifetime'. Now the realm would acquire a strong Navy, but 'unless his Majesty has the like power declared to raise a land army upon the same exigent of state, the Crown seems to me but to stand upon one leg, and to be considerable but by halves to foreign princes abroad.' These words of Thomas Wentworth, three years later to become Earl of Strafford, reveal the significance of Ship-Money to the Crown: it gave the King an important source of revenue independent of Parliament. Once the fleet was finished doubtless Ship-Money would be raised each year upon some pretext or other. For instance it might be used to maintain a small standing army, ostensibly for service at sea.

Yet these inviting prospects depended upon two facts: the opinions of the judges and the basic law-abiding characteristic of the English people. Charles had secured the first and counted upon the second. Certainly the advice of the judges swayed many waverers. By the autumn not more than about £20,000 remained outstanding in England and Wales. In Buckinghamshire, Sir Heneage Proby had collected all the assessment except £188.1s.11d., a sum which included the missing twenty shillings Hampden owed upon his Stoke Mandeville property.

The King had skilfully parried one thrust against Ship-Money. Lord Saye, a vigorous opponent of the tax, brought a legal action against the constable who sought to take away his goods to the value of the neglected assessment. The King replied by prosecuting him for various infringements of the forest laws, thus giving Saye no opportunity for preaching his well-known views on Ship-Money and the need for parliamentary authority for such a tax. Doubtless the King avoided a confrontation with Saye on this issue simply because he was a peer. Yet the opposition to Ship-Money could not be ignored. Most people knew that there would be a test case. By February 1637 it had become clear that John Hampden would fight it at his own expense, but on behalf of the nation.

The government had to pick up the gauntlet. Unless the refusers received punishment, those who had paid up would become unpopular with their neighbours, wrote Wentworth, and would feel 'extremely disheartened and out of liking with themselves'. If Hampden, the Puritan champion, wanted a fight he should have it. The authoritarian Lord Deputy, writing to Archbishop Laud, described his remedy: 'Mr Hampden is a great Brother and the very genius of that nation of people leads them always to oppose civilly as ecclesiastically, all that authority ever ordains for them; but in good faith, were they right served they should be whipped home into their right wits; and much beholden they should be to any that would thoroughly take pains with them in that sort.' In a later letter he repeated his suggestion that it would be charity if 'Mr Hampden and others of his likeness were well whipped into their right senses'. Wentworth had known Hampden in the 1628 Parliament, and he added: 'As well as I think of Mr Hampden's abilities, I take his will and peevishness to be full as great.'

Like a general marshalling his superior army before a small beleaguered town, King Charles made ready to crush Hampden in the law courts as thoroughly as he had dealt with Eliot in the Tower. The machinery of the great engine of law slowly began to turn. On 9 March the Court of Chancery sent a writ of *Certiorari* to Sir Heneage Proby. On 5 May the Court of Exchequer received a writ ordering that proceedings should be commenced there. Two weeks later that court issued a writ of *Scire Facias* against Hampden requiring him to show cause why he had not paid his assessment of twenty shillings for lands in the parish of Stoke Mandeville, adjoining Great Kimble. Hampden appeared in court during the Trinity term and made a general defence that he was not legally obliged to comply with the writs. The Barons of the Exchequer adjourned the case to the Court of Exchequer Chamber for a hearing in the autumn.

As Bulstrode Whitelocke of Fawley Court near Henley-on-Thames makes clear in his *Memorials*, Hampden determined the main lines of his argument himself in consultation with a group of lawyers. Thus his strategic mind lay behind the case, though others would serve as the orators in court: 'Mr John Hampden', writes Bulstrode Whitelocke, 'my countryman and kinsman, a gentleman of an ancient family in Buckinghamshire, and of great estates and parts, denied the payment of Ship-Money as an illegal tax. He often advised in this great business with Holborne, St John, myself and others of his friends and counsel.'

On 6 November the twelve judges arrayed in scarlet robes trimmed with ermine and heavy gilt chains of office took their seats and the court fell silent; Hampden's principal lawyer, Oliver St John, clad in his serjeant's robes, stepped forward to speak for his client. The thirty-nine-year-old lawyer of Lincoln's Inn was 'known to be of parts and industry, but untaken notice of for practice in Westminster Hall.' Clarendon continued: 'he was a man reserved, and of a dark and clouded countenance, very proud, and conversing with few, and those men of his own humour and inclinations.' He served as lawyer to the Russell family and also to the Providence Company. In 1629 the Privy Council had questioned and imprisoned St John for communicating a seditious paper he found in Sir Robert Cotton's library, and then brought him into Star Chamber for sentence, but the judges there discharged him on the grounds of insufficient evidence. Only weeks before Hampden's trial opened, royal officers ransacked St John's study for proof that he had prepared the defence speech in Star Chamber of Henry Burton, a minister who had joined William Prynne and physician John Bastwick in uttering sedition against the bishops such as Archbishop Laud, and endured with them public mutilation in the Palace Yard pillory on 30 June.

Oliver St John's address to the judges on behalf of Hampden lasted for three days and it forged a lifelong reputation for him. He rested the case against Ship-Money upon the broad history of the constitution and the evolved liberty of the subject. The ancient Magna Carta and the new Petition of Right shone brightly in the jewel-studded thick brocade of authorities, precedents and laws to which he appealed. Basically, he argued that Parliament alone could raise money beyond the normal revenue of the Crown.

Oliver St John began by conceding that the King was entrusted in law with the defence of the realm. 'My Lords,' said St John, in a rare metaphor, 'by the law the King is *Pater Familiae*, who by the law of economics is not only to keep peace at home, but to protect his wife and children, and whole families from injuries from abroad.' He conceded also that the King had the power, without recourse to Parliament, to confiscate the goods of his subjects when danger threatened. But what enemy, he asked, would have invaded England in 1635? If the writ issued on 4 August 1635 allowed seven months before the counties delivered their ships at Portsmouth, thus implying but a slight danger, why could not Parliament have been summoned to vote the necessary money in the customary way?

St John described how earlier sovereigns had paid for defence without recourse to Ship-Money, even borrowing heavily in order to do so. Would they have acted thus if Ship-Money had been thought legal? 'The non-claims, therefore, of so many kings and queens', he concluded, 'I shall present unto your Lordships as so many declarations of their general consents that, without assent in Parliament, they could not have laid the like assessments upon any of their subjects as is now laid upon my client.'

On 11 November, Sir Edmund Littleton, the Solicitor General, rose to reply for the Crown. In his three days' speech he counter-argued that parliaments since the time of Edward I had acknowledged the right of sovereigns not only to command military service from their subjects, but also to raise money to pay for defence. Parliaments could not always be summoned in time of national danger, because forty days must elapse after the issue of election writs before they could meet.

Robert Holborne of Lincoln's Inn spoke next on behalf of Hampden. Beginning his four days' speech on 2 December he again reviewed the precedents and statutes of the past. To his mind the crucial issue was whether or not the realm stood in real danger in August 1635, an external threat so pressing that the King had no time to summon Parliament. In the first writ, he pointed out, 'there is not a word of danger from any empire, but from pirates; not a word of danger to the kingdom, but to merchants. For aught that appears, a Parliament, even in the King's judgment, might have been called.' He then proceeded to question the centrepiece in the prosecution's case, namely that the King was always the sole judge of what constitutes national danger and how best to deal with it. This may be true in times of such sudden crisis that a Parliament could not be summoned, but that condition, Holborne claimed, had not existed in 1635.

Holborne allowed himself some flights of oratory. 'Before I enter into the argument further,' he said, 'I here profess for my client and myself, that while we speak of political advice, and how far a governor is subject to error . . . we do always with thankfulness to him acknowledge our present happiness to be blessed with so just a prince, and we fetch it from our hearts, and were his Majesty so immortal as he deserves, and that his successors might be heirs to his virtues and his Crown, we should wish that the regal power might be free from political advice and unlimited . . .' At this point Lord Keeper Finch interrupted to warn him that it 'was not agreeable to duty to have you bandy what is the hopes of succeeding princes when the King hath a blessed issue so hopeful to succeed him in his Crown and virtues.' To which Holborne replied – with some presence of mind – that he was thinking a long time ahead, perhaps five hundred years hence.

On 16 December the Attorney-General, Sir John Bankes, rose to summarize and present the final case for the Crown. Besides emphasizing the support of precedents, Bankes made much of the fairness and impartialitiy of the assessments for Ship-Money. He contrasted the paltry sum of twenty shillings with Hampden's broad acres. 'If he be too highly assessed he might call the sheriff in question. But the Sheriff of Bucks is rather to be fined for setting him at so low a rate as twenty shillings. We know what house Mr Hampden is of, and his estate too. For anything I know, it might as well be twenty pounds.' If Hampden had disagreed with the rating he could have appealed to the Sheriff of Buckinghamshire. Of course Bankes was entirely missing the point, and he must have known it, with this particular line of argument.

The Attorney-General moved briefly on to firmer ground by contending that the King alone could assess the degree of national danger. Then he wandered off into a still deeper bog by quoting a statute of Richard II to show that men held then the conviction that 'the King holds his empire immediately of the God of Heaven'. If the court accepted the argument of his opponents St John and Holborne, the consequence would be a fundamental restriction of the royal prerogative. 'Surely this argument is made by the people or to please the people. What will be the consequence of it but the introducing of a democratical government?' But England is a kingdom ruled by an 'absolute monarch' who possesses 'supreme jurisdiction by land and sea'. Therefore the King's command by writ must be obeyed. 'He is the first mover among these orbs of ours, and he is the centre of us all, wherein we all as the lines should meet. He is the soul of this body, whose proper act is to command. But I shall need no persuasions to your Lordships to do justice in this cause; and therefore I shall humbly desire judgment for the King.' With these eloquent words in their ears the judges adjourned until the Hilary term of 1638, when they promised to deliver their judgments.

In summary, the Crown had attempted to defend Ship-Money by confusing two lines of legal precedents. The King's lawyers argued that the relevant precedents were those which established that he could conscript ships and men in an emergency for national defence, not those different but equally valid ones which prohibited him from raising taxes without the consent of Parliament. He could compel people to contribute money towards the conscription of a ship, but such a vessel belonged legally to the donors and reverted to them after a period of six months' service with the royal fleet. In this form Ship-Money was indeed legal. In this case the people of Buckinghamshire would have owned their ship, and merely have lent it to the Crown. But the King wanted finance for the royal Navy and other uses, not ships provided on this temporary basis, and he was not legally entitled to raise it without Parliament's assent. The King therefore had to pretend that he was asking his subjects for a service rather than a tax. As this service of providing ships could only be required in an emergency, it became an issue who could determine if that dire state existed in 1634 or any other year. The Crown lawyers argued that the King alone could judge whether or not the nation faced a peril sufficient to require the military service of ships.

During the law terms of 1638 the judges gave their opinions by turn with much solemnity, beginning with the most junior and building up to a climax with the verdicts of the two Lord Chief Justices. Sir Francis Weston, Baron of the Court of Exchequer, and Sir Francis Crawley, Justice in the Court of Common Pleas, both found for the King early in the Hilary term. Before a crowded court Crawley indulged in some rhetoric of his own: 'You say, "That if the King doth move a war offensive, there's time enough to call a Parliament; if defensive, the cloud is seen long before." But Oh, good sir! is this always true? Is not the cloud sometimes even over the head before descried?' The King would not levy charges if there was no danger, therefore – ignoring the laws of logic – he concluded that present and imminent danger did exist. 'Must the King resort to Parliament? No. We see the danger is instant and admits to no delay. Shall we go home and sit in careless security? Not so. But let us resort unto our pious and just King, whose prerogative and sovereignty is to defend the realm, and to maintain his subjects' liberties. And so I give judgment for the King.'

On Saturday 10 February Sir Robert Berkeley, Justice of the King's Bench, declared that Holborne was utterly mistaken in believing that the monarch could not raise money without the consent of Parliament. 'The law knows no such King-yoking policy. The law is of itself an old and trusty servant of the King's.' It is not surprising in the light of such views that Berkeley gave his opinion in favour of the Crown.

The momentous national significance of the case had slowly dawned upon the shuttered mind of Sir George Vernon, Justice of the Court of Common Pleas. 'This is a cause of great consequence and is one of the greatest that ever came into question in this kingdom, and the records are infinite that have been cited on both sides . . .' He asked for more time to peruse the copious notes he had taken during the case and he held up a thick wad of them for all to see the evidence. In addition he pleaded his poor health as a reason for another week's delay before speaking. But his fellow judges saw through him and insisted that he delivered his opinion. The reluctant judge then gave judgment for the King on the unconvincing grounds that the sovereign could dispense with any law in situations of necessity.

Sir Thomas Trevor, Baron of the Court of the Exchequer, agreed upon the importance of the case 'for the sum is but 20s. but the weight thereof is of far greater extent: it concerns the whole kingdom'. He agreed that in normal circumstances it would be best for the King to summon Parliament to grant money for war, but cited the instances of the Armada in 1588 and the 'Gunpowder Treason' of 1605 as ground for preserving the Crown's independent powers. 'Alas, it is not Parliaments can keep us safe', he said.

Then Trevor firmly rejected any notion of popular control over the King. 'This Kingdom has been always monarchical: a democratical government was never in this Kingdom.' Parliament was too slow to be an instrument against danger, and could not supplant the King as the chief means of preventing it. Ships provided our best defence, and the royal fleet now contained ships of greater size and strength, all better furnished than ever before. 'All of which redounds to the King and Kingdom's honour. The ship, called the *Sovereign of the Seas*, may be termed the *Sovereign of all Ships*.' At least Trevor was right on that point, for the *Sovereign of the Seas*, launched the previous summer at Deptford, measured 254 feet long and carried 144 cannon. As for the Ship-Money tax, Trevor concluded: 'I wish it may be paid by all cheerfully.'

Five judges had now given judgment for the King, and a resounding royal victory was in sight when Sir George Croke, Justice of the King's Bench, rose to give his verdict. As a Buckinghamshire fellow-countryman of Hampden's and as one of the two doubtful justices in the 1636 consultation, Croke was a key figure in the trial. If he allowed himself to be swayed by the majority opinion, the case would turn into a triumph for King Charles. Whitelocke reported that his wife and nearest relations had brought pressure to bear upon him to speak from his conscience. More than any of the other judges, however, Croke showed that he had grasped the political and constitutional significance of the trial and his own brief part in it. 'I must confess, this cause is a very great cause, and the greatest cause that ever came into question before any judges,' he began. 'And for my own part

I am sorry it should come in question in this place; more requisite it was to have had it debated in a public assembly of the whole State, for on the one side, it concerns the King in his prerogative and power royal; and on the other side, the subject, in his lands, goods and liberty, in all that he has, besides his life.'

Doubtless to their delight, Hampden and his friends then heard Croke first apologize before proceeding to differ from his brother judges, which he must do because their views 'do much trouble me'. As for the apparently convincing case of the King's two counsels, he observed that when he had himself spoken as an advocate the argument had seemed clear-cut, but that it looked quite different from the judge's seat. Croke, who was probably a Puritan, then said he would follow 'God's direction and my own conscience', hardly legal language. 'I desire God to guide me to a true judgment, and though, for the reasons aforesaid, I doubt myself, yet I am not of the same opinion as my brothers, but according to my conscience, I think that judgment ought to be given to the defendant.'

We can only imagine the immense stir that these words must have caused in the Exchequer Chamber and later in the kingdom. Whatever the majority verdict, nothing could erase the fact that one judge, guided by God and his conscience, had declared in public in favour of John Hampden and the non-payment of Ship-Money. In the Inns of Court it would be said that the King had Ship-Money 'by hook but not by Croke'.

More excitement followed after the most hesitant opinion of Sir William Jones of the King's Bench in favour of the King. For Sir Richard Hutton, Justice of the Court of Common Pleas, the second doubtful judge in 1636, joined Croke in finding for Hampden. He could see no danger of actual invasion. Moreover, he could not forget that as a young bencher in the Inns of Court he had received back twenty shillings paid to Queen Elizabeth when the judges informed her that such a benevolence was technically illegal.

The real surprises, however, came with the next two verdicts. On 26 May Sir John Denham, Baron of the Exchequer Court, wrote from his rooms in Sergeant's Inn, Fleet Street, 'my old disease being upon me', giving his judgment in writing for the plaintiff. Sir Humphrey Davenport, Lord Chief Baron of the Exchequer, also found for the plaintiff on technical grounds, avoiding a general verdict on the large issue of prerogative versus law.

With six opinions for the King and four for Hampden it fell to Sir John Finch, Lord Chief Justice of the Court of Common Pleas, to tilt the case decisively for the Crown. According to Clarendon, Finch had led a 'licentious life in a restrained fortune' and had built his career 'upon the stock of a good wit and natural parts, without the superstructure of much knowledge in the profession by which he was to grow'. He had taken up Ship-Money from where Noy left it, and 'carried it up to that pinnacle from whence he almost broke his own neck'.

Finch began by reviewing the whole story, emphasizing that the judges had been consulted all along and had given their opinion in favour of its legality, 'which might have satisfied anyone that did not respect their own private benefit: and Mr Hampden, I think, of all has the least cause to complain, being affected but 20s. a contemptible sum, in respect of his annual revenues'. Perhaps aware of his own low stock of legal knowledge, Finch thought it not well to 'clog the case with so many precedents'. Instead he made loyalty the central issue, asserting roundly 'that for the excellency of the government of this Kingdom, through God's blessings, none are more happy than we', living under a King who ' is of God alone'.

The Lord Chief Justice then damned the House of Commons with faint praise. 'A Parliament is an honourable court, and I confess it is an excellent means of charging the subject, and defending the Kingdom, but yet it is only a means.' He recalled the honour bestowed upon him 'which never any shall with more respect remember than myself, whom they were pleased to choose as Speaker'. (Doubtless Finch also recollected that day nine years ealier when Holles and Valentine, ignoring his tears and protests, had held him firmly down in his chair while Eliot and his friends, including the plaintiff before him, had transacted their business.) As for the Petition of Right, passed when he was Speaker, it made no mention of Ship-Money, nor did it grant anything new.

Of course behind the case lay the very real possibility that Ship-Money would be used for purposes other than that for which it was intended; and in his judgment for the King Sir William Jones had specifically pointed out as a *caveat* that no part of the money should go to the privy purse. Finch sought to reassure the Court by informing all that the King had told him in the presence of Lord Chief Justice Bramston that 'it never entered his thoughts to make such a use of it'. In a story that must have caused a gust of laughter among the packed spectators, Finch went on to report the King's actual words: he had said 'he would rather eat the money than convert it to his own use'. He gave his judgment for the King.

On the slender grounds that a defence has to be prepared well before an enemy comes if it is to be effective Sir John Bramston, Lord Chief Justice of the King's Bench, made a careful examination of the terms of the writ, and because they specified that the money must be paid to Westminster, he concluded that Ship-Money was technically a tax and not a service. Thus he concurred with Davenport in deciding for the plaintiff on this procedural point, stemming from the wording of the writ, and avoided any pronouncement on the central constitutional issue of the case. On 11 June the Attorney-General moved the Court of Exchequer for a formal judgment for the King on the following day, which was duly given.

Yet the Crown had won by the narrowest possible margin of seven to five. Moreover, the arguments of Oliver St John and Holborne, which Whitelocke describes as 'full of rare and excellent learning', had become the talk of London. Even before the trial ended their effects, and still more the opinions of Sir George Croke and Sir John Hutton, had renewed the flagging opposition to Ship-Money. On 4 May a clerk named Thomas Harrison rushed to the bar of the Court of King's Bench in Westminster Hall, where Hutton and Crawley were sitting behind its marble table, and shouted, 'I do accuse Mr Justice Hutton of High Treason!' On examination, Harrison admitted that he had only heard the 'common report' of Hutton's judgment the preceding Saturday, but he believed the judge had denied the royal supremacy and excited the people to sedition. Near the place of his residence in Northamptonshire, he said, 'the people go on more and more in the stubbornness of refusing Ship-Money'. He alleged that Hutton, while on circuit, had encouraged them to such sedition. Yet an attack on one judge in this manner was held to be a contempt of all judges and the King whom they served. Harrison was fined £5,000, imprisoned and ordered to make submission in every court with a paper pinned to his hat describing his offence.

Yet the unwillingness to pay Ship-Money in the spring of 1638 had spread throughout the country, and it was especially strong in Essex, Oxfordshire, Buckinghamshire and Gloucestershire. The Privy Council heard reports that Sir Alexander Denton, the new Sheriff of Buckinghamshire, had not pressed the matter because he listened too much to his kindred and friends. Although men accepted that the judges had condemned Hampden on legal or technical grounds, they certainly felt that the true merits of his case had not been rejected. In 1639, when writs for Ship-Money went out again and Buckinghamshire was assessed for £4,500, no one seems to have paid. By 1640, only a third of Ship-Money was received by the Treasurer of the Navy, and sheriffs in almost every county encountered a stiffening resistance to it.

Ship-Money caused 'a wonderful murmuring', as Richard Baxter described it, because the nobility and gentry interpreted it as an attempt to overthrow the constitution of the kingdom and a threat to the concept of private property. Hampden lost the case and he duly paid up the sum for which he had been assessed. But the King had won a Pyrrhic victory. Hampden's 'carriage throughout that agitation', concluded Clarendon, 'was with that rare temper and modesty that they who watched him narrowly to find some advantage against his person, to make him less resolute in his cause, were compelled to give him a just testimony. And the judgment that was given against him infinitely more advanced him than the service for which it was given.'

Chapter Seven

WAR WITH SCOTLAND

The gain of civil wars will not allow
            Bay to the conqueror's brow.
At such a game what fool would venture in,
When one must lose, yet neither side can win?
            How justly would our neighbours smile
            At these mad quarrels of our isle
Swell'd with proud hopes to snatch the whole away,
Whilst we bet all, and yet for nothing play?

ABRAHAM COWLEY

By the beginning of June 1638, the month in which the Court of Exchequer Chamber gave its collective judgment against Hampden, the King's ecclesiastical policy had provoked a crisis in Scotland. The determined efforts of Charles, since 1635, to add the burden of an Anglican liturgy to the yoke of episcopacy already imposed by his father on the unwilling shoulders of Calvinist Scotland, produced at first murmurs of discontent and then riots in cathedral and church north of the border. The Bishop of Brechin, for example, took to preaching with a pair of loaded pistols on the pulpit top in front of him. Petitions flooded in from all over Scotland against the Laudian innovations, and in December 1637 Charles proclaimed these protests both illegal and treasonable. On Wednesday 28 February 1638 at the Mercat Cross of Edinburgh, the chief leaders of the Protesters bound themselves together in the National Covenant, a revised and amended form of the Confession of 1581 against the religion of Rome. With the exception of a small minority, the Scots people took the Covenant and swore to 'resist all those contrary errors and corruptions according to our vocation'.

A feeling of national exaltation gripped the presbyteries: it was, wrote one leader, 'the great marriage day of this nation with God'.

A year passed in fruitless negotiations between the King and the Covenanters. Charles delayed for as long as he could the act of summoning a Scottish Parliament and a General Assembly, and not until November 1638 did the latter meet in Glasgow, with a membership of 98 laymen and 140 ministers. In the following weeks, defying a royal command to disperse, the Assembly declared illegal episcopacy, the Court of High Commission, the Anglican prayer-book foisted upon them, and such novel practices as kneeling at Communion, the observance of Christmas, and confirmation by bishops. In place of diocese and deanery, the Assembly brought back the Presbyterian system: Kirk Sessions, Presbyteries, Synods, General Assemblies and all.

On 11 June 1638, the very day when the Attorney-General formally requested the judges to pronounce the majority verdict against Hampden, the King expressed his view to his Royal Commissioner in Scotland that force alone could reduce the Scots to obedience. The conduct of the Glasgow Assembly developed that tentative opinion into a firm conviction in the King's mind; at once he stepped up the preparations for an impressive military invasion to cow his Scottish opponents into a humble submission. He planned to enter Scotland himself at the head of 30,000 soldiers while at the same time two contingents from Wentworth's army in Ireland landed on the west coast. The *Sovereign of the Seas* and her sister ships would dominate the Firth of Forth, and another fleet would land a force of 5,000 men at Aberdeen to stir up the Highlands.

Yet the royal army which assembled around York in March 1639 mustered no more than 21,000 men. The King had raised some 3,000 cavalry by sending a feudal summons to the nobility to come in person with their troops, a method already ancient in the days of Flodden. Many nobles made plausible excuses for not taking the field, while Lord Saye and Lord Brooke presented themselves at York, but refused to swear an oath of obedience to fight against the Scots and returned home with their soldiers. The Earl of Essex, a man of Puritan sympathies and some military experience, who harboured no love for the Scots, received command over the 18,000 foot-soldiers, and did his best, with the help of veteran English officers from the Low Countries, to prepare them for the coming campaign. The Earl of Northumberland commanded the army in his capacity as Earl Marshal, and Lord Holland served as General of the Horse.

During March the Covenanters captured the castles of Edinburgh, Dalkeith, Douglas and Dumbarton, while in the north the forces of the Earl of Montrose brushed past the 3,000 soldiers of the loyal Marquess of Huntly, chief of Clan Gordon, and occupied Aberdeen. The English army marched north by way of Durham and Newcastle to Berwick, where the King pitched camp outside the walls and himself lived under canvas with the army. On 2 June news reached him that the Scots army of 20,000 men under General Alexander Leslie had reached Kelso, a day's march away. A few days later Charles watched the Scots army through his perspective glass as they marched along the opposite bank of the Tweed to face him, their unfurled colours bearing in large gold letters the proud motto: FOR CHRIST'S CROWN AND COVENANT.

Yet neither Charles nor the Covenanters wished to risk all on a pitched battle. A week of negotiations produced on 19 June the so-called Pacification of Berwick, which bought time for both sides by an agreement to hold a free Parliament in Scotland and another Assembly. When these bodies met later in the year they merely re-enacted the work of the Glasgow assembly, and once more both sides made preparations to continue their dispute on the battlefield. Wentworth, who returned to England in September, threw his considerable energy into these preparations. The King created him Earl of Strafford in 1640, and later in the year made him a Knight of the Garter.

Shortage of money bedevilled the royal strategists. Owing to Hampden's stand, the attempt to levy Ship-Money again in 1639 met with almost universal resistance, not least from the officers who were supposed to collect it. The Sheriff of Northamptonshire, for example, claimed that he could not proceed because the Grand Jury of his county had declared the tax illegal. The Sheriff of Yorkshire actively campaigned to persuade the gentry not to pay. Finch, now Lord Keeper of the Privy Seal, exhorted the judges before they went on circuit in the summer of 1640 to urge the prompt payment of the tax. 'I know not how it comes about', he told them, 'that there is not alacrity and cheerfulness given to the obedience of his Majesty's writs for Ship-Money.' If Finch spoke the words sincerely he must have been singularly lacking in any political acumen.

Such financial expedients as the now discredited Ship-Money could clearly not suffice for an invasion of Scotland. Confident of his ability to manage the House of Commons through an array of royal councillors and courtiers, Strafford persuaded the King to swallow his pride and summon a Parliament to vote him money for the forthcoming campaign. In March 1640 Strafford made a flying visit to Dublin and returned home with encouraging news that the Irish Parliament had voted money for the war, and agreed to expand the Irish army to 8,000 foot and 1,000 horse for use against the Scots. Doubtless Strafford believed that the English Parliament would follow suit when they heard the lengths to which the Scots were prepared to go in their revolt against their gracious monarch.

On Monday 13 April Parliament assembled at Westminster. In a short speech the King explained to both Houses why he had decided 'to renew his acquaintance with them.' Then, possibly on account of his speech impediment, the King left Lord Keeper Finch to give a full account of the Scottish rebellion. From the point of veiw of the House of Commons, a less suitable spokesman than the obnoxious Finch could hardly have been found. He soon confirmed that he was devoid of all political tact by comparing Charles to the Sun God of Greek myth, who was 'pleased at this time to lay aside his rays' and talk with them. With further classical and biblical allusions he warned them against attempting to seize the reins of government into their own hands. The King had summoned them so that 'the supplies of his subjects might be let down again like the precious dew'. To prove the treachery of the Scots, he brandished an intercepted letter from them to the French King asking for aid. It was addressed 'Au Roy', a phrase which in particular had incensed King Charles on the grounds that the Scots thereby regarded the French monarch as their natural sovereign rather than himself.

The House of Commons trooped back to St Stephen's Chapel and chose as their Speaker a king's serjeant named John Glanville. Business began in earnest on Thursday when the House met at the usual time of eight a.m. Most of the 493 elected members crowded the long tiers of benches. Eleven years had elapsed since Hampden, now one of two members for Buckinghamshire, had sat in that chamber, and the events of the intervening period, added to his former parliamentary experience, had uniquely qualified him for leadership. After a period of shuffling silence while the members gazed at each other, John Pym, member for Tavistock, rose to his feet and delivered a set-piece two-hour speech. He began with some courteous references to the King's justice and wisdom, but averred that many unwarrantable things had happened since Parliament last met. 'The powers of Parliament are to the body politic as the rational faculties of the soul to man', he declared in the course of his comprehensive survey of grievances such as the Ship-Money judgment and the profusion of illegal proclamations. Before voting subsidies, the Commons should confer with the House of Lords to determine 'the causes and remedies of these insupportable grievances' and then make petition to the King for their redress.

The next two speakers spoke specifically on the Ship-Money issue. Harbottle Grimston, Recorder of Colchester, commented upon that irregular business of the judges being asked to give their opinion in 1637 directly to the King. As for the judgment itself, Grimston felt sure that those who voted for the legality of Ship-Money had done so against their consciences. As Sir George Croke's son-in-law, Grimston may have had some inside information – or gossip – on that score. Another lawyer, George Peard of Barnstaple, whose mother had refused to pay her ten shillings in 1637 and again in 1639, spoke without mincing his words: he called the tax 'an abomination'.

Sir Edward Herbert, who owed his seat to Laud's influence, rose to reply for the King. One eye-witness of the scene recalled that Herbert took special care 'to stroke and commend Mr Hampden, who sat under him, for his great temper and modesty in the prosecution of that suit'. Then he elaborated on the theme of the King's responsible procedure of consulting the judges, and dwelt upon the length of the hearing and the fact that only two judges at a time had given their arguments in a single day. Having established this impression of royal fairness, Herbert then singled out Peard for calling Ship-Money 'an abomination' and demanded that he should be summoned to the bar to make apology. Some members old and new who owed their seats to Court influence took up the cry, a fact which led thirty-one-year-old Edward Hyde, who later became Lord Clarendon, sitting for the first time in the Commons, to conclude that the prevailing temper of the House was not opposed to the King.

During the mornings of the second week the debate continued on grievances. On Thursday 23 April, St George's Day, Secretary Windebanke made an eloquently patriotic appeal again for a handsome gift of money, but the Commons would not be diverted from their inquiry into the causes of the nation's troubles. The House arose at twelve each day and the committees met in the afternoon. Hampden exercised much of his leadership in these afternoon committees, sitting with a different one every day between Thursday 16 April and Friday 25 April except on Sunday. On the first two days the committees he attended met to look at election returns and the state of the parliamentary journals and records after the long intermission. Drawing up the necessary petition to the King on the violation of privilege at the end of the 1629 Parliament occupied two more afternoons.

On Monday 21 April his committee inquired into the effect of the commission granted to Convocation. Next day it was reported that Mr Dell, the secretary to the Archbishop of Canterbury, would have been brought to the bar of the House of Commons to make apology for misreporting what Pym had said, 'but for Mr Hampden that stood his friend'. Church matters continued to occupy much of his time. The petition of a Puritan clergyman, Dr Smart, for instance, who had been punished by Laud's court for protesting against the setting up of 'Babylonish ornaments' in Durham Cathedral where he served as a canon, came before his next committee on the same day that he interceded for Dell.

Hampden's standing now as a person of influence may be partly gauged by the fact that his distant kinsman John Williams, Bishop of Lincoln, asked him to move the House of Commons to take up his case as a breach of parliamentary privilege. Heavily fined and imprisoned in the Tower for suborning witnesses in 1637, the injudicious Bishop Williams again incurred the wrath of his inveterate enemy Laud when a letter from the headmaster of Westminster School was discovered in his possession referring to the primate, although not by name, as 'the little meddling hocus-pocus'. As a bishop not averse to the Puritan cause in the established Church, Williams may well have expected the Commons to act as advocate for him, but the pressure of business and certain tensions in Parliament between the two Houses would not allow it, as Hampden explained tactfully in his reply:

> My Lord – I should be very ready to serve you in anything I conceived good for you and fit for me; but in your Lordship's present commands I doubt that to make overture of your intentions, and be prevented by a sudden conclusion of the Parliament, which many fear, may render your condition worse than now it is.
>
> To begin with, our House is not the right place; the most important businesses of the King and the kingdom are pressed on with such expedition that any of a more particular nature will be but unwelcome and hardly prosecuted with effect. Besides that, there is at this instant a tenderness between the Lords and us about privilege. And for my own unfitness, I need mention no more but my disability to carry through a business of this nature, though your Lordship may easily conceive another incompetency in my person.
>
> In these regards I humbly desire your Lordship to excuse me and thereby to lay a new obligation upon me of being
>
> Your Lordship's most humble servant,
> JOHN HAMPDEN

Westminster, April 29, 1640

This 'tenderness' between the two Houses had arisen because the King and his advisers had persuaded the House of Lords to urge the Commons to vote subsidies before the redress of their grievances. Among the 149 lords spiritual and temporal eligible to sit in the Upper House, the 26 bishops and the 82 peers who had been created by Charles or his father formed a fairly solid core of support for the King, but not all of them were present at Westminster in April 1640. The small group of Puritan peers tended to be more diligent in attendance, and exerted an influence out of proportion to their small numbers. In the first week of this Parliament they compelled a bishop to beg forgiveness on his knees for referring to Lord Saye as 'one who savoured of a Scottish Covenanter'.

On Friday 24 April, after the King had spoken to them in person, the Lords obediently agreed (by 61 votes to 25) to seek a conference with the Commons and then to advise them to vote the money first. Hampden had sat on a committee the day before charged with preparing an agenda for a conference with the Lords based on the petitions for redress of grievances which members had carried up to London in their saddlebags. Six counties, for example, had petitioned against Ship-Money; many northern shires found the provision of coat-and-conduct money for the soldiers an especially objectionable burden. On Friday afternoon he attended this committee, and thus had advance warning of the vote in the Lords that morning. On Saturday he reported the outcome of the joint committee's deliberations in the Commons.

On Monday morning, 27 April, the Commons heard the motion passed by the Lords and at once took exception to it. For the right to initiate votes for supply belonged by immemorial tradition to their House, and not to the Lords. They requested an immediate consultation with the Upper House to discuss this breach of privilege. Hyde thought that the King, or rather his advisers, had made a tactical blunder; whereas the Commons had evinced no signs of hostility, now their 'whole temper was shaken'. The consultation restored equilibrium to some extent, for the Lords dropped their motion, but a 'tenderness' between the two Houses lingered longer below the surface.

Towards the end of the third week of the session the King offered to abolish Ship-Money in exchange for a vote of twelve subsidies amounting to £840,000. On Sunday 3 May, the Privy Council met to debate whether or not to lower the demand to eight or even six subsidies, but reached no conclusion. After prayers on Monday, the Commons heard the proposition read again, and a great debate on the King's offer developed. At length, feeling that a majority in the House had reached a consensus that anything given to the King should not be connected with Ship-Money, and thus the time was ripe for a vote, Hampden rose to his feet and proposed: 'Whether the House would consent to the proposition made by the King as it was contained in the message?'

As the House was sitting as a grand committee, with its own nominee, William Lenthall, in the Speaker's Chair, Serjeant Glanville could contribute to the debate. Twelve subsidies amounted to very little when spread over the country, he argued. Glanville's own share for his broad estates, which he quoted, certainly did not seem much. Leaning over backwards to carry his audience with him, the lawyer let slip in passing the admission that Ship-Money 'was against law, if he understood what law was'. After a short silence, others took up this line of argument. By now the House had sat long after noon, and many impatient voices called for Hampden's motion to be put to the vote. As Hyde observed, Hampden was 'the most popular man in the House'.

Hyde had enjoyed the King's favour during his undergraduate days at Oxford, and since then he had taken care to make himself known to those prominent at Court. Seeing now an opportunity to serve the King he stood up and denounced Hampden's motion as a captious question. For those members who wanted to give the King money, but not in the proportion or manner laid down, could not express their will by voting on such a motion. Instead he suggested that the House should vote first a 'yea or nay to supply', and then – if the affirmatives won – vote a second time on the means of raising the money. Glanville declared that his young fellow-countryman from Wiltshire had proposed a motion which agreed very well with what he had been trying to say. The House erupted in shouts and counter-shouts:

'Mr Hampden's question!' 'Mr Hyde's question!' Secretary Vane then rather spoilt Hyde's motion by stating that the King would not accept subsidies except in the manner he had laid down. The weary House, which had sat from eight a.m. until nearly five p.m., adjourned the debate until next morning.

A meeting of the Privy Council, hastily summoned at six o'clock the following morning (5 May), considered the probability that even if the Commons did vote money they would almost certainly make a condition that it should not be used against Scotland. Moreover, the Commons planned to debate the Scottish matter on Thursday and might conceivably express sympathy for the rebellious Covenanters. The King decided to take no chances and to dissolve Parliament. To avoid a repetition of the scene at the end of the 1629 Parliament, he sent for the Speaker to come to him at the House of Lords. Then the Commons received a summons to attend him in the Upper House. Here Hampden and his friends stood to hear Lord Keeper Finch announce the end of their sitting.

On Wednesday 6 May, royal officers arrested Pym, Hampden, Sir Walter Earle, the Earl of Warwick, Lord Brooke, and Lord Saye. In a search for incriminating correspondence with the Scots, the constables ransacked their lodgings and even turned out their pockets. A list of Hampden's papers seized on this occasion still survives. From such items on the list as 'certain confused notes of the parliament business written in several paper books with black lead', however, the royal inquisitors gleaned nothing and they set Hampden at liberty.

Hampden lived in a house that summer in Gray's Inn Lane, near to Pym's lodgings. In August, Secretary Windebanke reported to the King that Essex, Warwick, Bedford, Saye, Russell, Brooke, Pym and Hampden were meeting regularly. With these other opposition leaders Hampden corresponded with the Covenanters, offering them general support short of any action which could be possibly construed as treason. Later, royalist ballad-writers linked his name with the subsequent Scottish invasion of the north of

England. Sir John Denham put these words in Hampden's mouth:

> *Did I for this bring in the Scot?*
> *For 'tis no secret now – the plot*
> *Was Saye's and mine together.*
> *Did I for this return again,*
> *And spend a winter there in vain*
> *Once more to invite them hither?*

In a tract entitled *London's Farewell to the Parliament* there is a ballad which alludes, albeit in an unflattering way, to Hampden's intelligence and learning:

> *Farewell, John Hampden, with hey, with hey;*
> *Farewell, John Hampden, with hoe;*
> *He's a sly and subtle fox,*
> *Well read in Buchanan and Knox,*
> *With a hey, trolly, lolly, loe.*

Another song mentioned him in the same breath as Denzil Holles, and again accused him of bringing in the Scots:

> *'My venom swells,' qoth Holles,*
> *'And that his Majesty knows.'*
> *'And I,' quoth Hampden, 'fetch the Scots*
> *Whence all this mischief grows.'*

The ultimate responsibility, however, for drawing down the Scottish army upon his head must rest with King Charles and the policies which he attempted to force upon his northern subjects. The King left London for York on 20 August, the day that a Scottish army of 25,000 soldiers crossed the Tweed into England. A petition drawn up by Pym, Hampden, and their associates, but signed by Bedford, Warwick, Essex, Saye, Brooke, Mandeville, and six other peers, followed the King to York, reminding him of the strong feeling against his innovations in religion and favours to Roman Catholics. It asked for the abolition of such grievances as monopolies and Ship-Money and that 'the authors and counsellors of them may be brought to such legal trial and condign punishment as the nature of the several offences shall require'. On a new note, the peers implored him not to employ any Irish Papist soldiers in England. The petition concluded with the expressed desire that a speedy peace might be concluded with the Scots.

At least the last wish would be granted. For again both the King and the Covenanters chose to talk rather than fight. The two sides appointed commissioners to meet at Ripon on 2 October, and agreed that the Scots army would be paid £850 a day while the negotiations lasted. Faced with the presence of a hostile army on English soil, however, the King took the additional and proper step of summoning a new Parliament, which would meet on 3 November. Thus he set the stage for the work of the Long Parliament.

Chapter eight

THE LONG PARLIAMENT

I commend my humble suit to you and the rest of the 460 Kings who sit at Westminster to have regard to the honour of us soldiers.

EDMUND VERNEY

On the afternoon of Tuesday 3 November the King disembarked from his barge at Parliament-stairs and walked to the House of Lords in order to open what would become the most famous of all English parliaments. No gaily-caparisoned procession from Whitehall drew crowds to the streets on this occasion. Owing to the short interval between the issue of writs and the elections themselves, few members pressed into the House of Lords to hear the royal opening speech. In words coloured by hindsight Clarendon described it as a sad and melancholic scene, presaging the 'unusual and unnatural events' which lay ahead. Hampden was again returned for Buckinghamshire, the other county representative being Arthur Goodwin.

Seating himself on the state chair, the King informed Parliament that he now placed the whole affairs of the Kingdom in their hands. He had resolved to follow their advice on how to obtain peace with the Scots, whom he referred to twice as the 'rebels'. The exigencies of war had produced some grievances, the King airily admitted, but he would correct them with their assistance. Both in Church and State the accepted norms of Elizabethan times would be restored. With these promising words in their ears the Commons trooped away to elect William Lenthall as their speaker, and the King accepted him in the usual ceremony two days later. Before they received the Sacrament in St Margaret's

Church, however, the Commons ominously ordered the altar rails to be taken out and burned, and the table to be moved into the main body of the nave.

Hyde observed 'a marvellous elated countenance' in most of the members of the House of Commons. Doubtless they were pleased to see each other again so soon, for, if nothing else, a parliament was a great social occasion. But they also sensed the power and opportunity that events in the north had given into their hands. Hyde thought that they now spoke a more radical 'dialect', as he called it. In a conversation which took place in Westminster Hall, pacing up and down just before Parliament met, he claimed that John Pym had told him: 'We must now be of another temper than we were in the last Parliament. We must not only sweep the house clean below, but must pull down all the cobwebs which hung in top and corners, that they might not breed dust and so make a foul house hereafter.' Warming to his theme, Pym continued: 'We have now an opportunity to make our country happy, by removing all grievances and pulling up the causes of them by the roots, if all men would do their duties.'

Hyde held a different concept of duty, and he felt that the majority of members in the Commons shared it insofar as they were disposed to honour the King, obey the laws and uphold the traditional form of government in the Church. How then did the revolution come about? Through a combination of errors of judgment by the King and his advisers, Hyde argued, and the effective action of a small conspiracy of malcontents and extremists in Parliament who played upon the fears of the majority in order to achieve their ultimate aim of destroying the Court. Of course Hyde wrote his great *History* as a die-hard Royalist with a political purpose in mind. Therefore his interpretations are frequently biassed and his memory sometimes conveniently at fault. But he remains our chief eyewitness, and there is much truth in his view that a very small group of eight or nine men exercised the real leadership within the body of perhaps three to four hundred reformist members.

Hyde identified three 'great contrivers and designers' among the score or so of Puritan peers in the House of Lords:

the Earl of Bedford, Lord Saye and Lord Mandeville. On account of his lands, wealth, and rank, Bedford occupied the premier position, but it soon appeared to Hyde that this sensible and genial man sought no more than power at Court. Lord Saye had shown not only implacable opposition to such expedients as Ship-Money, but also disliked the bishops and episcopacy in general. In constrast to this rather reserved old peer, with his reputation for subtlety, the young Mandeville possessed the looks, manners and generosity (with other people's money) of a born courtier. Son and heir to the Earl of Manchester, the Lord Privy Seal, he had been married into the family of the Duke of Buckingham, and accompanied Charles on the Spanish adventure. As his relig-ion deepened, however, he withdrew from Court. After the death of his first wife he married the daughter of the Earl of Warwick, another great patron of the Puritans despite his somewhat dissolute personal habits, and thus moved into the leadership group. These three peers had the complete trust of the three chief managers in the House of Commons, whom Hyde named as Pym, Hampden, and St John.

John Pym was about fifty-six years of age, and therefore belonged to the older generation in the Commons. Like Hamp-den, more than ten years his junior, he had first become a member of the House in 1614. Although he owned some family estates in Somerset, Pym made his way in the world primarily as a man of business, as an officer in the Exchequer and as Treasurer of the Providence Company. His chief motive in politics seems to have been an opposition to the spread of Roman Catholicism. Like other Puritans born before the Armada, he did not distinguish between the Popish menace abroad and the insidious activities of Catholics and Arminians at home. Pym probably owed his seat at Tavistock to the Earl of Bedford.

Pym the manager is well known, but Pym the man remains an enigma. An official engraving by John Glover presents us with the bust of a man looking like a stout and prosperous Elizabethan merchant. Carefully-brushed hair curls inwards below the ears, framing a rather florid face decorated with an upturning moustache. A thick fold of flesh sags below the jaw-line. The eyes are half-closed, confident, shrewd and also cunning, with a hint of smile-lines at their corners. But in Samuel Cooper's less well-known miniature portrait the hair is unkempt and there is a defiant stare in Pym's dark brown eyes, accentuated by the lift of his head and downward curling lips. Both moustache and beard are thin and scraggy, and the linen collar is carelessly wrinkled. There are lined hollows below the high cheek-bones, and the double chin is much reduced in size. It is the portrait of a revolutionary.

Pym was the 'front man' of the opposition in the sense that he opened the debates with major set-piece speeches. Although not such a good orator as Sir John Eliot, he excelled as a manager of parliamentary business. But in modern terms he was more a Leader of the House than a Prime Minister. The higher direction of affairs probably lay in Hampden's hands. In contrast to Pym, Hyde wrote, 'Mr Hampden was a man of much greater cunning and it may be of the greatest address and insinuation to bring anything to pass which he desired of any man of that time, and who laid the design deepest.' In private conversations and meetings, he asserted, Pym was 'much governed' by Hampden. Thus Hampden may well have been the true architect of the English revolution.

A groundless attribution of Hampden's political opposition in 1640 to an unsatisfied ambition for a place at Court was merely Clarendon's method of reminding his contemporary readers in a tactful way how much King Charles had blundered by not encouraging and employing such 'a very extraordinary person.' Hyde knew Hampden well, though not as a friend, and he shared fully the national admiration for his character. For Clarendon it is Hampden and not Pym, still less Cromwell, who is the hero of the Puritans, the Ulysses of their Greek camp. Despite doubts that he might not be doing the Royalist cause much good by writing about Hampden in such glowing terms, it is to Clarendon's everlasting credit that he let his high testimony to the political and personal stature of the man stand unaltered:

> When this parliament began, the eyes of all men were fixed on him as their *Patriae pater*, and the pilot that must steer their vessel through the tempests and rocks which threatened it. And I am persuaded his power and interest at that time was greater to do good or hurt than any man's in the kingdom, or any man of his

rank hath had in any time: for his reputation for honesty was universal, and his affections seemed so publicly guided that no corrupt or private ends could bias them.

John Hampden's ability as a listener, and his sensitivity to the mood or common feeling of the House, made him an outstanding debater. Although he could speak briefly and effectively, he left the long opening set-piece orations to others. Hyde, who had often seen him at work, described his method thus:

> He was not a man of many words, and rarely began the discourse, or made the first entrance upon any business that was assumed; but a very weighty speaker, and, after he had heard a full debate and observed how the House was like to be inclined, took up the argument and shortly and clearly and craftily so stated it that he commonly conducted it to the conclusion he desired; and if he found he could not do that, he never was without the dexterity to divert the debate to another time, and to prevent the determining anything in the negative which might prove inconvenient in the future.

Outside the debating chamber, Hampden exerted a similar subtle influence on events through his winning personality. His natural cheerfulness and affability broke through the sobriety and strictness of his Puritan self-discipline in an engaging way. Despite a national reputation which could have induced pride in his own opinions, Hampden preferred to continue as himself: the self-effacing friend revealed in the letters to Sir John Eliot. Clarendon again:

> He made so great a show of civility and modesty and humility and always of mistrusting his own judgment and of esteeming his with whom he conferred for the present, that he seemed to have no opinions or resolutions but such as he contracted from the information and instruction he received upon the discourses of others, whom he had a wonderful art of governing and leading into his principles and inclinations whilst they believed that he wholly depended on their counsel and advice.

With his hindsight knowledge of Hampden's later inexorable firmness of purpose, Hyde accuses him of initially acting the part of a moderate out of deviousness: 'no man had ever a greater power over himself or was less the man that he seemed to be, which shortly after appeared to every body when he cared less to keep on the mask'. But the charge of play-acting in the first six months of the Long Parliament could better be levied far more effectively against those inseparable friends Mr Edward Hyde and Viscount Falkland. No, Hyde cannot disguise the fact that he liked Hampden as a man and respected him as a politician. To mollify his readers he has to hint that he perceptively saw through Hampden's disguise, while claiming to have resisted his evident charm. But Hyde gives himself away when he adds that even upon those who could not share his convictions, Hampden 'always left the character of an ingenious and conscientious man'. In sum, he was 'a very wise man, and of great parts, and possessed with the most absolute spirit of popularity, that is, the most absolute faculties to govern the people, of any man I knew.'

On 11 November Pym formally impeached the Earl of Strafford at the bar of the House of Lords. For the next six months the proceedings against 'Black Tom Tyrant' dominated the business of the Long Parliament. The Commons appointed a committee of twelve members to manage this 'first great design', as Hyde called it, consisting of Pym, Hampden, Holles, Lord Digby, Strode, Sir Walter Earle, Selden, St John, Maynard, Palmer, Glyn, and Whitelocke. As brother-in-law to the accused man, Holles successfully begged to be excused from the committee. Bulstrode Whitelocke, who now sat in Parliament for the Buckinghamshire constituency of Great Marlow, acted as their chairman. Whitelocke described Hampden as 'a most active and leading member' who spoke 'rationally and subtly'. Whitelocke also remarked on his popularity: 'he was well beloved in his country . . . as also in the House of Commons'.

While the Strafford committee, meeting in the afternoons, slowly drew up the particular charges and collected evidence, the House proceeded against the other personal 'instruments' of absolute rule. Falkland and Hyde led the attack on Lord Keeper Finch, the principal promoter of Ship-Money, an imposition which the House had made haste to declare illegal on 7 December. One morning, at the prompting of the two friends Falkland and Hyde, a committee of eight left St. Stephen's Chapel at ten o'clock, and working in pairs they interviewed the surprised judges in their chambers. Croke and one other admitted that Finch had pressed them to find for the King.

On 21 December, Finch was summoned to the bar of the House for examination. The Speaker told him that he could sit down in the chair placed there for him if he wished. From the benches Whitelocke observed his conduct closely: 'He made a low obeisance, and laying down the Seal, and his hat in the chair, himself leaning on the back side of it, made a very elegant, and ingenuous speech, in his own vindication . . . and delivered with an excellent grace, and gesture as well as words.' He assured the House of Commons that he would rather beg his bread from door to door with their blessing than be never so high and lie under their displeasure. 'If I may not live to serve you, I desire that I may die in your good opinion and favour.' His eloquence and bearing impressed the House, and many thought 'it was a sad sight to see a person of his greatness, parts, and favour, to appear in such a posture, before such an assembly, to plead for his life and fortunes'. Yet the Commons voted to impeach the Lord Keeper for treasonable offences such as 'soliciting, persuading and threatening the judges to deliver their opinions for the levying of Ship-Money'.

Hyde suspected that the debate over Finch was deliberately prolonged so that the accusation could not be made to the Lords that day. Possibly on account of Finch's Puritan daughter, the redoubtable Lady Anne who had married Sir William Waller in 1637, the leaders of the Commons may have dragged their heels. Be that as it may, Finch found that he had time to make good his escape. That night he took ship in the Thames and sailed to France, where he lived in exile until his death in 1660. Subsequently all the other judges who gave opinions in favour of the King, except for Vernon who was dead, and Jones who had expressed much doubt about it, lost their judicial offices and suffered impeachment as well.

Secretary Windebanke, a notorious patron of Papists, had already fled overseas, and several lesser servants of the Crown followed his lead. On 18 December, the House appointed Hampden to a committee to draw up charges against Archbishop Laud. Having secured agreement for the articles on 24 February, two days later Pym, Hampden and the lawyer Maynard impeached the Archbishop of Canterbury, the first subject of the King, at the bar of the House of Lords. On 1 March the Lords committed the Archbishop to the Tower, and would allow him no conversation with his old friend Strafford, who was now awaiting trial in that prison.

The forty-eight-year-old Earl, racked by painful gout and the stone, had been ferried up the river to hear the charges against him read in the Lords on 4 February. Back in the Tower that evening he wrote to his wife a letter which breathes his over-confident spirit:

> Sweet Harte.
>
> It is long since I writ unto you, for I am here in such a trouble as gives me little or no respite. The charge is now come in, and I am now able, praise God, to tell you that I conceive there is nothing capital, and for the rest I know at the worst his Majesty will pardon all, without hurting my fortune, and then we shall be happy by God's grace. Therefore comfort yourself, for I trust these clouds will away, and that we shall have fair weather afterwards.
>
> Your loving husband,
STRAFFORD

When a soldier in the Tower showed him the new beheading axe, fashioned for state prisoners with a short silver-mounted handle, Strafford merely smiled.

On 22 March the great trial of the Earl of Strafford opened in Westminster Hall. The House of Commons occupied most of the tiers of seats in the two grandstands on either side of the Hall, with the Scottish Commissioners, a committee from Ireland, and some favoured friends squeezed in among them. In return for being allowed to attend as a House the members had agreed to sit uncovered, that is without their hats on. The peers, in their ermine robes and hats, sat according to rank on benches covered in red cloth in the pool of the court. The law lords clustered on the centre square of woolsacks, like survivors lining a raft. Clerks knelt around a second set of low woolsacks to drive their feathered quills over their papers to record the trial, but they looked like monks at prayer. The public crowd in the gallery ate and drank noisily, and aroused much adverse comment because of their unwillingness to go out from the Hall into the streets to perform other natural functions.

The Earl of Arundel as Lord High Steward deputized for the sick Lord Keeper, and perched high on a woolsack presiding over the proceedings. The King and Queen sat in a latticed and curtained box in the wooden gallery erected behind an empty chair of state; as the trial proceeded it was observed that the King drew back the curtains in order to gain a better view. At the other end of the Hall, on a raised wooden dais, surrounded by lawyers and guarded by the Lieutenant of the Tower, Sir William Balfour, stood Strafford. He was dressed in a black gown and close-fitting cap, and wore his George on a gold chain. The unshaven chin and stooping shoulders told their tale, but Strafford's bright black eyes and restless long hands spoke volumes about his intelligence and energy.

The two most serious charges of the nine general ones against Strafford alleged that he had 'endeavoured to subvert the fundamental laws and government of England and Ireland, and instead thereof to introduce an arbitrary and tyrannical government against law', and that 'he had laboured to subvert the rights of Parliaments and the ancient course of parliamentary proceedings'. Twenty-eight more specific counts, drawn from Strafford's rule as Lord President of the Council of the North and as Lord Deputy in Ireland, completed the case of the Commons. During the eighteen days of the trial Whitelocke's committee concentrated their attention strategically on the general charges while Strafford and his lawyers attempted to fight the battle on the refutable particular incidents.

Although the participants and onlookers alike came to admire Strafford's resourceful self-defence on points of law, a damning picture of him as a high-handed and imperious ruler began to emerge. For example, on one occasion he had whacked a page with a cane for dropping a stool on his gouty foot, in itself a trivial incident. But a kinsman of that page, Lord Mountnorris, boasted at a Dublin dinner party that 'the gentleman had a brother who would not have taken such a blow'. Hearing of it, Strafford had Mountnorris tried by a court-martial, who sentenced him to death. It is true that Strafford subsequently procured for him a royal pardon and claimed that the young lord 'was an insolent person, and that he took this course to humble him'. Allowances could be made for Strafford in this particular instance and in many others, but the general impression created by such cumulative evidence looked less and less favourable. Sir Thomas Knyvet, one of the country gentry up in London who spent a day or two at the trial, respected the courtesy, calmness and courage of the defendant, but saw him as one whom the prosecution had 'laid open to be so foul a man'.

The Commons accused Strafford of declaring to the King in an inner committee of state (called the Cabinet Council) held after the dissolution of the Short Parliament: 'Sir, you have now done your duty, and your subjects have failed in theirs; and therefore you are absolved from the rules of government, and may supply yourself by extraordinary ways; you must prosecute the war vigorously; you have an army in Ireland, with which you may reduce this kingdom.' Strafford denied that he had uttered these last words, and produced four of the seven privy councillors then present to bear witness to that fact. Even if he had said these words, he added, *'this* kingdom' clearly referred to Scotland. Moreover, even if he had meant the kingdom of England, the testimony of one witness – Secretary Vane, his inveterate enemy – would be insufficient to prove him guilty. For it was well established that more than one witness was required to prove guilt in cases of treason.

On 10 April Strafford blocked an attempt by the prosecution to introduce new evidence in order to reopen this crucial twenty-third accusation. He watched the lawyers leave the Hall with another smile on his face, while the King in his box could be seen openly laughing. The so-called 'evidence' turned out to be a copy which Vane's son had made of his father's original minute of the fatal meeting, which the younger Vane had conveniently come across in a small red velvet box when rifling through his father's papers in search of some legal document. It proved disappointing even when produced outside the court. Lord Digby for one said that he would not send a man to his death on such evidence. As Digby, a member of the prosecuting committee, sent a copy of Vane's new evidence to the King, it is clear that the unsuspecting Pym and Hampden had a traitor in their camp.

That afternoon the House of Commons gave a first reading to a Bill of Attainder .against Strafford. Whereas impeachment was essentially a judicial process, requiring legal proof of the alleged crimes, this alternative method could lead to an Act of Parliament declaring that the safety of the state made the death of the accused a necessity. It allowed those who were convinced of Strafford's moral and political guilt, but thought him technically innocent on narrowly legal grounds, to vote with a better conscience for his death. The Bill received a second reading in the Commons on 14 April, hard on the heels of the news that the King still refused to disband the Irish army. The following day Lord Falkland announced that his scruples of conscience had been removed by the switch to the Bill of Attainder approach.

On 16 April the House debated whether or not to proceed with the trial. Oliver St John asserted that their Bill made them the judges now, and therefore it would be a dishonour to hear counsel anywhere but at their own bar, and Sir John Colepeper supported him by urging 'if we reply to Lord Strafford's counsel before the Lords, we prejudice our cause in taking away the power of treason.' Sir Ralph Verney noted that Hampden alone spoke for continuing with the trial. 'The Bill now depending does not tie us to go by bill,' he argued. 'Our counsel has been heard. *Ergo*, in justice we must hear his. No more prejudice to go to hear matter of law, than to hear counsel to matter of fact.' Hampden suggested a compromise: 'Our members appointed to manage the evidence might speak first to matter of law, and then retire from the bar to their places among us. The Earl of Strafford's counsel having spoken at the bar on the left side of the earl, our members might again come down to their former place, and answer them what they thought material to be answered.' His reasoning prevailed, and Strafford's counsel spoke in Westminster Hall the following day. But the trial had virtually ended. On 21 April the Commons passed the Bill of Attainder by 204 to 59. Pym voted for the motion, but Hampden significantly abstained.

On the afternoon of 26 April Hyde went to a place called Piccadilly, where there stood a fair house for entertainment and gambling in grounds well-shaded, with gravel walks and two bowling greens. The Earl of Bedford came up to him and they fell into a discussion about public affairs. 'This business concerning the Earl of Strafford is a rock upon which we should all split,' Bedford said, arguing that the passion of Parliament would destroy the kingdom. The King had of course accepted that Strafford had made himself unemploy-able in the royal service, but his conscience would not allow him to give assent to an Act ordaining his execution. Accord-ing to Hyde, Bedford then asked him to do his best to persuade Essex to support a move for clemency. Following Bedford's directions, Hyde found Essex strolling with Hert-ford beside a bowling green on the lower terrace. When Hertford had tactfully left them alone, Hyde put the case for a punishment of Strafford short of death. Essex merely shook his solid head and answered, 'Stone-dead has no fellow.' The King, he claimed, could always pardon Strafford later and restore him to his service after the dissolution of this Parlia-ment. Clearly Essex had made up his mind, and he told Hyde 'familiarly' to stop talking about it for he was tired of the argument for that day.

Three days later St John addressed the re-assembled court in Westminster Hall in favour of proceeding by the Bill of Attainder, which had already received a second reading in the Lords. 'It is true we give law to hares and deer, because they be beasts of chase,' he said, 'but it was never accounted either cruelty or foul play to knock foxes and wolves on the head as they can be found, because they be beasts of prey.' It was not the most convincing legal argument, but it illus-trates the desperate resolve of those who sought Strafford's death at any price.

At this crucial juncture the Earl of Bedford – perhaps the one man who could have saved Strafford's life – fell ill and died within days. Bereft of his moderate counsels, the King took the unwise step of speaking to both Houses on Saturday

1 May in a personal bid to save Strafford's life. His conscience, he declared, would never allow him to give the royal assent to such a bill. As it appeared as if Charles was declaring that the ultimate court of appeal in England lay in his own personal conscience, not in Parliament as the nation's council, his intervention did more harm than good.

During the following week the pressures mounted on those peers who still attended the Upper House, shouldering their way through a mob shouting 'Justice! Justice!' Threatening rumours circulated rapidly in the emotional atmosphere of Westminster. On Monday 3 May the Commons drew up a declaration stating that they would live and die for the true Protestant religion, the liberties and rights of the subject and the freedom and privilege of Parliament. That day Hampden, Goodwin, Verney, and many others signed the Protestation, as it came to be called. On Wednesday 5 May Pym disclosed details of a rather vague plot by Whitehall courtiers who had served in the Bishop's War in league with some army officers, including some members of the House of Commons, to seize strategic ports and strong-points. Behind these rumours borne upon the winds of nervous alarm lay the fear of a conspiracy between the army in the north and the Catholic interest. So tense became the House of Commons that when a board in the gallery cracked under the weight of two fat spectators, Sir John Wray called out that he smelt gunpowder and the members rushed out into the lobby. The City militia, who were also known as the trained-bands, hearing the rumour, marched as far as Covent Garden before they heard that it was false. Thus it was against the backcloth of suspicion and fear that the House of Lords voted on Saturday 8 May in favour of the Bill of Attainder. Now only the resolution of the King stood between Strafford and the headsman's axe.

Charles spent Sunday 9 May in a personal garden of Gethsemane made worse by contradictory advice of his bishops. Archbishop Ussher and Bishop Juxon counselled him to follow his conscience, while Bishop Williams of Lincoln argued casuistically that he must distinguish between his personal and public conscience. On 4 May Strafford had written to the King releasing him from any obligation to save

his life. It was perhaps the finest gesture of loyalty ever made
by an English minister to his sovereign. Williams urged the
King to weigh in the balance his responsibility to Strafford
against his care for his people, his wife and his children. The
King hesitated and then made his moral judgment. Next
morning he signed an order granting authority to three
commissioners to give the royal assent to Strafford's execution. 'My Lord Strafford's condition is happier than mine,'
he said, in some self-pity. But the King's lack of wisdom had
brought about this situation. Nor had he yet learnt his
lesson.

In vain on Tuesday 11 May the King sent the Prince of
Wales to plead in the House of Lords for the life of Strafford –
the carpenters were already at work erecting the scaffold and
public stands on Tower Hill. Just before noon on Wednesday 12 May, before perhaps the largest crowd ever assembled in one place in England, Strafford stepped out of the
Tower to meet death with characteristic disdain. A deep
silence descended upon the thousands of people, standing
densely packed behind the trained-band soldiers, sitting in
the stands or perched like crows upon every vantage point.
Then, at that awful moment when the executioner raised the
severed head with the words 'God save the King!', a mighty
roar broke from the lips of the vast throng and sounded
across London. Strafford had despised the common people:
it was his fatal mistake.

During the late spring and summer of 1641, during and after
the trial of Strafford, the King had made some half-hearted
attempts to win over the opposition by taking them into the
bosom of the government. Bedford, Bristol, Saye, Mandeville,
and Essex all became privy councillors in the early spring, and
the last-named was subsequently made commander of all
military forces south of the Trent and Lord Chamberlain at
Court. In the legal promotions after the flight of Finch, Oliver
St John received the coveted office of Solicitor-General. There
were rumours that Pym might become Chancellor of the
Exchequer and Denzil Holles the principal Secretary of State in
place of Windebanke. Such appointments, however, would
have served only to reduce the numbers of those bound to the

King by office without in any way placating the opposition.

The King's advisers considered several possible offices for Hampden. According to Hyde, these possibilities for his satisfaction and promotion were 'very far driven'. In July, for example, it was rumoured that Hampden would be a Secretary of State, and Edward Nicholas mentioned him during that month as about to be admitted into the office of Chancellor of the Duchy of Lancaster. Yet the Member of Parliament for Radnor, Sir Philip Warwick, informs us in his *Memoirs* that Hampden's own desire was to be Governor of the Prince of Wales. As a natural teacher or tutor, Hampden would have excelled as a guide to the future King of England. Moreover, the statement – if it is true – confirms the impression of Hampden as a man who preferred a self-effacing influence behind the scenes to political power in the open stage. The office of the Prince's Governor, however, passed to the incompetent and ill-educated Marquess of Hertford, who certainly did not imbue his charge with the values and ideals of Puritan England.

Already by the summer of 1641 the Commons had initiated much of the legislation designed to prevent a repetition of the eleven years when Charles ruled without Parliament. Shortly before Christmas 1640 an Act of Edward III's reign, long since ignored by kings, appeared again in the form of a bill for annual parliaments. Committees of both Houses gradually converted it into a Triennial Bill, which laid down a procedure for ensuring that intervals between parliaments should not exceed three years and that each should sit for a minimum period of fifty days. A Subsidy Bill which accompanied it to Whitehall for the royal assent on 16 February contained clauses prohibiting payment of any moneys into the King's privy purse. As both the English soldiers at York and the Scots army at Newcastle cried out for money, the Subsidy Bill could not be lightly foregone on account of some objectionable clauses. In a speech to both Houses the King told the assembled peers and commoners that having taken his government to bits like a watch they should now put it together again and make it go. Pym and Hampden, the chief watchmakers, however, had not finished their work of dismantling the cogs and wheels of arbitrary government.

On 8 June the Commons passed without division Bills abolishing the Courts of High Commission and Star Chamber, and the Councils of Wales and of the North, along with other lesser prerogative courts. A month later these measures received the royal assent. During that summer the King also touched with his sceptre Bills declaring the proceedings in Hampden's case null and void and making Ship-Money illegal. He also agreed to laws limiting the boundaries of royal forests, abolishing knighthood fines and replacing the antique system of subsidies with a poll-tax. A Tonnage and Poundage Bill, accepted on 22 June, at long last granted the King these taxes, but for a few weeks only and with the clear understanding that they could not be collected in future without parliamentary consent.

These concessions from the King failed to create the new atmosphere of trust he intended that they should. For Charles imagined that deeds by themselves could make confidence, while his opponents looked rather at the relationship between King and subject which lay behind them. Not without reason they sensed that Charles might be playing for time by making outward gestures, while behind the scenes he was marshalling his forces for an effective assertion of his regal authority. Inflated rumours, imbedded with sparse facts like currants in a pudding, kept London on tiptoe waiting for a military *coup d'état*.

Meanwhile the King hardly advanced the cause of conciliation by making a peer in June of Lord George Digby, a member for Dorset and an erstwhile friend of Bedford. Digby, at thirty years of age a 'graceful and beautiful person' with good looks and ready conversation, may perhaps have reminded Charles of his dearest friend the Duke of Buckingham. Thenceforth Digby became one of the King's chief advisers. The new favourite enlisted Lord Falkland and Edward Hyde to the royal council chamber. But Hyde soon found Digby's ambition, his overweening confidence, and his corresponding carelessness about communication with his fellow councillors, extremely irritating. He remarked that Digby's own propensity for acting fitfully, and without a proper survey of the consequence of the various courses of action, should have been enough to disqualify him from acting as an adviser to King Charles who was by nature anyway 'too easily inclined to sudden enterprises'.

Never did a more half-hearted minister serve a king than Lord Falkland. His irresolution culminated in what amounted to his suicide at the first Battle of Newbury in September 1643, when he deliberately guided his horse to a hedge gap swept by enemy musket shot. Hyde explained Falkland's long delay in declaring unequivocally for the King by stating that the 'great opinion he held of the uprightness and integrity of those persons who appeared most active, especially of Mr Hampden, kept him longer from suspecting any design against the peace of the kingdom; and though he differed commonly from them in conclusions, he believed long their purposes were honest.'

Among the issues pressing upon the attention of the House of Commons in the summer of 1641 was the future of the bishops. On 28 November in the preceding year those martyrs of episcopal discipline, Prynne and Burton, had made a triumphal entry into London by way of Charing Cross, accompanied by ten thousand persons on horseback or foot with boughs and flowers in their hands, crowds strewing the road before them with more flowers and herbs. Next month ten or a dozen ministers presented a petition from seven hundred clergymen in London and the home counties, supported by another in the hands of Alderman Pennington signed by twenty thousand laymen, calling for the abolition of the episcopal government of the Church of England, 'with all its dependencies, roots and branches . . . and all laws in their behalf made void'. As counter-petitions from such counties as Cheshire revealed, not all the clergy or laity of England wanted such a radical solution and this division of opinion was reflected in the Commons as the debates on the 'root-and-branch' petitions, held in February 1641, soon revealed. In the middle of March, however, the House resolved to bring in a Bill to exclude the bishops from participation in judicial or civil administration, including the House of Lords.

Probably referring to this period, Clarendon wrote of

Hampden that 'they who conversed nearly with him found him growing into a dislike of the ecclesiastical government of the church, yet most believed it rather a dislike of some churchmen'. Clarendon had a habit of insinuating such personal animosities as the motives for men's words or deeds, alongside ambition, envy and vanity, and these hints and imputations, nods and winks, tell us far more about Edward Hyde, Earl of Clarendon, than about Hampden.

As for Hampden's views on the subject of episcopacy, he doubtless shared the widespread Puritan distaste for some of the bishops who gloried in the temporal privileges and wealth of their offices, like little popes in their dioceses. But there is no solid evidence that he disliked any particular churchman, or that he objected to episcopacy as such. The problem of restoring the office of bishop to the pristine simplicity of the New Testament must, however, have seemed insurmountable when one contemplated the facts of episcopal pride, their vested interests and the apparently limitless support promised to them by the royal prerogative. Bishops appeared to be both products of the whole system of national government and its chief bulwarks, as indeed they were: to change the part would demand a re-shaping of the whole. The combination of the well-intentioned but stupid leadership of Laud and the stubborn, vacillating and devious conduct of King Charles would precipitate just that crisis of revolution upon England.

On 30 March 1641 a Bill for the abolition of the temporal powers of episcopacy had been introduced into the Lower House and caused much heated debate. Owing to the trial of Strafford, it did not pass in the Commons until 1 May, and then almost four weeks elapsed before the Lords agreed that the bishops should cease from all temporal power but that they should retain their seats in the Upper House. On that day (27 May) Oliver Cromwell and the younger Vane introduced a 'root-and-branch' Bill calling for the total extirpation of episcopacy, which passed its second reading by a small majority. Ten days later, however, the Lords again rejected the move to exclude the bishops from their number. Various measures to reform episcopacy or to place the powers of bishops in commission were initiated in both

Houses but none commanded general approval. The Lords threw out a Bill, for example, proposing a test of Protestant faith for all office holders, for that would have excluded the Catholic peers as well as their Laudian bishops. The Commons replied by impeaching thirteen bishops for their voting in favour of the canons framed in the Convocation of 1640. Although the Lower House did not slacken in its efforts to remove 'the dregs of Popery' from the Church of England, they dropped their attempts to reform or abolish episcopacy for a time.

Hampden's part in the 'root-and-branch' debates is difficult to determine. Hyde says that Nathaniel Fiennes and the younger Vane were believed to be for the Bill, 'and shortly after Mr Hampden (who had not before owned it)', but Pym, Holles, the northern members and lawyers such as Selden opposed it. To the consternation of his inseparable friend Hyde – they always sat next to each other in the House – Falkland spoke in favour of the exclusion of the bishops from the Lords when the matter came up first, probably in December. Six months later, however, he altered his opinion and said that he had been deceived, claiming that 'Mr Hampden had assured him that if that Bill might pass, there would be nothing more attempted to the prejudice of the Church'. It is possible that Falkland's reception into royal favour during the late spring played a major part in this change of mind. Certainly Hampden did not mean to deceive him, for he probably did think that matters would stop with the exclusion of the bishops from the House of Lords. In all probability he wanted to see bishops reformed and not abolished, although he may have sided with the abolitionists to prevent a political rift from opening up within the opposition.

Hyde may have had these private discussions about epsicopacy in mind when he wrote of Hampden as a man

of that rare affability and temper in debate, and of that seeming humility and submission of judgment, as if he brought no opinions with him, but a desire of information and instruction; yet he had so subtle a way of interrogating, and under the notion of doubts insinuating his objections, that he left his opinions with those from whom he pretended to learn and receive them.

During these debates of the Long Parliament Hampden showed more than once his ability to sense the feeling or consensus of the House. He could read the mood of the Commons. Hyde noted that Hampden sometimes did not vote with the majority, a fact which he attributed to his deviousness, while stating that others regarded it more as a sign of integrity. Hampden, he said, 'begat many opinions and motions, the education whereof he committed to other men, so far disguising his own designs that he seemed seldom to wish more than was concluded; and in many gross conclusions, which would hereafter contribute to designs not yet set on foot, when he found them sufficiently backed by a majority of voices, he would withdraw himself before the question, that he might not seem to consent to so much visible unreasonableness; which produced as great a doubt in some as it did approbation in others of his integrity.'

Despite these characteristic suggestions of Clarendon, designed to sow some doubts about Hampden as well as to breed confidence in his own astuteness, it is more likely that Hampden deliberately conserved his influence by not tilting at every windmill or leading every charge. Like an intelligent shepherd, he knew when the flock were moving on the right path and would then leave them at that point. On the other hand, Hampden may have withdrawn from motions he had initially favoured if he sensed that the balance of rational arguments had changed his mind or if the time for that measure had not come.

The King signed a treaty with the Scots and secured the necessary money from Parliament to pay off his debt to the Scottish army camped on English soil. Then Charles resolved to visit Scotland. The Commons felt an immediate suspicion that the King might do some sort of deal with his northern subjects in order to bring a Scottish host down upon his opponents in England. On 24 June the House in some haste voted through a political manifesto of ten propositions. In them the Commons called for the banishment of evil counsellors, the removal of Papists from Court, the delay of the King's journey north, the disbanding of the army, and the placing of military arsenals and forts in safe custody. Charles agreed to disband the army, but denied the existence of evil counsellors. As for postponing his visit, he ignored the request and departed without more ado for Scotland on 10 August.

Ten days later both Houses appointed Hampden to a commission of two peers and four commoners with orders to attend the King in Scotland. Lord Howard of Escrick, seventh son of the Earl of Suffolk (who had married Buckingham's niece and thus been made a baron), and the young Earl of Bedford served for the Lords. Nathaniel Fiennes, the second son of Lord Saye, Sir William Armine and Sir Philip Stapleton completed the commission.

The King received Hampden· and his colleagues courteously at Holyrood Palace on 30 August. Their main task was to enter into negotiations with the Scots concerning the ratification of the peace treaty. In the middle of October they reported by letter to Parliament the exposure of a conspiracy to assassinate the Marquess of Hamilton and the Earl of Argyle, which came to be known as 'The Incident'. It seems doubtful that King Charles or the Earl of Montrose, now his supporter, had allowed themselves to be involved in this design, but it stirred up the smouldering embers of suspicion, mistrust and fear in both kingdoms. 'This plot', wrote the commissioners to Parliament on 14 October, 'has put not only ours but all other business to a stand, and may be an occasion of many and great troubles in this kingdom if Almighty God in his great mercy do not prevent it.'

Yet larger and more troubles had broken out elsewhere in the King's domains. Towards the end of October tidings reached both London and Edinburgh of a bloody insurrection in Ireland. The Irish Papists, tribal chieftains at the head of wild skin-clad natives of bog and moor, had risen up and cruelly slaughtered thousands of Protestant settlers. Men said that the Shannon ran red with blood. Almost at once Hampden set out for London ahead of the other commissioners. He wanted to face with Parliament this crisis in Ireland so fraught with political implications for England.

Chapter Nine

THE FIVE MEMBERS

I hope those gentlemen the King would have from your House shall be safe; they stand so much for the general good that it was a miserable thing they should suffer.

LADY SUSSEX

Parliament faced a dark and menacing situation in that autumn of 1641. Insurrection in Ireland, intrigue in Scotland, hostility in France and plague, debt and mistrust in England: so ran the inventory of troubles. Moreover, the King was known to be negotiating with Holland and Denmark to obtain soldiers, arms and ammunition for use against his subjects, should need arise. Clearly the conflict between the King and Parliament had already begun to move towards its climax of war.

On 20 October Parliament re-assembled under the elaborate protection of the Westminster Trained-Band, and three days later passed a second Bill for the exclusion of bishops from the Upper House. Meanwhile Charles wrote a letter from Scotland protesting against any changes in the discipline and doctrine of the Church of England, and expressing his resolution 'to die in the maintenance of it'. The Lords obediently shelved the Bill and put aside the request for sequestration. The indignant House of Commons, goaded yet further by fresh news of plots against them among the disbanded officers, resolved to draw up a Remonstrance on the state of the kingdom.

On 1 November, the day fixed for the discussion of the Remonstrance, a reading of the first official dispatches of the Irish rebellion stunned the House of Commons into a deep silence. Besides inflaming Protestant feeling to a white heat, the tidings raised a momentous question. An army would be needed to suppress the rising, but could such a weapon be entrusted to the hands of the King? The Commons edged towards the precipice of civil war by asking the King to employ only such counsellors as should be approved by Parliament, and threatened – if he refused – to proceed against the Irish rebels through agents of their own choosing.

Hampden reached London in time to support the Remonstrance, during the debates which shaped it which took place in November. The Remonstrance asserted that from the beginning of His Majesty's reign there had been a design to subvert the fundamental laws and principles of government, upon which the religion and justice of the kingdom was established, inspired by Jesuits, the bishops, the corrupt part of the clergy, and those counsellors and courtiers who were receiving pensions from foreign powers. Such men had created a division between the King and his people over the questions of the royal prerogative and the liberty of the subject and had sought to suppress the purity of religion by promoting those opinions and ceremonies in the Church which came close to Popery. As evidence to support this general case, the framers of the Remonstrance listed all the objectionable practices and acts of the royal government since 1625, including the imprisonment of Sir John Eliot who 'died for want of refreshment, whose blood still cried out for vengeance'. In contrast, the Remonstrance presented the impressive record of the present Parliament: the abolition of Ship-Money, monopolies and the royal arbitrary power to tax the subject; the justice done on such 'living grievances' as Strafford and Laud; and such reforms as the removal of the prerogative courts and the Triennial Act.

The Remonstrance, however, not only reviewed the past: it set forth a manifesto for the future. While disclaiming any desire 'to let loose the golden reins of discipline and government in the Church', it declared an intention to 'reduce within bounds that exorbitant power which the prelates have assumed'. Both Houses would be asked to petition the King to deprive the bishops of their temporal powers and to prohibit 'unnecessary ceremonies by which divers weak

consciences have been scrupled'. To bring about the reformation, the King should summon a synod of divines and,
purging his council of those with contrary views, employ
henceforth persons in whom Parliament had confidence.

At nine a.m. on 22 November the Commons began a long
debate on the Remonstrance, taking its 204 clauses one by
one. Characteristically Hampden waited until late in the day
before speaking. At nine p.m. when he rose to his feet, the
candles had burned low and many of the older and more
infirm members had made their way home. Yet some three
hundred members heard him describe the Remonstrance as
'wholly true in substance and a very necessary vindication of
the parliament'. Replying to Edmund Waller's criticism of
the clause declaring that the Commons might have occasion
in the future to take exception to some men being royal
counsellors without charging them as criminals, Hampden
asked, 'What is the objection to this declaration? When this
House discovers ill counsels, may it not say there are evil
counsellors and complain of them? When any man is
accused, may he not say he has done his endeavour? And we
say no more in this.'

A previous speaker had defended episcopacy on the
grounds that without a few large prizes in the lottery of
preferment few men would take holy orders. 'If any man
could cut the moon out into little stars', he had argued, 'we
might still have the same moon, or as much in small pieces,
yet we should want both light and influence.' Hampden now
replied to him by asking by what authority they should
suppose that God valued the moon more than the stars.
Were the clergy less useful to the Church than the bishops?
Quoting the Book of Revelation, he spoke of the vision of the
Church as the Bride of Christ, clothed with the sun, with the
moon as a footstool and the stars as a crown about her head.

At about two a.m. the Remonstrance was put to the House
and passed by 159 to 148, a majority of only eleven votes. As
soon as the result was declared, Hampden moved that the
Remonstrance should be printed. In other words, he
intended to make it an appeal to the people. This possibility
infuriated those who had already opposed the Bill, and may
have alarmed some who had supported it. Hyde stood up

and asked for leave to register a formal protestation against this unprecedented action. A friend of his, Geoffrey Palmer, then shouted out 'I do protest!' and others called out 'All! All!' Weariness and hunger had frayed tempers to a breaking-point. Members were on their feet, hurling their hats in the air; some took their swords in their scabbards from their belts and rested them on the ground with their hands on the pommels. Palmer argued that the chorus of 'All! All!' meant that he spoke for all the rest and justified a protestation.

In the dim candle-lit chapel with its dark lofty cavernous roof above them, 'I thought', wrote Sir Philip Warwick, 'we had all sat in the valley of the shadow of death; for we, like Joab's and Abner's young men, had catch't at each others locks, and sheathed our swords in each others bowels, had not the sagacity and great calmness of Mr Hampden by a short speech prevented it.' Hampden began by quietly asking how Palmer could know other men's minds. His brief speech brought silence to the House, and it was agreed to leave the matter of printing the Remonstrance undetermined until the morrow.

As the members tumbled out of St Stephen's Chapel into the cold morning, Falkland walked beside Oliver Cromwell. On the previous morning Cromwell had asked Falkland why he had wanted to postpone the debate on the Remonstrance until the next day. 'There would not have been time enough, for sure it would take some debate,' replied Falkland. 'A very sorry one,' commented Cromwell. Now, with fourteen hours of debate behind them Falkland could not resist asking Cromwell if he was now satisfied. Cromwell answered that he would take Falkland's word another time, and whispered in his ear that if the Remonstrance had been rejected he would have sold all he had next morning and never seen England again, and he knew many other honest men of the same resolution. It is possible that Oliver Cromwell meant this conspiritorial stage whisper to the King's over-serious adviser as a piece of heavy humour, but Hyde caps his account of their conversation by exclaiming, 'So near was the poor kingdom at that time to its deliverance!'

At this time few men perceived the worth of Oliver Cromwell. The courtly young Sir Philip Warwick had noticed him in November:

> I came one morning into the House well clad, and perceived a gentleman speaking . . . very ordinarily apparelled; for it was a plain cloth suit, which seemed to have been made by an ill country tailor; his linen was plain, and not very clean; and I remember a speck or two of blood upon his little band which was not much larger than his collar; his hat was without a hatband: his stature was of a good size, his sword stuck close to his side, his countenance swollen and reddish, his voice sharp and untunable and his eloquence full of fervour . . .

Such men as Warwick prized exquisite clothes, polished manners and silver oratory: the Huntingdonshire squire jarred upon both their eyes and ears. The most elegant member in the House, Lord George Digby, laughed derisively at 'that sloven', with his untidy suit and harsh voice. 'Pray, Mr Hampden, who is that man? For I see that he is on your side by his speaking so warmly today.' Hampden answered: 'That sloven whom you see before you has no ornament in his speech; but that sloven, I say, if we should ever come to breach with the King (which God forbid!), in such a case, I say, that sloven will be the greatest man in England.'

The Commons introduced a Bill authorizing the raising of soldiers for use in Ireland, but forbidding the compulsory impressment of men for military service outside their counties except in time of foreign invasion. When the Lords objected to this provision, the Commons replied by bringing in a Militia Bill which took the supreme command of the military forces to be raised out of the King's gift. A Lord General and Lord Admiral would be nominated in the Bill. It was a revolutionary proposal.

Although the Militia Bill went no further at that time, it illustrates the frame of mind engendered by the growing conviction that the rumours of plots in the army during the previous summer had foundations of fact. Sir John Conyers told the Commons committee investigating the matter that a senior officer had come to him from the King and attempted to persuade or threaten him to agree to a plan to march on London and dominate the Parliament. On 25 November Hampden had produced the torn fragments of a letter found upon a Papist called Adam Courtney, arrested at Fingest and now in Aylesbury gaol, which contained yet further evidence of the army plot. He suggested that the Committee should piece the letter together again and then order Courtney to be brought up to London for interrogation. What became of the matter is not known, but it shows that Hampden was active in the work of unravelling the plots.

On 23 December the King made a general and evasive answer to the Remonstrance, although he did express willingness to call a synod of divines. The publication of that document in the week before, however, may well have influenced the elections in London, for the citizens returned a Puritan majority to the Common Council. Stirred up by more horrid news from Ireland and rumours of an enormous Popish threat at home, multitudes of poor people invaded the Palace of Westminster shouting 'No bishops! No bishops! No Popish lords!' and man-handling any of the 'Popish innovators' they spotted coming in or out. Twelve bishops, headed by Williams, now Archbishop of York, signed a protest claiming that as the crowds had prevented them from attending the Upper House, all proceedings of Parliament were henceforth null and void. The Commons impeached them, and the Lords concurred, for they regarded the protest as a grave interference with their own privilege. That day the Lords committed the twelve bishops to prison.

On their way to Westminster the mobs paused to shout their slogans outside Whitehall Palace where the King was in residence. Some roared out 'that they would have no more porter's lodge, but would speak with the King when they pleased'. In these circumstances Charles thought fit to accept an offer from several hundred disbanded officers to serve as his bodyguard at Whitehall. These men, many of them hard-bitten swordsmen of the Continental wars, had come to London to claim their arrears of pay and to petition for employment in the army for Ireland. These bored and idle officers loudly professed their contempt for the 'Roundheads', as they called the crop-haired apprentices in the passing mob. Such insults led to fights outside Whitehall, so that some lads had cuts and slashes to show at Westminster. As word spread back in London about the swordsmen, the apprentices came back in ever larger numbers and jeered at the 'Cavaliers' before drifting off to Westminster.

On the afternoon of 3 January, Sir Edward Herbert, the Attorney-General, announced to the House of Lords that the King had commanded him to accuse Lord Mandeville and five members of the Commons on the charge of high treason. They were accused of casting aspersions on the King and his government, encouraging the Scots to invade England, raising tumults to coerce Parliament, levying war against the King, and, like Strafford, endeavouring to subvert the fundamental laws and government of the kingdom. The King had himself written the seven articles and named Pym, Hampden, Denzil Holles, Sir Arthur Heselrige and William Strode in the charge. A short time afterwards a sergeant-at-arms appeared at the bar of the Lower House and demanded in the King's name that the five should be delivered to him. Forewarned by the action of some royal servants, who were busy sealing up the studies and trunks of the accused that morning, the Commons passed an order authorizing the arrest of such investigators and affirming the right of a member to resist arrest in cases where the House had not been consulted. Now they contented themselves by sending a message to the King that the members would be forthcoming as soon as proper legal charges had been made. The House then adjourned for the day, the five members taking home a copy of the order with them.

The next day in the afternoon, the King came down from Whitehall to Westminster accompanied by his halberdiers, and the bodyguard of Cavaliers, about five hundred in number, armed with swords and pocket pistols. The Countess of Carlisle, a lady in the Queen's Household, had told the Earl of Holland of the design, and he had already sent an advance warning to Pym. To avoid bloodshed, the House directed the five members to withdraw. The young and unmarried Devon member William Strode, much given to violent language and impulsive action at the best of times, protested that he would rather die at the door of the House than leave, and Sir Walter Earle dragged him away by the cloak to a boat waiting at Parliament-stairs, where he joined the other four accused members in a short journey downstream to the City.

Barely thirty minutes later, at about three o'clock, the doors of St Stephen's Chapel swung open and King Charles stood there to the great amazement of the House. The doors were kept open, and the Earl of Roxburgh stood within the door, leaning upon it. Leaving the men outside, the King and his nephew Charles, Prince Palatine, walked into the chamber. Everyone stood up and removed their hats. The King also took off his hat, and bowed to the members on the left and right as he walked; they bowed towards him. The intruders approached the Speaker's chair. 'Mr Speaker, I must for a time make bold with your Chair,' the King said. Lenthall vacated it, and Charles stood before it. He asked if Pym was present. Silence. He asked if Holles was here. Silence. The kneeling Speaker asked the King to pardon him, for he could neither see nor speak except by command of the House. 'Well, well, 'tis no matter,' replied Charles. 'I think my eyes are as good as another's.' He scanned the benches for a few minutes. After a pause the King said, 'I perceive my birds have flown.' He told the House that he expected that they should be sent to him as soon as they returned. If not, he would seek them himself, for their treason was foul. Upon his word as a king, he intended no violence, but would proceed against the five accused in a fair and legal way. With that Charles walked out of the House amid ringing shouts of 'Privilege! Privilege!'

Like the victim of a violent blow, the House of Commons now experienced something akin to a delayed corporate shock. After the King's exit the House had immediately adjourned until the following afternoon. Sir Simonds D'Ewes spent the rest of the day in his lodgings making his will. Then they voted to continue their adjournment but to appoint a standing committee of privileges, which would confer with the Lords and meet in the City for its better safety. All the previous night the citizens had stood to arms, with messengers running from gate to gate crying out 'The Cavaliers are coming to fire the City!' At ten o'clock the following morning, accompanied by three or four lords-in-waiting, the King rode to the Guildhall and told the assembled Common Council that he presumed that they would not give shelter to men accused of high treason. Having dined with the Lord Mayor and Sheriffs the King drove back to Whitehall through crowds shouting 'Privilege of Parliament! Privilege of Parliament!' Among those who followed the coach walked a fellow calling out in a very loud voice, 'To your tents, O Israel!', the title of a pamphlet which the King later took to be a clear sign of a rebellious intent.

The five members had taken refuge in a house in Coleman Street, or possibly at an inn called the Red Lion in Watling Street, near its junction with Bread Street. From there they conferred daily with the committee for privileges, which met in the halls of the livery companies guarded by the London trained-bands. The House then resumed its sitting and sent word to the committee and the accused members to attend again at Westminster. On 10 January the first trickles of a vast flood of people, expected next day at Westminster to hail the return of the five members in triumph, passed the gates of Whitehall Palace. That morning the King left for Hampton Court, accompanied by the Queen and their elder children and his household servants. 'What has become of the King and his Cavaliers? Where has he gone?' called out the people.

On 11 January at about two o'clock in the afternoon the five members emerged from hiding and walked through cheering crowds lined with pikemen and musketeers down to the river where they embarked in a barge. The oarsmen rowed them past over a hundred lighters and long-boats armed with light cannon, decked with bunting and streamers. These gun boats were a lively testimony of the support of the 'Navy Royal' for the cause of Parliament. Meanwhile the City trained-bands marched to Westminster behind their new Sergeant-Major-General, Philip Skippon, with copies of the Grand Remonstrance spiked upon the tops of their pikes or pinned upon their hats.

Once in Parliament House the five members joined their colleagues in giving thanks to the citizen soldiers and the mariners. Then they heard that at the door was a petition which had been carried up to London by about five thousand inhabitants of Buckinghamshire, also wearing the Grand Remonstrance as a badge in their hats. In it they offered their lives in defence of the persons and privileges of Parliament, and begged that Popish lords and bishops should now be excluded and evil counsellors punished, without which 'they had not the least hope of Israel's peace'. This political demonstration by the gentry and yeomen of Buckinghamshire is witness of Hampden's remarkable popularity in both his own county and in the kingdom at large.

The men from Buckinghamshire brought with them another petition for the King, and it was entrusted to a small deputation who found him some days later at Windsor Castle. By virtue of a royal writ, the petition ran, having 'chosen John Hampden Knight for our shire, in whose loyalty we, his countrymen and neighbours, have ever had good cause to confide, of late we, to our no less amazement than grief, find him with other members of parliament accused of treason'. The petition blamed the deed on the malice which their good deeds had aroused, and prayed that they should be restored to the just privileges of Parliament. The King in answer took notice of their views and agreed to lay aside his proceedings against the accused members for the time being, and later to adopt methods less open to legal questions 'when the minds of men were composed'.

Yet the rude shock inflicted upon the body politic by the impeachment and attempted arrest of the five members could not be overcome by the mere passage of a few weeks or months. The whole episode had confirmed the worst fears entertained by the leaders of Parliament about the intentions and character of King Charles. This abortive act, wrote Sir William Waller in his *Vindication*, 'was interpreted as such a horrid violation of privilege that although his Majesty was pleased to withdraw the prosecuting of it and to promise a more tender respect for the time to come, yet nevertheless this spark (as his Majesty terms it) kindled such flames of discontent as gave occasion first to the raising of guards and afterwards to the levying of an army.' The experience certainly taught Hampden to disguise his good nature with a firmer and more determined demeanour. Clarendon observed that after the impeachment Hampden 'was much altered, his nature and carriage seeming much fiercer than it did before'.

On 12 January Lord Digby had attended a muster, held at Kingston-on-Thames, of several troops of mounted Cavaliers commanded by the notorious Sir Thomas Lunsford, whom initially the King had appointed Lieutenant of the Tower in place of Balfour until vigorous protests from Parliament and City caused him to change his mind. Digby and Lunsford apparently asked for volunteers and thanked those who joined them in the King's name. The Commons promptly accused Digby to his fellow peers of treason, and he fled to Holland to avoid arrest. Now thoroughly alarmed, the Commons reached out for the tangible symbols of security. On 20 January Hampden successfully moved the first reading of a Bill for 'the putting all the forts, castles and garrisons into the hands of such persons as they could confide in'.

In particular Parliament wished to control the great arsenals of Hull and the Tower. The artillery, arms and ammunition of the disbanded army raised for service in Scotland had been stored in Hull. By secret commission the King appointed the Earl of Newcastle to be governor of that magazine. As soon as Newcastle arrived in Hull, however, he received a summons to attend the House of Lords immediately in London, and he judged it wise that he should obey it. On 31 January 1642 Sir John Hotham, member of the House of Commons for Beverley and also a veteran soldier, occupied the town at the head of the trained-bands of the East Riding in the interest of Parliament, despite the fact that Hampden's Bill for securing the forts had yet to be passed in both Houses. Twelve days later the King agreed to replace Sir John Byron as Lieutenant of the Tower with Sir John Conyers, an officer whom Parliament felt that it could trust.

On 5 February the Lords finally passed the Bill for excluding the bishops from their House, and the King gave his assent to it a week later. On that day 'the ordinance of both Houses of Parliament for the ordering of the militia' also came before him, which in effect would take from him the power of appointing the lords-lieutenants in the counties. Although the King had promised some days earlier to agree to it, providing he could have the power of taking exception to any of the nominated lords-lieutenants if he so desired, he now temporized and said he would reply upon his return from Dover, where he went to embark the Queen for Holland. The Commons, in return, countenanced the unofficial mustering of the county trained-bands, the men choosing their officers, listing themselves and training as volunteers. On 23 February the Queen sailed to join Digby in his efforts to raise money and soldiers in support of the King. Soon afterwards, Hyde claimed that he saw Hampden embrace a member of the House of Commons who had abandoned his support of the Court. This member, an unsavoury young Welshman named John Griffith, had informed the House of the whereabouts of the Prince of Wales. According to Hyde, Hampden told Griffith that 'his soul rejoiced to see that God had put it in his heart to take the right way'. But this tale was probably hearsay.

On 28 February the King replied concerning the militia ordinance. He would agree to Parliament nominating the lords-lieutenant except in the case of London and other corporations protected by royal charter. But he could not accept such a surrender of his just powers in a matter concerning the defence of the realm for an indefinite time. Both Houses sent a commission to the King at the palace of Theobald's in Hertfordshire with an ultimatum that unless he assented they would be forced 'to dispose of the militia by the authority of both Houses'. They could never feel secure, they added, until the King sent away from his presence 'those wicked and unfaithful counsellors' who had advised him to reply as he had done. For good measure, Parliament asked him to continue to live near London and not go northwards to reside in remoter parts. Recovering from a genuine pained surprise at the rebuff of his compromise solution, the King replied in sharp tones that he would not alter his answer over the militia on any point.

The following day, 2 March, both Houses ordered the Earl of Northumberland, Lord High Admiral, to put the fleet in a state of readiness. Five days later their commissioners caught up with the King, now on his journey northwards, at Newmarket and presented a Declaration specifying the causes of their 'fears and jealousies'. In the designs to alter England's religion, the war with Scotland and the rebellion in Ireland, they saw evidence of a concerted and long-standing Popish plot, hatched long ago in this country and nurtured by the Catholic Queen's agents. From evidence garnered in foreign capitals, they knew that the King had some design in hand for altering England's religion and 'breaking the neck of his Parliaments' to be effected with the aid of 4,000 men apiece from France and Spain. His words alone could not now create trust, but the dismissal of mischievous advisers and a return to London might be a happy beginning of a new chapter in his relations with his people.

The King listened to this petition with mounting anger. 'That's false,' he interjected over one point; and, when it was explained to him, he added testily: 'It might have been better expressed then; it is a high thing to tax a King with breach of promise.' When the Earl of Holland had finished reading it, the King made a short vehement speech asserting that he feared more for 'the true Protestant profession, my people and laws than for my own rights or safety'. In indignant tones, he insisted that he had done his part, asserting the integrity of his own thoughts and intentions for the maintenance of religion and laws. 'There is a judgment from heaven upon this nation if these distractions continue,' he added. Would he at least agree to reside near to Parliament, asked Holland. 'I would you had given me cause, but I am sure this Declaration is not the way,' answered Charles. Might the militia be granted for a time as Parliament wished, asked Pembroke? 'By God, not for an hour!' exclaimed the King. 'You have asked that of me in this [which] was never asked of a king, and with which I will not trust my wife and children.' Once more he tried to divert their attention to Ireland. Only one man with the necessary authority and power could accomplish the task of suppressing the Catholic rising, not four hundred members and peers. The King assured the commissioners that he would pawn his head to complete that work.

The King continued upon his journey towards York. In the meantime Parliament set about raising money for the suppression of the Irish rebellion by encouraging men to be 'adventurers' in lending money in return for the promise of confiscated lands, so many acres for so much money. Clearly Pym and his colleagues were employing the same broad method to finance a war in Ireland as they had used to forward Puritan settlement in the New World. Hampden subscribed £1,000 to the Irish adventure, compared to Arthur Goodwin's £1,800, Pym's £600 and Cromwell's £500. When one member offered to give £50 a year without reward as long as the rebellion lasted, Hampden proposed that the offer and its acceptance should be recorded in the Journal of the House of Commons as a significant public service. This 'Adventurer's Army' of six to eight thousand men would be commanded by Lord Wharton. Significantly it would receive its orders not from the Lord Lieutenant of Ireland but from a committee of seven peers and fourteen commoners appointed to manage the war.

Parliament had asked Scotland for 'brotherly assistance' in the Irish affair. Hampden, Fiennes and Stapleton also served as commissioners appointed by the House of Commons in January 1642 to treat with the Scots about the supply and victualling of 2,500 soldiers they promised for this service. The Scots sold their aid for £16,000, the town and castle of Carrickfergus being delivered to them as a pledge.

The King reached York on 19 March 1642, where he received a heart-warming welcome from his northern subjects. Hardly had he published his detailed and reasonable reply to the Declaration presented at Newmarket when another arrived from Westminster in support of it. The King sent back a hasty answer to it point by point. As for their proposal of a militia ordinance rather than a Bill, 'what is this but to introduce an arbitrary way of government?' He denied any knowledge of a 'design' at home or of an attempt to procure a foreign invasion. Confident that he had done all that could be expected of him since this Parliament began, and that he had made sufficient amends for such admitted breaches of privilege as the attempted arrest of the five members, the King made it clear that he would not be pushed further into any more concessions.

These paper skirmishes were not without their small victories. The Earl of Essex, for example, succumbed in so far as he expressed a desire that Parliament should moderate its approach in light of the King's evident willingness to satisfy the most part of their demands. With singular lack of judgment, however, Charles chose this time to implement a promise he had made some weeks earlier to the Queen, to dismiss Essex and Holland from their offices of Lord Chamberlain and Groom of the Stole. Meanwhile Parliament secured control of the Navy by persuading Northumberland, the Lord High Admiral, to appoint the Earl of Warwick to command the sea-going fleet that year, rather than the present incumbent, Admiral Sir John Pennington, whom the King had nominated.

In April Charles resolved to seize the great magazine of arms and ammunition at Hull before they could be transferred by sea to the Tower, which (admitted Hyde) 'in truth was the sole motive of his journey into those parts'. On the 23rd he appeared before the town with a cavalcade of three or four hundred horsemen, only to find the gates shut, the drawbridge up and the walls manned. Sir John Hotham shouted from the walls that 'he dare not open the gates, being trusted by the Parliament', nor would he descend for a parley. The King ordered him to be proclaimed a traitor on the spot and then, full of trouble and indignation at the public affront, he returned to York.

When the Commons heard the news of the King's abortive attempt on Hull they appointed Hampden to manage a conference with the Lords on the subject. As a result both Houses concurred in a vote that Hotham had acted in obedience to Parliament, and that to declare a member of the House of Commons a traitor without any legal process was a high breach of privilege, both against the liberty of the subject and the law of the land.

As the King had by now refused his assent to a compromise Bill for placing the militia under lords-lieutenants trusted by Parliament for the period of two years, both

Houses published on 5 May a Declaration announcing their decision to put into execution the ordinance. The King replied with a broadsheet commanding his 'loving subjects' not to cause the trained-bands to rise, muster or march under colour of this pretended ordinance. Loyal gentry began to flock to York. In Holland, the Queen sold or pawned her own and some of the Crown jewels in order to buy gunpowder and arms. Seeing the storm ahead, the King now began serious preparations for a war to be waged with steel and shot rather than paper and words. In the middle of May he ordered a bodyguard of horse to be raised, and also took one regiment of the Yorkshire trained-bands into his pay. Some forty thousand men of the north country flocked to Heyworth Moor to see and hear the King.

On 10 May the first muster of trained-bands under the new ordinance took place in Finsbury fields. Before a great crowd, including many members of both Houses sitting in a tent specially pitched for them, Sergeant-Major-General Philip Skippon marshalled his six London regiments of some eight thousand pikemen and musketeers. During the Civil War these citizen soldiers under their merchant colonels and tradesmen captains played a vital role as Parliament's strategic reserve.

Hampden wrote to Sir John Hotham on behalf of Parliament on 17 May, in reply to a letter from him read that morning. He referred to a report about the naval captains: 'When we first heard that the captains suspended their obedience to the commands of the Houses, it did something amuse us, but, when their own letter was read to my Lord Admiral, which was soon after yours, the House received very good satisfaction.' He hoped that things were not 'in so ill a posture' as Hotham judged, and that it was vigilancy and tender care for the peace of the kingdom that made Sir John suspect the worse. 'And no doubt it is the part of a wise man to foresee and be prepared.' In the Commons they were every day entertained with messages or news of occurrences from York, which took up all the time. 'God put an end to these distractions in his own way and season, which are the best. The Lords and Commons go on unanimously, and the countries hereabouts are like to give a cheerful obedience to

the Ordinance of the Militia, which is now putting in execution . . .' Hampden did not sign his name, explaining in a
postscript, 'We suspect the opening of letters.'

Eleven days later Hampden wrote again to Hotham:

> I went from this town into Buckinghamshire where I have been
> until now about the militia of that county. During this absence I
> find you have been pleased to favour me with two of your letters,
> which my brother Pym read when I was away, and the latter of
> them he imparted to the House as it was necessary he should,
> and is even now returning you the sense of the House in answer
> to it. I see God has showed himself wonderful in his deliverance
> of you from treachery, and he that has done it will still deliver. I
> know not what has passed in the House in my absence, having
> been here but about an hour. But I may tell you they seem
> confident and secure above what I could expect, considering
> how great a noise the withdrawing of those Lords made in the
> country. The deputy lieutenants of our county and the soldiers
> have performed their parts very well, and besides our trained
> bands we have many volunteers that have armed themselves at
> their own charge and formed themselves into bands. I have no
> more to write of at this present being such a stranger here, but
> now you shall find me ready to serve you here . . .

Clearly Hotham reposed considerable confidence in Hampden. On 7 June Hampden sent him an order from the Houses
he had requested, adding some words of caution. Yesterday
the Houses received information of 'the great meeting at
York upon which no conclusion can be made, since nothing
was required of the people nor anything declared by them.
But the Houses are much affected with the carriage of my
Lord Lindsey and my Lord Savile that so violently hindered
the delivery of the country's petition.' Parliament was very
apprehensive of the danger in which the kingdom now stood,
and would do the best it could for keeping the peace 'which I
assure myself is your principal aim'.

Now the inexorable logic of conflict began to sweep the two
parties towards the very brink of civil war. On 1 June both
Houses passed another last-ditch petition with nineteen
propositions summarizing their requests; the King offered
some concessions in a published answer eighteen days later,
but as for his right to control the militia, 'he would no more

part with that than his crown'. Meanwhile, on 9 June, Parliament had offered an interest rate of eight per cent for those who loaned money, plate, horses or equipped horsemen for their defence. Goodwin gave £100 and promised four horses, while Hampden for his part sent in 802 ounces of silver plate worth £214.3s.8d. and £100 in coin, besides three horses with their furnishings. In all, this 'Proposition Money' produced £76,000 by the end of the year. Buckinghamshire headed the county list with a tender of £30,000 for the public service. But the merchant companies and the City of London made separate loans of far larger sums.

Shortly afterwards, the King issued Commissions of Array to secure the militia for himself. The local supporters of the Lion and the Unicorn began their struggle to win the loyalty of the county trained-bands, or, failing that, the possession of their armour and weapons in the shire magazines.

Lord Paget, the Lord-Lieutenant of Buckinghamshire, went northwards to join the King early in June. But Hampden wrote to Hotham on 14 June that:

> . . . there be, God be thanked, those noble Lords that will live and die in doing their duty to the utmost. The towns, also, are more entire than ever. More of them than I could have imagined have declared themselves to assist in the last propositions, which I am sure you have seen. The City, likewise, continues full of affection for the Parliament; they lent £100,000 very lately and when these propositions of horse and plate were made to them in a great assembly at Guild Hall, there were large testimonies of approbation.

As a member for the shire, Hampden promptly asked the Commons to name a new lord-lieutenant or to give the deputy-lieutenants power to proceed with the muster planned for the following Friday. Consequently he took down with him to Aylesbury a militia ordinance appointing the thirty-two deputy-lieutenants of the county to be the Committee of Buckinghamshire. Parliament entrusted to a quorum of five or more members of this committee the responsibility for collecting money for the support of a garrison at Aylesbury. They would take it in turns, three weeks at a time, to live in the town at the 'George' inn, so that a committee of five would always be there to muster and pay the garrison once a month. If need arose, they should also summon aid from the rest of the county for the strengthening of the garrison. Neither Hampden nor Arthur Goodwin were members of the committee, although the latter's son-in-law, Lord Wharton, became Lord-Lieutenant in Paget's place.

On 2 July Captain Straughan ran his fourth-rate warship *Providence* aground up a creek in the Humber, having narrowly evaded capture by Warwick's ships. He unloaded that evening the supplies purchased by the Queen in Holland: about two hundred barrels of powder, seven or eight brass field-pieces, eight hundred muskets and some two thousand pikes. Much encouraged, the King now granted commissions to raise regiments of horse and foot. He made the veteran Earl of Lindsey his General, with Sir Jacob Astley as Major-General of Foot and Prince Rupert in command of the Horse. These generals addressed themselves to the task of creating an army of cavalry and dragoons, foot regiments and artillery sufficient to defeat any forces that Parliament could put into the field against them.

On 4 July Parliament appointed a committee of five peers and ten commoners to take care of the safety of the kingdom and its defence. For their part the Commons appointed to this Committee of Safety the following members: Pym, Hampden, Denzil Holles, Sir Philip Stapleton, Sir John Merrick, Nathaniel Fiennes, William Pierrepoint, John Glyn, and Sir William Waller. A week later both Houses voted that an army of ten thousand men should be raised in London and the neighbourhood under the command of the Earl of Essex. Thus in July 1642 both sides were arming for the battle that had now become entirely predictable.

In his last letter to Sir John Hotham that summer, dated 18 July, Hampden mentioned the new Committee of Safety and said that it was 'extremely full of business'. He could inform Hotham, however, that orders had been issued that morning to send him six pieces of ordnance and that many of the men intended to reinforce the garrison had already set out by sea. The King and his army had reconnoitred Hull earlier that month, and Hampden referred to the incident: 'Your courage and constancy have demonstrated that Hull is tenable for above five hours, which has been opposed by divers arguments.' But, he continued, 'we are of opinion the King's forces will not stay long before Hull, but that he will march southward . . . They speak from Court of great forces, and no less confidence, but we are not easily induced to believe it. Yet there are persons ill affected enough to Parliament working in every corner, but the Lord in heaven will plead for his poor servant, and either give us peace or preserve us from violence.'

Chapter Ten

COLONEL JOHN HAMPDEN

I see him lead the Pikes! What will he do?
        Defend him God! Ah whither will he go?
Up to the cannon mouth he leads; in vain,
        They speak loud Death, and threaten till they're ta'en.

ABRAHAM COWLEY

On 26 July about ten thousand volunteers paraded in the Moorfields and five days later they were assigned to regiments. By order of the Committee of Safety on 6 August a grant of seventeen shillings was made for equipping each man with coat, shoes, shirt and cap. Within a few weeks the army of the Earl of Essex began to take shape. With the exception of John Pym, all of the five members who had become national heroes in January received commissions to raise regiments for Parliament, for it was doubtless felt that their popularity would attract men to the colours.

Thus Hampden began forming his famous regiment of Greencoats. A regiment of foot, composed of ten companies, should have numbered twelve hundred soldiers, besides officers. The colonel's company, by custom the largest in the regiment, was placed under the day-to-day command of Captain-Lieutenant Henry Isham. As his lieutenant-colonel Hampden chose an experienced veteran named Joseph Wagstaffe, who had served with distinction as a major in the French service. Subsequently in 1643 Wagstaffe was captured by the Royalists, changed sides and earned a knighthood from his new employers. Thus Hampden must have chosen him on the grounds of his military merits, not because he was a Puritan at heart.

Sergeant-Major William Barriffe, commanding officer of

the third company of Greencoats, had the distinction of being an author. His drill manual, entitled *Militarie Discipline, or the Young Artilleryman, wherein is discoursed and showne the postures both of musket and pike*, had appeared in 1635 and came out in a third edition in 1643. Richard Ingoldsby, the senior captain, was the son of Sir Richard Ingoldsby of Lenborough, one of the deputy-lieutenants of Buckinghamshire. Captains Nicholls, Arriett, John Stiles, John Raymond, Robert Harrington, and Morris, received commissions to command the other six companies.

Each company commander had under him a lieutenant, ensign, two sergeants, three corporals and two drummers, with perhaps one or two gentleman volunteers. The regiments tended to dwindle as the war progressed. Hampden's Greencoats, for example, mustered 893 soldiers on 21 January 1643 and 44 men less on 21 June that year. His regimental staff included a quarter-master, William Spurstow as chaplain, a provost-marshal, a 'chirurgion' and his mate, a carriage-master and a drum-major. Each company included both pikemen and musketeers, possibly in the proportion of two of the former to one of the latter.

The musketeers carried a matchlock, a piece not fired by the clash of flint on steel as in the flintlock, but by clamping to the touch-hole a burning length of rope soaked in saltpetre. Thus before an action the musketeers had to light this match until it smouldered and spluttered, and then carry it wrapped around their arms. Some musketeers also bore a long rest, spiked at one end and forked at the other, to support the musket when firing, but its use was in decline. They had at their side a bullet bag – twelve bullets weighed a pound – a flask of fine powder for priming, and a bandolier with twelve to twenty charges of powder dangling ready in wooden cylinders from it.

The pikemen were armed with a full pike, a cumbersome ash pole of as much as eighteen feet or more long with a sharpened steel head, and poor quality swords or knives. Unlike the musketeers, who wore coats and felt hats, most of the pikemen were equipped with breastplate and helmet. When marching, they trailed their pikes behind them on the road; in action, they levelled them or rested the butt against the instep of their right foot drawn back. The pikemen provided a defence for the musketeers, who at close quarters could only upturn their pieces and wield them as clubs. Rival bodies of pikemen on the battlefield would close upon each other and come to 'push of pike', like stags locking their antlers in struggle.

Parliament's nominal rates of pay were a little higher than those of the Royalists, and in addition there were small variations between regiments. The standard rates for a regiment of foot in Parliament's service were as follows:

	£	s.	d.	
Colonel	2	5	0	per day
Lieutenant-Colonel	1	10	0	per day
Major	1	4	0	per day
7 Captains	5	5	0	per day
10 Lieutenants	2	0	0	per day
10 Ensigns	1	10	0	per day
20 Sergeants	1	11	6	per day
1 Drum Major	0	1	6	per day
20 Drums	1	0	0	per day
10 Gentlemen	0	10	0	per day
30 Corporals	1	10	0	per day
Chaplain and Man	0	8	8	per day
Chirurgion and 2 Mates	0	9	0	per day
Marshal and his Man	0	4	8	per day
Quartermaster and Man	0	4	8	per day
All Officers, per day	19	14	0	
1000 Soldiers, per day	33	6	8	
Regiment complete, per day	£ 53	0	8	

Hampden's own colours were white with a green and white fringe. The other companies bore versions of it as laid down by the prevailing custom. 'The Colonel's Colours in the first place is of a pure and clean colour, without any mixture', wrote Captain Venn, a veteran of the English Civil War. 'The Lieutenant Colonel's only with Saint George's arms in the upper corner next the staff, the Major's the same, but in the lower and outmost corner with a little stream blazant. And every captain with Saint George's arms alone, but with so many spots or several devices as pertain to the dignity of their several places.' These colours of painted taffeta measured six feet square, and served as rallying points for the soldiers in quarters or on the battlefield.

During August the Greencoats made ready to march to the rendezvous at Northampton appointed by the Lord General. The letters of Nehemiah Wharton, a sergeant in the Redcoats of Colonel Denzil Holles, give a vivid picture of life in Parliament's regiments of foot at this time. On 8 August the Redcoats set out from London on the long march to Northampton. At Chiswick they burned the altar rails in the church and at Hillingdon they tore up the vicar's white surplice for use as handkerchiefs.

After entering Buckinghamshire ('the sweetest country that ever I saw') Wharton notes the burning of more altar rails, and the accidental death of a maid, shot by a careless musketeer in Captain Francis's company, on Saturday 14 August at Wendover. 'From hence we marched very sadly two miles, where Colonel Hampden, accompanied with many gentlemen well horsed, met us, and with great joy saluted and welcomed us, and conducted us unto Aylesbury, where we have a regiment of foot and several troops of horse to join with us.' In better spirits, with loaves and cheeses looted from Papist houses stuck on their swords, the Redcoats thus entered Aylesbury. The regiment awaiting them was probably Hampden's own, while the troops belonged to Colonel Arthur Goodwin's Regiment of Horse, also raised like the Greencoats in Buckinghamshire.

At about this time Hampden received intelligence that the Earl of Berkshire and other Royalist gentlemen had gathered at Ascott, a mansion near the village of Chalgrove in Oxfordshire, some sixteen miles south-west by way of Thame, with the intention of executing the Commission of Array in that county. On Monday 16 August he marched out of Aylesbury with a hundred horse and four hundred musketeers towards Ascott. Once near their destination Hampden sent the soldiers forwards under a guide – his servant William Liddall – to take up a position on Chalgrove Field, a flat plain of large open cornfields not two miles from the house.

Probably with an escort of a troop of horse and the other officers Hampden rode forwards to Ascott. A newsletter, written three days later, described the arrest: 'Mr Hampden, without much ceremony, entered the house and apprehended the Earl, who affirmed that he was innocent and had done nothing; to whom Mr Hampden replied he was therefore sent to protect him.' The Earl protested that he and the other gentlemen, most of whom had fled, were meeting as magistrates to settle the peace of the county, not upon the Commission of Array. But nonetheless Hampden sent the Earl and Sir John Curzon to London as prisoners.

The Redcoats marched on towards Northampton by way of Buckingham, with the Bluecoats of Colonel Sir Henry Cholmley's regiment, also raised in London, now making clouds of dust on the road not far behind them. Wharton killed a fat buck in the park of Hillesden House, home of the Royalist Sir Alexander Denton. He speared its head as a trophy on top of his sergeant's halberd and marched on to Buckingham. That night in Buckingham he entertained his captain, Captain Beacon, Captain Parker, and Hampden's son John, who was possibly a gentleman volunteer with the Redcoats at this time, to a welcome feast of roast venison. From Buckingham the regiments marched northwards seventeen miles to Northampton.

In July Lord Brooke, as the Lord Lieutenant of Warwickshire and Staffordshire, had garrisoned Warwick Castle which lay some thirty miles to the west of Northampton, and defeated a force sent against him under the command of the Earl of Northampton at Kineton, near Banbury. Later the Earl of Northampton had returned with the Earl of Derby, the Earl of Berkshire and Lord Dunsmore, and laid siege to the castle. The garrison hung out the bloody flag, a symbol of defiance, and kept up a brisk fire on the Cavaliers. One of Northampton's men, going over the street with a shoulder of mutton in his hand, provocatively held it up and said, 'Look here, you round-heads, you would be glad of a bit presently.' A musketeer on the castle walls fired his piece and shot the man dead. The governor Captain John Bridges then displayed his own winding-sheet as a sign of his determination to resist to the end. Also he held up a Bible, lest the Cavaliers should be in any doubt as to what the war was about.

Early in August the King led his army south towards Warwick Castle, pausing to bombard Coventry some ten miles north of it, where his guns soon breached the medieval walls of the town. To relieve the pressure upon Coventry, the Parliamentarians hastily assembled on 21 August three thousand foot and four hundred horse at Southam, a market town in Warwickshire twenty-one miles west of Northampton and ten miles from Warwick Castle. Here Hampden and Goodwin with their own regiments and the Redcoats made a rendezvous with Lord Brooke and his Purplecoats and Lord Saye's Bluecoats, commanded by the Scots veteran Sir John Meldrum, and a small train of six field guns. Hearing that the Earl of Northampton, with eight hundred horse and three hundred foot, was at hand, the Parliamentarians 'gave a great shout, with flinging up of their hats and clattering their arms, till the town rang again with the sound thereof, and, casting aside all desires of meat and lodging provided for them, went immediately into the fields adjoining to the town, ready for battle.' At daybreak they found Northampton's men drawn up, and 'being on fire to be at them', advanced under Hampden's command. After a brief skirmish the Royalist foot companies fled and their cavalry trotted away.

On 26 and 27 August a part of the force marched to the environs of Coventry, and again encoutered a body of Cavalier horse on Dunsmore Heath who seemed to be offering them a fight. Once in range, the Parliamentarians let fly with a cannon that ploughed a lane through the Royalist troops, making the frightened horses plunge and rear in disorder. Hampden rode at the head of his regiment with 'wonderful courage and shouts of joy' as the forces advanced and skirmished. The Royalist cavalry under Commissary-General Lord Wilmot, however, decided not to hurl themselves against the hedgehogs of twelve hundred pikemen and musketeers; they turned away and rode off northwards. The Parliamentarians lost none killed, but one untrained trooper shot a companion through the back while another had fired a pistol bullet into his own foot. On Monday 31 August the regiments set out on the thirty-mile march back to Northampton, pillaging Papists and poaching deer on the way.

Meanwhile the King had abandoned his design on Warwick Castle and Coventry and withdrawn to Nottingham
where his standard, bearing the Royal Arms quartered with
a hand pointing to the Crown above the motto *Give Caesar his
due*, was unfurled on 22 August in a formal declaration of
war. Clarendon paints a depressing picture of the ceremony:

> The standard was erected, about six of the clock in the evening
> of a very stormy and tempestuous day. The King himself, with a
> small train, rode to the top of the castle-hill, Verney the Knight
> Marshal, who was standard-bearer, carrying the standard,
> which was then erected in that place, with little other ceremony
> than the sound of drums and trumpets. Melancholic men
> observed many ill presages about that time . . . and a general
> sadness covered the whole town, and the King himself appeared
> more melancholic than he used to be. The standard itself was
> blown down the same night it had been set up, by a very strong
> and unruly wind, and could not be fixed again in a day or two till
> the tempest was allayed.

Sir Edmund Verney, Hampden's countryman, would die
defending the royal standard at Edgehill. Verney shared
Hampden's Puritan convictions, and heartily wished that
the King would yield to Parliament's desires. Yet as Knight
Marshal his sense of honour and gratitude to the King weigh-
ted the scales in his conscience. As he plainly told Edward
Hyde: 'I have eaten his bread and served him near thirty
years, and will not to do so base a thing as to forsake him,
and choose rather to lose my life – which I am sure I shall do
– to preserve and defend those things which are against my
conscience to preserve and defend; for I will deal freely with
you. I have no reverence for bishops, for whom this quarrel
subsists.'

The King could count upon much support in the northern
and western parts of the country, while on the whole the
south and east sided with Parliament. Only about one-
seventh of the national population of perhaps five million
people lived in the Royalist areas north of the Trent. By
contrast London, which was mainly pro-Parliament, contained nearly half a million inhabitants. Norwich and Bristol, the next cities in size, mustered less than about 30,000

Reade in this Image him, whose dearest blood
Is thought noe price to buy his Countryes good,
Whose name shall flourish, till the blast of ffame
Shall want a Trumpet, or true Worth, a name.

Edw: Bower pinxit   G: Glover fecit

John Pym

ROBERT DEVEREUX EARLE OF ESSEX HIS EXCELLENCY. LORD GENERALL OF
the Forces raised by the Authority of the Parliament. For the defence of the King and Kingdom.

Printed for John Partridge

One of a series of engravings by Wenceslas Hollar commemorating
Parliament's military successes in 1643

Arthur Goodwin, Hampden's friend and fellow Member of Parliament, painted by Anthony Van Dyck

Sala Regalis cum Curia Westmonasterij vulgo Westminster haall

New Palace Yard, with Westminster Hall, and the Clock House, from an engraving by Wenceslas Hollar

Part of Westminster, with Parliament House, Westminster Hall, and the Abbey, from an engraving by Wenceslas Hollar

Hampden, from an engraving made in 1740 by Jacobus Houbraken

Oliver Cromwell – Hampden's cousin – by Robert Walker

The statue of Hampden in Aylesbury

citizens apiece. The country's wealth, as well as the bulk of its population, lay in parts loyal to Parliament, as the Ship-Money assessments reveal. The counties which lay south and east of a line between Hull and Bristol were assessed for about three-quarters of the total sum. Most of the large towns and all the major ports (after the capitulation of Portsmouth early in September) declared for Parliament. Last but not least, the royal fleet of sixteen warships in the Downs, two in Irish waters and twenty-four transport ships, many of them built with the proceeds of Ship-Money, sided with Parliament. Yet wars are not won by counting heads or acres or tax returns. Charles possessed that intangible mystique of kingship on his side and also the practical advantage of an unchallenged authority to make all the big decisions himself. Moreover, depite his inferior share of the nation's resources, he succeeded in maintaining his armies on virtually an equal footing with the Parliamentary forces for two years, which was itself an extraordinary achievement.

Back in the crowded streets of Northampton, where Essex had concentrated his army, the grumbles and complaints to which soldiers are prone began to break the surface of early enthusiasm. The Redcoats had already succeeded in getting their unpopular Lieutenant-Colonel Henry Billingsley cashiered. A professional soldier, Billingsley's rough manners and oaths obviously did not appeal to the Puritan Londoners: Wharton dismissed him as a 'Godamme blade, and doubtless [he will] hatch in hell'. On 7 September the foot soldiers asked for more pay, an extra five shillings a month per head which had been promised to them by the London Committee, or else they said they would surrender their arms. Hampden and other officers laboured to appease them but could not. Wharton thought that if there was no more money forthcoming there would be trouble.

Meanwhile, the foot-soldiers found themselves abused and looked down upon by the cavalry troopers, and brawling broke out between them over the spoils of pillage. Wharton stopped 'the base blew coats' of Cholmley's Regiment from plundering a well-affected justice, only to be robbed himself of the confiscated goods and his own sword by the troop of Colonel Fiennes, who were supposed to be on guard. Whar-

ton had his revenge when his company stood guard on one of
the gates: he searched all of Fiennes' troopers to the skin
whenever they came in and took anything of value.

Nobody seems to have held undisputed command over the
thousands of soldiers in and around Northampton. Sir John
Merrick, the Sergeant-Major-General of Foot, had appeared
in Aylesbury when the Redcoats were there, and declared
that the command had been given to him, but he failed to
impose his will upon the army. Hampden saw the need to
establish martial law in the army immediately, and also to
get the soldiers on the march so that the devil did not find
work for their idle hands. With other senior officers of the
army – Sir Arthur Heselrige, Colonel Thomas Ballard, Colonel Sir Henry Cholmley, Captain Nathaniel Fiennes and
Captain James Sheffield of the Lord General's own Regiment of Horse – Hampden wrote to the Earl of Essex in
London:

> The soldiers are grown so outrageous that they plunder every
> place. Even this morning, five or six gentlemen's houses have
> been ransacked by them, of which we conceive one great cause
> to be the malignity of the country people who instigate and
> direct the soldiers in what places they should exercise this
> insolency. We use all means to suppress it, sending out squad-
> rons of horse, who do their duty very well. But the truth is that,
> unless we are able to execute some exemplary punishment upon
> the principal malefactors, we have no hope to redress this horrid
> enormity.
>
> We beseech your Excellency to take this into your present and
> serious consideration, for if this go on awhile the army will grow
> as odious to the country as the Cavaliers. And, though we take
> not upon us to advise the Parliament, yet we that are eye-
> witnesses of that state of the Army do verily believe that without
> Martial Law (to extend to the soldiers only) it may prove a ruin
> as likely as a remedy to this kingdom.
>
> My Lord, we dispatched an express on Saturday to give
> notice that we had stayed my Lord of Newport here, who
> alleged that he was employed with my Lord Falkland and my
> Lord Spencer to carry his Majesty's message to Parliament;
> but, finding no testimony of this more than his own word, we
> held it fit to stay him here until the pleasure of the Houses were
> known. My Lord thinks the time long that he is stayed here, but
> that is no warrant for us to discharge him. Tomorrow my Lord

Montague and divers other prisoners are upon their way for London.

My Lord, once more let us beseech your Lordship to put those unruly upon present action, which, being commanded by your Excellency, shall with all obedience be performed by your Excellency's humble servants.

Next day senior officers judged the situation to be getting worse, and Hampden wrote again to Essex on their behalf:

We are so perplexed with the insolencies of the soldiers already committed, and of which the apprehension is greater if they be not prevented forthwith, that we thought it absolutely necessary to desire Sir Arthur Heselrige to take this journey that he might inform your Excellency of the particulars which are fitter to be related by a friend than to be read by an enemy, as they may be if they should be committed to paper.

He will likewise acquaint your Excellency with the importunate desires of the soldiers to have an increase of allowance, which they do not only pretend to as reasonable in regard to the great prices they are forced to pay for all their victual, but they challenge it also as just, upon the grounds of a promise made unto them by the Committee of London that they should have 5 shillings every month besides their ordinary pay – which divers of the soldiers do confidently affirm, and the truth is we do not see how they can possibly live without some such addition as they desire.

My Lord, the officers are very desirous to know your pleasure about the wagon money; for here they could provide themselves well of wagons and cannot hereafter when they are marched from home. And to provide carriages in the manner now we do is both an excessive charge and will fail us when we shall stand in need.

My Lord, we have no more, but to desire your Excellency's hastening to us, which we hope would be a means to appease these disorders and would be a great satisfaction to the longing desires of your Excellency's most humble servants.

The Lord General arrived at Northampton shortly afterwards, bringing his own coffin and winding-sheet with him. The watchword in Northampton that night was 'Welcome'. On Wednesday 14 September he reviewed the army in the fields outside the town. Next day, after the code of martial laws had been read out at the head of every regiment, the army began its march towards the King, heading by way of Rugby into Warwickshire. On Tuesday 19 September the

Redcoats met Colonel Hampden, his Greencoats and three other regiments at a rendezvous on Dunsmore Heath and marched behind the Lord General to Warwick. The Redcoats arrived too late to claim beds; they slept on straw and became lousy with fleas and bugs. The drill-conscious Sergeant Wharton says that these 'backbiters' seemed to march 'six on breast and eight deep at their open order'.

From Warwick the army trudged some twenty-eight miles westwards through incessant rain to Worcester. Wharton notes 'such foul weather that before I had marched one mile I was wet to the skin'. The King had fallen back from Nottingham to Chester, but Prince Rupert and his Cavaliers roamed abroad. On 23 September they inflicted a sharp defeat upon the Parliamentarian cavalry at Powick Bridge, not two miles south of Worcester. Young Edmund Ludlow serving in the Lord General's orange-coated Life-guard saw some of the routed fugitives 'riding very hard towards us with drawn swords and many of them without hats', crying out that the enemy was hard by in pursuit. The inexperienced Life-guard was much alarmed by the report. Some offered to ride forward as scouts to confirm the news.

> But our captain Sir Philip Stapleton not being then with us, his Lieutenant one Bainham, an old soldier (a generation of men much cried up at that time) drawing us into a field, where he pretended we might more advantageously charge if there should be occasion, commanded us to wheel about; but our gentlemen not yet well understanding the difference between wheeling about, and shifting for themselves, their backs being now towards the enemy, whom they thought to be close in the rear, retired . . . in a very dishonourable manner, and the next morning rallied at the head-quarters, where we received but cold welcome from the general, as we well deserved.

In the city of Worcester the soldiers refreshed themselves on perry made from Worcestershire pears at one penny a quart, and wandered around the streets looking over the cathedral and the churches. Wharton compared this Royalist city to Sodom and Gomorrah: he considered it to be rather more heathen than Algiers or Malta. But he was even more shocked by the Welsh oaths in the streets of Hereford, whither he marched in September with a commanded party of nine hundred soldiers. The men attended the Laudian clergy's morning service in Hereford Cathedral and danced to the organ music in the choir while the 'puppets' of the choir sang away. When a robed canon prayed for the King a soldier roared out, 'What! Never a bit for the Parliament?' After this 'human service' conducted by the Baalists, wrote Wharton, the men then marched off to a 'divine service' where they heard a rousing sermon from the chaplain of the Redcoats, the eminent Puritan divine Mr Obadiah Sedgewick. Back in Worcester once more, Wharton and his men helped to construct fortifications around the city.

On 4 October Hampden wrote to Sir John Hotham, presumably from Worcester. Hotham had come under criticism from two members in the House, and Hampden wrote to assure him that

> . . . the evidence you have given to all the world by your noble actions of that judgment and honesty which is in you shall never be called in question by me upon slight grounds. And therefore let me desire this justice from you that you will not believe me otherwise than what I now profess upon any misinformation until you do me the favour to let me answer for myself. I shall only desire you to manage the business concerning those persons with that tenderness that without absolute necessity no public discouragements may fall upon them who have ventured far in the public [service] and have incurred . . . a very high degree of displeasure of the Court. But your wisdom I doubt not will so moderate these things as will give very good satisfaction to all observing. We are sending horse and foot to your noble son with all speed, and think ourselves not well dealt with to the late pacification made in Yorkshire, as by declaration will appear. I shall trouble you no further at this time . . .

Yet in December that year the Hothams, father and son, began a secret communication with the Marquess of Newcastle which would lead to their execution in 1645 as traitors to Parliament.

On 12 October the King, with his army, began his march towards London. The Royalists had come into Warwickshire when they heard that Essex had departed from Worcester and was closing rapidly upon them. After some debate the King resolved to turn and offer him battle at Edgehill on

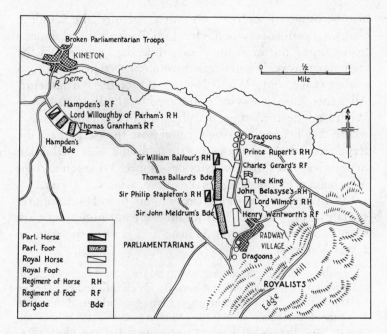

The Battle of Edgehill: situation at about 4.30 p.m.

the following day, Sunday 23 October. Owing to a shortage of draught horses, the heavier Parliamentarian guns had not been able to move fast enough, and so Essex left them behind to follow on the road from Stratford-upon-Avon under the guard of Hampden with two regiments of foot.

The armies at Edgehill were about equal in size. The King's cavalry of some 2,800 horse and 1,000 dragoons slightly outnumbered the estimated 2,150 horse and 720 dragoons of Parliament. On the other hand, the twelve Parliamentarian regiments of foot who took part in the battle comprised about 12,000 men compared to the King's infantry forces of some 10,500 pikemen and musketeers. The King's field officers arrayed his forces at the foot of the steep north slopes of Edgehill. Essex drew out his men from Kineton into a great broad field half a mile away, and also made ready for battle. In plain buff-coat and black armour, wearing an orange sash, Essex rode about the lines, accompanied by his Life-guard in their red cloaks. For his part, 'the King was that day in a black velvet coat lin'd with ermine, and a steel cap covered with velvet', wrote young **Richard** Bulstrode of the Prince of Wales' Regiment of Horse. 'He rode to every brigade of horse, and to all the tertia's of foot, to encourage them to their duty, being accompanied by the great officers of the army. His Majesty spoke to them with great courage and cheerfulness, which causes "Huzzas!" thro' the whole army.'

Both generals disposed their foot in the centre with clumps of horse on both wings. After a preliminary exchange of cannon fire lasting about one hour, the shouting and cheering Cavaliers charged home and easily chased away the Parliamentarians on the wings. On the Parliament's left, Prince Rupert swept away twenty-four troops of horse under Commissary-General Sir James Ramsey, while Lord Wilmot with ten troops scattered a regiment of horse on their right wing but significantly missed two others under Balfour, who stood further back and partly shielded by the embattled phalanxes of foot in the centre. While the Cavaliers wildly pursued their broken opponents into Kineton and beyond, the Royalist infantry in five brigades advanced and engaged Parliament's foot, now reduced to the two large brigades of Sir John Meldrum and Colonel Thomas Ballard by the running away of the third brigade of Colonel Charles Essex. The terrible fight ebbed and flowed as the sudden fury of charge and counter-charge gave way to moments of respite. White smoke enveloped the field and the cries of wounded men sounded among the incessant bangs and cracks of cannon and small arms fire, while swords threshed yet more noise from steel and armour. Gradually more of Prince Rupert's troopers drifted back, and it looked as if the bristling hedgehogs of pikemen and musketeers under Essex, who fought manfully himself with a halberd, might yet be broken before nightfall.

As daylight began to fade and the battle raged on, however, Colonel John Hampden came at last into the field at the head of a brigade made up of the Greencoats and Colonel Thomas Grantham's russet-coated Regiment of Foot, accompanied by Lord Willoughby of Parham's Regiment of Horse with their black colours fluttering at the head of every troop. In a letter published shortly after the battle, Captain Nathaniel Fiennes says that his brother John, also captain of a troop of horse, succeeded in rallying his men and those of Captain Robert Vivers of Goodwin's regiment after their flight on the left wing. Having stopped the runaways he

> made two or three stands, and at length gathered a pretty body upon a hill together, and with them (there being Captain [Edward] Keightly's and Captain [Oliver] Cromwell's Troops at length came to them also) he marched towards the town [of Kineton]; and hearing the enemy was there (as indeed they were with the greatest part of their horse) they made a stand, and sending forth their scouts to give them intelligence of Colonel Hampden's Brigade that was coming another way to the town, and so joining themselves unto them, they came to the Army together.

Whether Cromwell's troop had already been in action or had simply arrived late for the battle is not known, but certainly he marched for a time under Hampden's command at his first major battle.

According to Whitelocke, the three fresh colonels, with Sir Philip Stapleton and others, pressed for a new assault or a renewal of the battle on the following day. But Essex was inclined to listen to the veteran professional officers. Whitelocke mentions the Frenchman Dalbier, Quarter-Master-General of Horse, as the leading spokesman of the 'old soldiers of fortune' who successfully urged Essex to stand on the defensive.

The Parliamentarian army stood shivering that night as a bitter north wind blew over the white-frosted fields at the foot of Edgehill. Edmund Ludlow describes their hardship:

> The night after the battle our army quartered upon the same ground that the enemy fought on the day before. No man nor horse got any meat that night, and I had touched none since the
> · Saturday before, neither could I find my servant who had my cloak, so that having nothing to keep me warm but a suit of iron, I was obliged to walk about all night, which proved very cold by reason of a sharp frost.

After allowing the army to take breakfast in Kineton, Essex drew out the weary regiments to stand in battle order again for three or four more hours next morning facing the Royalist army who occupied the brow of Edgehill. At noon the King dined in the field off a drumhead. His herald had returned that morning from the Parliamentarian army claiming to have seen 'trouble and disorder' in the faces of Essex and his principal officers and dejection in the ranks of soldiers who 'looked like men who had no farther ambition than to keep what they had left'. According to Bulstrode Whitelocke, Hampden and others again urged Essex to attack, while Quarter-Master-General Dalbier led the opposition in favour of calling it a day. Whitelocke is not generally accurate on the battle, and he may possibly be retailing common Puritan gossip on this incident.

After burying their dead, the Parliamentarian army marched to Warwick, where the soldiers rested and refreshed themselves. The King's army marched to Banbury, from thence by easy stages to Oxford, which he entered in triumph one week after the battle. Meanwhile, the Parliamentarian regiments turned their faces towards London. Edmund Ludlow, who fought in Essex's Life-guard at Edgehill, observed their low morale now, for they appeared not as an 'army that had obtained a victory but as if they had been beaten'.

Doubtless the Puritan leaders in the army felt as dejected as the common soldiers. They had expected the issue to be settled in one great battle, with God vindicating their cause by granting them a clear victory. What had gone wrong? Cromwell blamed the poor quality of the Parliamentarian cavalry. Years later, speaking in the Commons, he recalled a conversation which he had with Hampden about this time:

> I had a very worthy friend then; and he was a very noble person, and I know his memory is very grateful to all – Mr John Hampden. At my first going into this engagement, I saw our men were beaten at every hand. I did indeed; and desired him that he would make some additions to my Lord Essex's army, of some new regiments; and I told him I would be serviceable to him in bringing such men in as I thought had a spirit that would do something in the work.
>
> This is very true that I tell you; God knows I lie not. 'Your troops', said I, 'are most of them old decayed serving-men and tapsters and such kind of fellows; and', said I, 'their troops are gentlemen's sons, younger sons and persons of quality: Do you

think that the spirits of such base and mean fellows will ever be able to encounter gentlemen, that have honour and courage and resolution in them?' Truly I did represent to him in this manner conscientiously; and truly I did tell him: 'You must get men of spirit, and take it not ill what I say – I know you will not – of a spirit that is likely to go on as far as gentlemen will go – or else you will be beaten still.' I told him so; I did truly. He was a wise and worthy person; and he did think that I talked a good notion, but an impractical one. The result was I raised such men as had the fear of God before them, as made some conscience of what they did.

This famous conversation tells us something about Hampden as well as Cromwell. Again we see him acting as a good listener. Although senior in rank he treats Cromwell as an equal. With the two opposing armies marching southwards towards London, perhaps heading for a decisive battle outside the city, Cromwell's idea of adding some new regiments of horse to Essex's cavalry was clearly impracticable. But Hampden dealt as gently with the suggestion as he had done previously with Sir John Eliot's turgid manuscript. Yet Cromwell's idea had fallen on good ground. Later that year the Committee of Safety began to form associations of counties for mutal defence, which provided the necessary financial support for new regiments of horse. As a leading member of that committee, Hampden may well have been the person who pressed for the raising of these county association forces.

A week after Edgehill, the Parliamentarian army reached Northampton while at the same time the Royalists entered Oxford. From thence the King despatched cavalry forces both to harry the flank of Essex's army as it moved towards London and also to forage deep in the Buckinghamshire countryside. The Parliamentarian committee in Aylesbury had withdrawn their forces from that town as being indefensible when Prince Rupert bore down upon them. Hampden had not heard this news for he wrote to the committee assuring them of support:

GENTLEMEN – The army is now at Northampton, moving every day nearer to you. If you disband not, we may be a mutual succour to each other; but if you disperse, you make yourselves and your country a prey.

You shall hear daily from

Your servant,

JOHN HAMPDEN

Northampton
Octob. 31

I wrote this enclosed letter yesterday and thought it would have come to you then; but the messenger had occasion to stay till this morning.

We cannot be ready to march till to-morrow; and then, I believe, we shall. I desire you will be pleased to send to me again, as soon as you can, to the army, that we may know what posture you are in, and then you will hear which way we go. You shall do me a favour to certify me what you hear of the King's forces; for I believe your intelligence is better from Oxford and those parts than ours can be.

Your humble servant,

JOHN HAMPDEN

Northampton, Nov.1

On 1 November Prince Rupert sat in Aylesbury while his troopers collected forage and drove in cattle. That day six troops of Sir William Balfour's horse arrived to stiffen the Buckinghamshire levies, and they fought stoutly against the Cavaliers at Holman's Bridge, a half-mile north of the town. The townsfolk threatened the rear of Prince Rupert's forces, and he retreated towards Thame.

Both armies marched on towards the capital. On 4 November the King had entered Reading, rather nearer to London than the Earl of Essex at Woburn in Bedfordshire. Yet the Parliamentarians, marching down Watling Street, reached the capital ahead of their rivals. The Royalist advance continued. On 7 November Prince Rupert summoned Windsor Castle to surrender, but the garrison made ready for a siege. Two days later, when the main body of the Royalist army occupied Colnbrook, less than twenty miles from the capital, Parliament gave directions for the Earl of Essex to take the field again with his army.

On the same day that the Royalist army marched into Oxford, a group in both Houses who favoured immediate peace negotiations had persuaded the more militant members to agree to their proposal for a petition to the King. In return, however, they secured from the peace group an agreement that more recruits should be found for Essex's army and that Parliament should send a formal message to the Scots asking them for speedy and powerful succour. The King took exception to one member of the proposed commission of emissaries, which held matters up for several days. On 11 November the commission of two peers and three commoners finally presented their petition to the King at Colnbrook, asking him to reside near London while committees of both Houses came to him with their propositions to secure peace. They took back with them the King's answer in which he agreed to reside 'at our own castle of Windsor if the forces there shall be removed', until the committees had occasion to bring him their peace propositions.

Edward Hyde, who was with the King at Colnbrook as an adviser, believed that if the Royalist army had withdrawn to Reading, or even stayed still, Parliament might have handed over Windsor Castle as a gesture of good will. He blamed the excitable and over-confident Prince Rupert for the amazing decision to march on the capital next morning. Having advanced with the horse and dragoons to Hounslow, Hyde declares, the Prince impudently sent word to the King to march with the foot to support him. But it is nearly impossible to believe Hyde on this point. Why did not the King order his impetuous nephew to heel, like a disobedient dog? In order for a whole army to march some preliminary orders must have been issued on the evening of the day before. Nothing can quite clear the shifty King Charles from the charge that he used the peace overtures as a cover for making a surprise attack on London.

Having received the King's gracious reply to their petition, both Houses had issued orders to their army to cease hostilities. On Friday 12 November they sent a messenger towards Colnbrook with news to that effect coupled with a request that the Royalists should reciprocate this step. The messenger never delivered his letter. As the Earl of Essex spoke in the House of Lords, the peers suddenly heard the dramatic thunder of great guns away to the west. Essex hastily left the House and rode at a gallop across Hyde Park

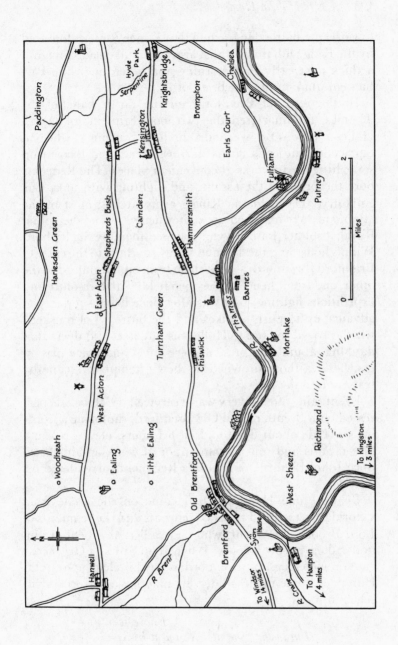

Brentford and Turnham Green

towards the battle. He learned that Prince Rupert, followed by the King with the Royalist army, had taken advantage of a thick mist early that morning and fallen upon the Parliamentarian outpost at Brentford.

In the town of Brentford, on the north bank of the Thames, lay quartered the two foot regiments of Denzil Holles and Lord Brooke, and a small party of horse, who had barricaded the ends of the narrow streets and thrown up some little breastworks at convenient places. The Redcoats bore the brunt of the assault and, fighting with tenacious gallantry, they held the King's army at bay most of the afternoon. 'We marched up to the enemy', wrote the young Royalist soldier John Gwyn, 'engaged them by Sir Richard Winn's house and the Thames side, beat them to retreat into Brainford [Brentford], – beat them from one Brainford to the other, and from thence to the open field, with a resolute and expeditious fighting, that was after once firing suddenly to advance up to push of pikes and the butt-end of muskets, which proved so fatal to Holles his butchers and dyers that day, that abundance of them were killed and taken prisoners, besides those drowned in their attempt to escape by leaping into the river.'

Eventually, after 'a very warm service', the Royalists possessed both Brentford and Old Brentford, capturing according to Hyde about five hundred prisoners, eleven colours, fifteen guns and much ammunition. Even Captain 'Freeborn John' Lilburne of Brooke's Regiment surrendered his sword.

By this time Hampden had come on the scene from Uxbridge at the head of his Greencoats and the remnants of Lord Brooke's regiment, who had rallied also behind him under their purple colours. When John Stiles, a Greencoat captain who fought at Brentford, wrote his elegy upon John Hampden some months later, he may have had this vivid scene in mind:

> *I have seen*
> *Him in the front of's Regiment-in-Green,*
> *When Death about him did in ambush lie*
> *And whizzing shot, like showers of arrows, fly,*
> *Waving his conqu'ring steel, as if that he*

From Mars had got the sole monopoly
Of never-failing courage.

Hampden's Greencoats held the Royalists at bay until the
other regiments of Essex's army could come up. By providence or chance, Essex had ordered his army to muster in
Chelsea fields that afternoon anyway. Rather than attempt
to hold Brentford, the King decided to withdraw his army
some distance westwards where the weary soldiers camped
for the night. Next day the Royalist commanders marched
their men towards London once more along the road to
Hammersmith. A mile beyond Brentford, however, they
caught sight of the full armed might of both Parliament and
the City of London, a solid wall of some 24,000 soldiers who
had been standing in battle order on Turnham Green.

Resplendent in their burnished armour, with drums beating and colours flying, the Londoners – many of them
apprentices – had marched about nine miles that day, 'very
cheerfully' thanks to Sergeant-Major-General Philip Skippon's inspiring leadership. For he went all the way along
with the soldiers talking to them, sometimes to one company
and sometimes to another; and the soldiers seemed to be
more taken with his informal words than a set formal ora-
tion. 'Come on, my boys, my brave boys!' he said, 'let us pray
heartily and fight heartily. I will run the same hazards with
you. Rember the cause is for God and for the defence of
yourselves, your wives and children. Come, my honest brave
boys, pray heartily and fight heartily, and God will bless us.'
The Earl of Holland, who was the field marshal that day,
drew up the twenty-four thousand men, wisely interleaving
City regiments with those of the army. Horse stood on both
wings, and the regiments of Sir Philip Stapleton and Arthur
Goodwin took their station forward in the van. The guns
waited in a lane near Hammersmith, with a strongly-
guarded wagon park in a field nearby. As the Lord General
rode from regiment to regiment the soldiers threw up their
caps and shouted, 'Hey for old Robin!'

After the opening exchange of cannon fire, Essex sent a
brigade of two regiments of horse and four of foot to dislodge
a party of Royalists occupying the hill at Acton. 'Hampden's

regiment being one of that party which were to go about, I marched with them,' wrote Bulstrode Whitelocke. 'They had the van next to the horse, and after we had marched about a mile on our way, and the enemy began to gaze on us, Sir John Merrick, Major-General to Essex, rode galloping after us.' Merrick told them that the Lord General had changed his mind and wanted them to return to the main body of the army. Of course he should have let them continue in order to threaten the King's line of retreat. 'At which', added Whitelocke, 'we were exceedingly troubled and wondered how this should come to pass, that we should be recalled and lose so great an advantage against the enemy, and it was feared that some who were false had given this advice to the General.'

As the day passed the armies stood on their guard and looked at each other. Every time the Royalists stirred, a crowd of spectators who had ridden out from the City were seen to gallop off in alarm, and then return somewhat sheepishly. Cartloads of provisions, wine and ale, were sent out of London to the army, but towards late afternoon some of the citizen-soldiers began to slip off homewards. Meanwhile there were signs that the King's army intended to march away. It is said that Hampden, Holles and Skippon pleaded with Essex to advance. But the Earl of Holland and Quarter-Master-General Dalbier counselled him not to fight until the arrival of three thousand soldiers from Kingston and Windsor, who were on their march by way of London to join him. Yet even when these regiments appeared in sight, Essex still would not stir. As the Cavalier officer Gwyn wrote, 'I cannot omit observing that had Essex's right wing of horse, which stood upon more ground than the King had horse to face them, wheeled to the left to join with the foot that came from Windsor and Kingston, and fallen on the King's rear, he might have gone to London *nolens volens*,' i.e. whether he liked it or not.

Leaving a body of horse to face the enemy between the two Brentfords, the King drew back his main army to Kingston-on-Thames and he rested for a night at Hampton Court. Next day he gave orders for all his forces to pull back to Reading. In a message to Parliament he excused the

attack on Brentford as a defensive move against being hem-
med in by the Earl of Essex's forces. On 24 November,
however, Parliament voted that only one proposition should
now be made to the King, namely that he should come to
them in London, alone, having dismissed his evil counsellors. Upon receiving the expected refusal, Parliament
directed Essex to march forwards with his army and make
his headquarters at Windsor.

When the King realized that Brentford had killed the chance
of peace negotiations for a time, he left a garrison of over two
thousand foot and a regiment of horse under the command of
Commissary-General Sir Arthur Aston in Reading, and took
the rest of the army to Oxford. His tentacles stretched out
from the city. Thus he placed a strong garrison in Wallingford, thirteen miles away, and another at Brill on the
escarpment of the Chilterns. On their march southwards
from Edgehill the Royalists had already secured Banbury,
some twenty-two miles north of Oxford. With his cavalry
quartered in and around Abingdon, the King had surrounded his new capital with a defensive and offensive system of outposts.

These new dispositions placed west Buckinghamshire in a
vulnerable position. On 29 November, the day on which the
King was expected at Oxford, Edward Hyde writing from
that city forwarded a paper to Viscount Falkland. 'My intelligence added', he wrote, 'that Mr Hampden and Mr Goodwin are at their houses, and our calvary here think it a very
easy matter to take them if His Majesty will give such
directions either to these forces which are near those parts, or
to their lordships here what shall be done. It is a pity the
gentlemen should not be visited.' Certainly the county
would receive many such 'courtesy calls' from the Cavalier
horse in the next two years. Indeed their depredations spoilt
the prosperity of Buckinghamshire for a decade or more.

What it meant to be 'visited' by the Cavaliers is vividly
described by Bulstrode Whitelocke, who lived at Fawley
Court in Buckinghamshire, some twelve miles south of Great
Hampden. During the Royalist advance on London early in
November the locusts had swarmed into his property:

Sir John Byron and his brothers commanded those horse, and gave order that they should commit no insolence at my house, nor plunder my goods; but soldiers are not easily governed against their plunder, or persuaded to restrain it, for there being about a thousand of the King's Horse quartered in and about the house, and none but servants there, there was no insolence or outrage usually committed by common soldiers on a reputed enemy, which was not committed by these brutish fellows at my house. Then they had their whores with them, they spent and consumed a hundred load of corn and hay, littered their horses with sheaves of good wheat, and gave them all sorts of corn in the straw; divers writings of consequence, and books which were left in my study,some of them they tore to pieces, others they burnt to light their tobacco, and some they carried away with them, to my extreme great loss and prejudice, in wanting the writings of my estate, and losing very many excellent manuscripts of my father's and others', and some of my own labours.

They broke down my park pales, killed most of my deer, though rascal and carrion, and let out all the rest, only a tame young stag, they carried away and presented to Prince Rupert, and my hounds which were extraordinary good. They eat and drank up all that the house could afford, broke up all the trunks, chests, and places; and where they found linen or any household stuff they took it away with them, and cutting the beds, let out the feathers, and took away the ticks. They likewise carried away my coach, and four good horses, and all my saddle horses, and did put all the mischief and spoil, that malice and enmity could provoke barbarous mercenaries to commit, and so they parted.

The Lord General took some action to curb the foraging raids from Oxford. Early in December a body of Cavalier horse and dragoons pillaged and burned the Wiltshire market town of Marlborough. Essex despatched four regiments of horse and two of dragoons under Colonel Sir William Waller to drive them out. Waller's force eventually surrounded the Cavaliers in Winchester and captured them all. In the next weeks Waller siezed Arundel Castle and Chichester as well. Portsmouth had fallen to him in the previous September, and Farnham Castle in late November. Thus when Waller entered London to resume his seat as the member of Andover in the Commons the people gave him a warm welcome, hailing him as 'William the Conqueror.'

Thus the year 1642 ended with the two opposing main armies in winter quarters. The great decisive pitched battle, for which the Puritan leaders in the House of Commons and the field had worked so hard, had not materialized. Certainly the war would not now be settled in a matter of weeks. Why had the Cause failed to triumph? As no Puritans could suppose that God the Lord of Hosts had failed Israel or would do so, some of them tended to look for scapegoats in an obvious place, namely those Scots, Dutch, German and French officers who had enlisted for wages in the Lord General's army. Had not these men counselled delay for their own base ends? In a speech delivered to the newly-chosen officers of Warwick Castle and published before the Edgehill campaign, Lord Brooke had sounded a clear warning:

> In Germany they fought only for spoil, rapine and destruction, merely money it was and hope of gain that excited the soldier to that service. It is not here so required of us as the Cause stands with us. We must rather employ men who will fight merely for the Cause's sake, and bear their own charges, than those who expect rewards and salaries, for by such means we shall never have a conclusion of these wars. For mercenaries, whose end is merely their pay . . . rather covet to spin out the wars to a prodigious length, as they have done in other countries, than to see them quickly brought to a conclusion. We must despatch this great work in a short time or be all liable to inevitable ruin. I shall therefore freely speak by conscience. I had rather have a thousand or two thousand honest citizens that can only handle their arms, whose hearts go with their hands, than two thousand of mercenary soldiers that boast of their foreign experience.

Foremost among these mercenaries, both in numbers and experience, stood the large clan of Scots professional officers. They were doubly suspect, being members of that unpopular nation. Moreover, their dogmatic Presbyterian opinions and cock-sure manners probably grated as much as their sense of military superiority. Trouble between the Scots and English became well-nigh inevitable. The House of Commons on 16 March 1643 learned of a shouting match between Colonel Jeremy Horton and two Scottish commanders, Colonel Ogleby and Lieutenant-Colonel Marshall, in which Horton had called them both 'Rascals!' In the brawl that followed, a hundred swords had leapt from their scabbards and Ogleby for one received a nasty slash wound. This conflict between the English and the Scots remained endemic, until in 1644 – after another major row – some senior Scots officers led an exodus to Sir William Waller's army, where at least they found a general who loved their nation, admired their courage in battle and respected their steadfast loyalty to the Covenant.

From Cromwell's conversation with Hampden after Edgehill it appears that he placed the blame on the quality of the rank and file, whom he regarded as wage-earners rather than God-servers. But his remarks in August 1643 to the Suffolk Committee make it clear that Cromwell thought that a troop of horse was the lengthened shadow of its commander:

> If you choose godly honest men to be captains of horse, honest men will follow them . . . I had rather have a plain russet-coated captain that knows what he fights for, and loves what he knows, than that which you call a gentleman and is nothing else. I honour a gentleman that is so indeed.

A number of troop commanders at Edgehill came up to this standard, including Oliver himself, and so there must have been many 'honest men' in Essex's cavalry. But the Parliamentarian horse adopted the wrong tactics, sitting and firing carbines and pistols rather than charging home. Moreover, the cavalry as yet largely lacked the more settled regimental structure of the foot. Nor did its generals inspire the confidence of the Puritans. Parliament found it difficult to find even six colonels of horse in July 1642, possibly because it expected them to a large extent to 'bear their own charges'. The titular Lord General of the Horse, the twenty-nine-year-old Earl of Bedford, fought well at Edgehill, but quitted the service of Parliament soon afterwards. Scottish mercenaries dominated the cavalry. Sir William Balfour commanded it as Lieutenant-General of the Horse, with Sir James Ramsey as Commissary-General and Major Gilbert Blare as Adjutant-General, while Captain John Dalbier served as Quarter-Master-General. Ramsey returned to Scotland after a court-martial had held him responsible for the collapse of Parliamentarians' left wing at Edgehill.

Thus the failure to win the grand battle could be attributed more to the senior officers of the army than to the quality of Parliamentarian captains and troopers. Indeed it was the combined cavalry of Balfour and Waller, whose troops had been swept away at Edgehill, who inflicted the first major defeat upon the Cavalier horse (at Cheriton in March 1644). Eventually Cromwell and others would come to blame the most senior officers of all, the Earls of Essex and Manchester, for the repeated frustrations in the efforts towards bringing the King to battle and then inflicting that great decisive defeat upon him in one day.

Essex had allayed any Puritan doubts about him by attempting to settle matters at Edgehill. Parliament had made him a little king, with his own prerogatives as Captain-General which he guarded jealously. In order to preserve unity, no criticism of him was allowed, and so – as in the case of the King – his mistakes and delays were at first blamed upon his advisers in the council of war, a group of senior officers which a general summoned in times of difficult decision. Contemporaries portray Hampden as the Puritan leader in this council, pressing for the crucial battle. Essex became more identified with the policy of caution, put to him either by peers such as the Earl of Holland at Turnham Green (who showed his true colours by going over to the King in 1643) or else by professionals such as Dalbier, whom the Puritans suspected of wanting to prolong the general conflict out of a vested interest in war itself.

If Hampden did play this role, which seems likely, it is interesting to speculate on his relations with Essex. We may be sure that Hampden showed every sign of respect for the Earl's social status and military rank; his loyalty was never in doubt. Essex trusted him implicitly and may have liked him personally, for he named him in his will, drawn up in 1642, as an executor. He may also have recognized Hampden's abilities as a soldier and his wisdom in the field. Yet the Lord General was a vain man. He loved his title and position as 'His Excellency', and would brook no rivals. In May 1643, six months after Edgehill, Hampden's name was being mentioned as a possible successor to the Lord General.

In November 1642 a design to raise an independent army under a more avowedly Puritan commander, the Earl of Warwick, came to naught, but the more extreme Puritans in Parliament and City would try again in the summer of 1643 with Waller as their hero. Meanwhile, the new regiments of the associated counties began to take shape, many of them under Puritan officers. Early in 1643, for example, Colonel Cromwell raised his 'Ironsides' in the Eastern Association, while Sir Arthur Heselrige mustered his well-mounted regiment of cuirassiers (nick-named the 'Lobsters' by the Cavaliers) for service with Waller in the army of the Western Association.

Therefore by the end of 1642 almost all the leading Puritans had departed from the army of the Earl of Essex, except for Hampden. Unlike Brooke, Cromwell, Waller, and the others, he had no strong regional connections to draw him elsewhere. Indeed Essex's army was developing into the extra-mural army of London and of the home counties. It stood on the southern flank of his own county. As Hampden possessed considerable influence both in London and in these counties, it was natural for him to remain in Essex's army. He threw himself with considerable energy into the task of securing recruits for the remaining regiments and reinforcements from London and the home counties.

Thus Hampden had proved his worth in the field as well as in the debating chamber; the same qualities served him well in both arenas. Clarendon wrote:

In the first entrance into the troubles he undertook the command of a regiment of foot, and performed the duty of a colonel on all occasions most punctually. He was very temperate in diet, and a supreme governor over all his passions and affections, and had thereby a great power over other men's. He was of an industry and vigilance not to be tired out or wearied by the most laborious, and of parts not to be imposed upon by the most subtle or sharp; and of a personal courage equal to his best parts; so that he was an enemy not to be wished wherever he might have been made a friend, and as much to be apprehended where he was so as any man could deserve to be.

With Hampden standing at the side of Essex, Pym and his colleagues could entertain no doubts that the army would shortly seek out the King's army in Oxford and defeat it. For his part, Essex could rely upon Hampden to secure him recruits and money. Moreover, Hampden possessed real power in the House of Commons, far more than Sir Philip Stapleton, also a member of the Committee of Safety. Thus Hampden had become the chief link between Essex and Pym's group. As a colonel he had led his regiment successfully in action and shown himself worthy to command a brigade. Prompt and intelligent in a crisis, he was also wise in the council of war. Above all, nobody doubted Hampden's spirit or his will to win. 'And without question', concluded Clarendon, 'when he first drew the sword he threw away the scabbard.'

Chapter Eleven

THE SIEGE OF READING

O blessed Peace,
To thy soft arms through death itself we flee;
Battles and camps and fields and victorie
Are but the rugged steps that lead to thee!

RICHARD LOVELACE

The Civil War spread over the whole country, and ceased not for the winter snows of December 1642 and January 1643. With Essex's army quartered between them and the King's much enlarged forces around Oxford, the citizens of London and their families could sleep secure. But tidings reached the capital from the west, the north and the midlands which removed the hopes of an early victory for Parliament in the spring, that biblical time when 'the kings go forth to war'. The King's Lieutenant-General in the west, the Marquess of Hertford, had left Sherborne Castle after the surrender of Portsmouth in August 1642 and gone to south Wales were he had recruited some regiments of foot with which he returned to Oxford. Meanwhile his horse and dragoons rode down into Cornwall, where they helped Sir Ralph Hopton and his Cornish trained-bands to secure that county for the King. As these Cornishmen would not march across the river Tamar, Hopton raised some stout volunteer regiments of foot and carried the war into Devon, where he routed the local Parliamentarians at Braddock Down on 19 January 1643. He then made ready to besiege Plymouth. Thus Hopton had not followed the conventions of war and gone into winter quarters. On 5 December a critic of the Lord General's inactivity could sarcastically inquire why 'it was summer in Devonshire and only winter at Windsor'?

In Yorkshire the forces of Parliament under Lord Fairfax faced another formidable and active Royalist army in the eight thousand soldiers under the Earl of Newcastle. The Cavaliers crossed the Tees on 1 December and relieved York, compelling Fairfax to fall back to Selby. The Earl of Newcastle occupied Leeds and Wakefield, but met with a repulse at Bradford. The younger Fairfax, Sir Thomas, already noted for his enthusiasm and dash, had made his way there and given some inspired leadership to the townsmen. On 23 January he recovered Leeds. But Newcastle had placed a strong garrison in the strategically well-situated town of Newark, which gave him a foothold south of the Trent and not a hundred miles from Oxford. In summary, the Royalists had secured much advantage for themselves in these winter campaigns.

Hampden did what he could to encourage action in the south. Colonel Arthur Goodwin wrote to him in January to obtain the Lord General's permission for an attack upon the Royalist quarter at Brill, a fortified village on the Chiltern escarpment some ten miles west of Aylesbury:

> My Lord General by your letters finds your good intention to fall upon Brill, which his Excellency is well pleased you should do, and hath therefore commanded me to let you know that you should attempt that place if you find your strength fit for it, which, in regard of the nearness of that garrison, you must know better than he can; and that his pleasure is you should put this in execution upon Thursday next in the morning by break of day rather than at any other time. But, if that cannot be, at such time as you shall find most convenient.
> Your faithful friend and humble servant,
>
> JOHN HAMPDEN
>
> Windsor, January 24th, 1643.

> I am directed to desire you presently to send hither, twenty Reading men out of Captain Forteglaus' company. They must be here to-morrow by noon or within an hour or two after, at the farthest. This you will do with as little noise as such a business can be. You may do well to provide them horses before the men know anything; then send them from Aylesbury about five o'clock in the morning. Direct them to come into Windsor, but three or four in a company at the most.

These latter men were needed for a design against Reading.

Hampden presumably knew that town well, for his second wife Lady Letitia, whom he had married in 1641, was the widow of a former Sheriff of Berkshire named Sir Thomas Vachell of Coley, on the outskirts of Reading, who had died in 1638. Little is known about this lady, beyond the fact that she was the daughter of Sir Francis Knollys, and continued to reside at Coley House after her marriage to Hampden. Reading contained many supporters of Parliament, and so Hampden may have counted upon them to rise against the garrison when he appeared before the town.

In the last week of January, Hampden marched some nineteen miles to Reading with a force which included his regiment and a cavalry troop under a leading Scots officer called John Urry. But, as he related to Arthur Goodwin, the adventure came to nothing:

> It grieves me much you had no better success at Brill, and that it should deprive us of that valiant Captain Jermyn.
>
> The enterprise intended against Reading took not effect the first day for want of a bridge over the Kennet, where some of our forces were to have passed; and, though it was considered of to be put in execution the second day, yet upon serious debate it was thought better to be forborne.
>
> I read your letter to my Lord General, who was very sensible of that passage in it where you express trouble that he should think you disobedient to his commands – concerning which, he purposing to write with his own hand, I need say no more but that you will be assured that he neither hath nor ever had the least jealousy of your obedience.
>
> Since it hath pleased God to deny our desires in this attempt upon Brill, we have great cause to bless him that so many of our worthy friends are yet preserved, among whom, that yourself is come off with so much honour and safety, it is a great comfort to
>
> Your assured friend and servant,
>
> JOHN HAMPDEN
>
> I thank you for your favour to Robert Pye, to whom I beseech you to continue it and add your own counsel.

Arthur Goodwin's scruples about offending the Lord General and Hampden's assurances are significant. In July that year Goodwin and Sir Philip Stapleton defended Essex in the House of Commons against the intemperate attacks of the younger Henry Vane, William Strode and Henry Marten, 'who did snarl at every one'. D'Ewes observed that these 'violent spirits' in the House of Commons made haste to 'pluck their hats over their eyes' at the mention of Essex's name. Stapleton and Goodwin forced the Lord General's arch-enemy Vane to retract his insulting references to the Lord General and make an apology. So close a friend of Hampden was Arthur Goodwin that it is impossible to believe that this action did not reflect Hampden's own policy.

Young Sir Robert Pye, a captain of a troop of horse, had married Hampden's seventeen-year-old daughter Anne. His son-in-law's wealthy father, also named Sir Robert, a member of the House of Commons, chose this month of January to write to the King desiring to make his peace with him, declaring that if the war continued for only a few months more destruction and famine must fall upon the kingdom. D'Ewes noted that when the intercepted letter was read in the Commons, 'although divers enemies of the House had been put out of the House for less offences, the fiery spirits, out of respect for their chief captain and ringleader, Mr Hampden, did pass no vote against Sir Robert Pye, the father, neither at that time nor at any time afterwards'.

This difficult position of his son-in-law stands least in the catalogue of Hampden's personal troubles. John, his eldest son, had either been killed or had died in his winter quarters. Hampden's beloved eldest daughter Elizabeth Knightley had also died in childbirth. If *Mercurius Aulicus*, the Royal newspaper, is to be trusted, there were other afflictions as well. In a report dated 15 April 1643 the Oxford editor wrote:

> It is advertised by some who have been curious in the observation that Mr Hampden, one of the five members so much talked of, hath had many great misfortunes since the beginning of the present troubles, whereof he hath been a principal mover: particularly that he hath buried since that time two of his daughters, one grandchild which he had by a daughter married to Sir Rob. Pye the younger, and his own eldest son and heir: there being only two sons surviving, whereof the one is said to be a Cripple, and the other a Lunatick. Of which, whatever use may be made by others, 'tis not unfit that the party whom it most concerns would lay it close unto his heart, and make such use thereof, as the sad case invites him to.

Many others, who could no longer bear to see their country wasted by civil war, now earnestly desired an accommodation with the King. Prompted by a small minority of Royalist merchants, a peace group in the Common Council of the City secured a majority vote for making another petition to the King. The House of Lords took up the proposal and prepared some propositions. The House of Commons had considered them in late December and agreed to begin negotiations, laying down as a preliminary condition the disbandment of both armies. They also passed a motion for the abolition of episcopacy, to which the Lords assented on 30 January 1643.

The peace negotiations opened in Oxford on 1 February. Parliament's proposals closely resembled the nineteen propositions put forward in the preceding June, with some important additions. For example, episcopacy would be abolished in the Church of England and replaced by another system to be devised in consultation with an assembly of Puritan divines. As another example, Parliament now sought control over the royal ships as well as the land forces and forts.

The Parliamentarian commissioners spent some pleasant weeks in Oxford. On being first received by the King in Christ Church gardens they kissed his hand. They also had the honour of being presented to the Prince of Wales. The senior commissioner, the Earl of Northumberland, had brought with him his own silver plate, household stuff, provisions and wine, and he kept a good table in his lodgings. On one occasion he even sent across delicacies for the King's table. Yet the two sides had not even agreed to an armistice, and the fighting continued all over the country. On 8 April the King raised the stakes by asking that his castles, arsenals and ships should be restored to him, and that Parliament should both admit back the expelled members and adjourn to some place outside London. Parliament rejected these strange proposals on 14 April, and thus the discussion for a 'Treaty of Oxford' proved as insubstantial as a masque in a college garden.

In the Commons debates upon these peace proposals,

Hampden stood firmly opposed to a surrender on the King's terms. The diarist Sir Simonds D'Ewes, who would pay any price for peace, listed 'Pym, Hampden, Strode, Marten and other fiery spirits', who 'accounting their own condition desperate, did not care though they hazarded the whole kingdom to save themselves'.

On 17 February, for example, an amendment was desired by Sir Philip Stapleton in a debate on the propositions, namely that the articles touching the disbandment of both armies and those concerning the restoration of forts, ships and magazines to the King, should be first agreed upon, and then the other clauses discussed. Hampden 'and some other violent spirits' at first seconded the motion, writes D'Ewes, but, seeing that the peace group in the House agreed to it, 'then did Mr Hampden stand up again, and, like a subtle fox, would have diverted us from the question, after he saw that young Sir Henry Vane and Mr Rigby disliked this addition, fearing that it would cause the whole question to pass with the less opposition'. The matter was put to the vote, and the 'ayes' carried the motion by three voices. All the 'fiery spirits' stayed in the chamber with the negatives, and many who were for peace also voted against it, fearing some hidden poison.

On 20 February Pym wrote to Sir John Hotham expressing sympathy for his financial straits, but so little money had come in recently that the whole army was ready to disband. Other good garrisons had received even less than Hull, but he hoped to send a good sum soon. Pym added that he was pleased to hear of Hotham's son's successes and that he concurred so well with Lord Fairfax. He wrote also that he was one of a committee to confer with Essex about conditions for ceasing hostilities, which he hoped might be contrived. But until it was, there must be no slackening in 'the industry of the Army there'.

Hampden's exacting double role as the Puritan watchdog at the side of the Lord General and as the leader of equal standing with Pym in the Commons had become public knowledge. His frequent journeys between the headquarters of the Earl of Essex at Windsor and the chamber of the House at Westminster aroused comment even in Oxford. In a lampoon entitled *Mr Hampden's Speech on the London Petition for Peace*, written by the Royalist poet Sir John Denham and published about this time, Hampden says:

> *Have I so often passed between*
> *Windsor and Westminster, unseen,*
> *And did myself divide,*
> *To keep His Excellence in awe,*
> *And give the Parliament the law?*
> *For they knew none beside.*

The skirmishes of winter grew into larger actions as the spring of 1643 brought better weather. At the end of January Sir William Brereton defeated the Royalists of Cheshire and Lancashire at Nantwich. Prince Rupert seized Cirencester on 2 February, but Sir William Waller – now Sergeant-Major-General of the newly-formed Western Association – brilliantly surprised Malmesbury and then captured a 'mushroom army' of Welsh Royalists who were blockading Gloucester. Lichfield fell to Parliament on 4 March, albeit with the loss of Lord Brooke, commander of the forces in Warwickshire and Staffordshire, who was shot by a musketeer from the cathedral tower.

Incessant Cavalier raids made the Buckinghamshire Parliamentarians deeply aware of their exposed position. In February they had unsuccessfully asked the Eastern Association to admit them as a member. On 19 March the Lord General informed the Commons that Prince Rupert was marching on Aylesbury, Henley or London, and asked that Sir Philip Stapleton and Hampden should come to him at Windsor. Three days later Prince Rupert appeared before Aylesbury with six thousand horse and foot. Colonel Goodwin, who commanded the garrison, twice sallied out. On 23 March Goodwin, who had been appointed commander of the Buckinghamshire forces by Essex in January, told the House in a letter how the Lord General had shown his care by sending Colonel Hampden and Stapleton, who came up sooner than expected. The Cavaliers withdrew towards Oxford, plundering Wendover and pillaging the countryside as they rode homewards.

In March the King sent a force to attempt the capture of Bristol, and Parliament countered by ordering Essex to open the spring campaign with his army. D'Ewes noted that Essex had done little for four or five months 'to the dislike of all men', and that 'Mr Hampden and some other fiery spirits about him', who saw a greater prospect of peace if there was a cessation of fighting, therefore pushed for an advance. A cessation would only have led to the discouragement of Parliament's friends and the accession of more recruits to the King. D'Ewes states that when the proposed articles of peace came under discussion again on 18 March, Hampden and others deliberately absented themselves 'because they easily foresaw it would not lie in their power to stop the said articles'. But D'Ewes was wrong on this last point: Hampden had been summoned back for active service with the army.

In the second week in April the Royalists in Oxford heard rumours that the armed forces of Parliament would shortly converge on them. They expected Essex to march from Windsor, while Lord Grey of Wark would descend upon them from St Albans with the men of Norfolk, Suffolk and Essex. Colonel Cromwell would arrive with the soldiers of Cambridgeshire and Huntingdonshire, at the same time as Sir William Waller approached out of Gloucestershire with his western army. But Prince Maurice relieved the anxiety somewhat by inflicting a sharp reversal upon Sir William Waller's brigade at Ripple Field on 13 April.

Meanwhile the army of Essex stood idle around Windsor. The Puritans in London grew increasingly impatient. On 11 April the King's *Mercurius Aulicus* carried this news:

> It was this day reported exceedingly confidently by some who came from London lately, how it was noised in the City that the Earl of Essex was to leave the place of General unto Mr Hampden, as one more active and so by consequence more capable of the style of Excellency.

Clarendon states that there was a deep division among the Parliamentarian commanders over whether their army should march on Reading or Oxford. Had they resolved on the latter, he states, 'as Mr Hampden and all they who desired still to strike at the root very earnestly insisted upon, without doubt they had put the King's affairs into great confusion'. For Oxford lacked proper fortifications and a well-found garrison. The city held a multitude of nobles and gentlemen with their families, who 'bore any alarm very ill'. But other counsellors argued that the Reading quarter could not be left untaken in the rear of the army, and that the new levies who now comprised its bulk would not prove equal to the tests of such an enterprise. Essex's own views are not known for sure, but they may be deduced from the decision to march on Reading.

On Saturday, 15 April, the day the peace commissioners returned empty-handed from Oxford, the army set out westwards from Windsor. One column of four or five regiments of foot with four pieces of cannon passed down the road which led through Wokingham, while a second brigade of two regiments with twelve guns took the road to Twyford. On 12 April the Royalist governor of Reading, Sir Arthur Aston, sent intelligence of these forces northwards to Prince Rupert. The Prince had stormed Birmingham on 3 April, and was now besieging a Parliamentarian force in the close of Lichfield Cathedral. Aston complained about the quality of his soldiers; rather than command them he wished that the Prince had sentenced 'me to have lost my head, for I doubt, with these men, I shall lose it and my reputation both at once'. Aston had clearly lost his stomach for the war, for he wrote: 'I am grown weary of my life with perpetual trouble and vexation.'

Many soldiers in the Lord General's regiments on the northern route believed the rumour that they were marching on Oxford, but the column wheeled southwards at Twyford and came before Reading on Saturday evening. To the summons for surrender, the war-weary Aston gave a resolute reply: 'He would keep the town or starve in it.' He refused the chivalrous offer of Essex to allow him to send out the women and children and made ready for a siege.

After a great debate in the council of war between the alternative courses of taking the town by assault or approach, Essex decided upon the latter method. He placed the bulk of his army on the west side of Reading in order to prevent the King from sending reinforcements into the beleaguered town from Oxford. Under Sergeant-Major-General Skippon's direction the soldiers entrenched themselves and then began to dig siege approaches towards the town. They also dug their way towards a Royalist fortified redoubt on Caversham Hill, a mile north of Reading, which would give their guns a commanding position against both the town and Caversham bridge over the Thames if they could take it. By Monday the Parliamentarians had gained control over part of Caversham Hill, and they dragged up some guns to begin the bombardment of the town. Their cannon opened fire and knocked down the tower of Caversham church on the wooded hillside below, where the Royalists had mounted two light guns. On Sunday 16 April the army of Essex had been joined by Lord Grey of Wark, together with six troops of horse, two companies of dragoons, three regiments of foot and three guns from the newly-formed forces of the Eastern Association. These forces, supplemented by some of Essex's horse and foot, took up positions on the other three sides of Reading, thus completing the investment of the town.

By Wednesday 19 April the besiegers had captured the earthwork redoubt on Caversham Hill and driven away the enemy from the church in the bottom. On Monday or Tuesday, Aston hung out the white flag for a parley and offered to surrender the town if he could march away with his baggage, but 'it was answered that we came for the men not the town'. Hope burgeoned in Puritan hearts. In a letter from 'the Leaguer', dated on Wednesday, one of Essex's soldiers wrote to a London friend:

> that it is all the camp talk that if the Cavaliers come not out of Oxford to meet us here, that we shall speedily find them at Oxford, except they run for it, for we hope to play them such loud music with our camp organs as shall make their best bulwarks quake. We expect to meet Sir William Waller at Oxford with 8,000 men. Be confident in a week's time you shall see the scales turn: if we remove from Reading, Sergeant Major Skippon shall be left to continue this siege. I pray God teach our hearts to pray, and our fingers to fight.

There spoke a true Puritan.

Yet the siege dragged on for another week full of incident.

The Royalist defenders received powder and reinforcements of three or four hundred soldiers one night by barge
from Oxford. On Sunday, a party of Parliamentarians under
Colonel John Middleton beat up the quarters of two Royalist
regiments at Dorchester. A cannon ball dislodged a tile or
brick from a roof and it fell on the head of the luckless Sir
Arthur Aston, knocking him senseless. The Parliamentarians staged a public hanging of a deserter from Lord
Robartes' Regiment of Foot, who had accepted a bribe of £5
to explode the powder magazine. In another attempt to blow
up the magazine with forty pounds of gunpowder, a servant
of the Royalist officer swam the River Kennet both ways, but
was taken by a drummer of the Bluecoats. The new recruits
found themselves digging and fighting every day. 'It is something of a hot service for young soldiers,' wrote one officer in
a letter home, 'but custom will make it easy.'

If Essex and Hampden were using Reading as a bait to
lure the main Royalist army out of Oxford, it looked as if
their plan would succeed. On Tuesday 25 April, the King,
accompanied by Prince Rupert and Prince Maurice with
some forty-five troops of horse, nine weak regiments of foot
and twelve pieces of cannon, marched from their outpost at
Wallingford towards Caversham bridge in order to relieve
Reading. Essex had placed two regiments of foot to guard
this vital wooden bridge. Colonel Barclay's Regiment of
Foot had been newly raised, and four companies of the
inexperienced soldiers were placed in the earthworks on top
of Caversham Hill. Lieutenant-Colonel William Hunter
drew out his veteran Redcoats of Lord Robartes' regiment
in two divisions on the north bank of the river, barring the
entrance to the bridge. The right-hand division was supported by Barclay and his remaining six companies. With
considerable good sense the two commanders allowed their
musketeers to take up firing positions in the plentiful ditches
and hedgerows.

At about four o'clock in the afternoon a great body of
enemy appeared on a rise, not a cannon-shot away. The
King sent forwards the veteran Patrick Ruthven, Earl of
Forth, with a thousand musketeers to clear a way over the
bridge. Two Royalist regiments – 'a Green and a Red' –

marched forward and attacked. But the Parliamentarian musketeers, lying in the ditches which ran like trenches across the fields, had the wind behind them and they fired with good effect. White smoke rose as volley after volley cracked out across the meadows into the hesitant companies of Royalist foot edging forward in close-order formations. But they could not get near enough to their partly hidden enemy who lay in those natural trenches plying their pieces until the barrels grew hot under their hands. After the futile skirmish, lasing some ninety minutes, the Royalist generals ordered a withdrawal towards Wallingford. Hearing the glad tidings, many soldiers in the Green regiment of Cavaliers threw away their weapons and ran for it. Some of the Redcoats had fired their muskets more than thirty times, but now they fell to looting. A common soldier in Lord Robartes' Regiment picked £30 from the pocket of a slain Royalist major called Smith. The Parliamentarians lost only four men dead, while Colonel Barclay received a slight wound in the arm.

'Many would say their wounds have brought them more joy and comfort than ever they had in their lives,' wrote one of Barclay's officers. 'I could hear nothing but encouraging words from the soldiers one to another, some saying "God fights for us", "God will preserve us", "God will make good his promise to us, to cover our heads in the day of battle" etc. And when the enemy fled, very many cried out, "Let God have all the glory!" '

The King may have retired from Caversham because he heard that the acting governor of Reading, Colonel Richard Feilding, had already hung out the white flag and begun to negotiate for the surrender of the town. Moreover, he had exchanged hostages with Essex. After a debate in the council of war, the Lord General decided to accept the proffered surrender terms, allowing the garrison to march away with arms, ammunition, four cannon and baggage, and with their colours flying. Doubtless Hampden vehemently opposed this feeble course of action.

The decision did not prove to be popular with the Puritan rank and file. The same correspondent in Barclay's gallant regiment reported a 'great distraction in our army, for that we fear an unworthy accord will be agreed between our council of war and the town.' Certainly the terms of surrender pleased neither the King nor Parliament. Feilding subsequently asked for a court martial to clear his name; for his pains he was found guilty, but dramatically reprieved on the scaffold. Because the soldiers so disliked the terms of the agreement and it looked as if they might pillage the town anyway, Essex promised them a donation of twelve shillings each.

About four o'clock in the afternoon of Thursday, 27 April, Aston was carried out of Reading in a horse litter, draped with red cloth and lined with white linen. After him came the coaches and wagons, and then about forty troopers and dragoons with trumpets sounding, and nine sparse regiments of foot beneath white, blue and red colours, 'most of them bare and beggarly rogues', marching with drums beating and matches burning, followed by their many whores. The curious soldiers of Essex's army snatched at their hats and coats, or seized weapons from them, contrary to the articles of surrender. Next day Essex was called out three times to restore discipline in person, on one occasion leaving his dinner to grow cold in his absence.

With Essex and Skippon, Hampden had made an entry into Reading on Thursday afternoon, and shortly afterwards he wrote with Sir Philip Stapleton and others the somewhat reserved official report for Parliament. Probably he carried it up to London so that he could explain what had happened and press for a more active strategy. 'Some of our commanders are at London,' wrote one correspondent in Essex's army to *Mercurius Bellicus* on 30 April, 'I need not tell you their errand, only suggest better anything on this side ruin done or suffered, than we lie still at this present.'

News of Waller's capture of Hereford on 27 April reached the dissatisfied Puritans in Essex's army. The same correspondent made the painful comparison and drew a Puritan's moral from it. Waller had obtained all the arms, ammunition and colours of the Hereford garrison for small loss of life, 'so wonderfully does God go along with the endeavours of this valiant and vigilant commander'. The writer warned the public against gratifying the enemy's desire to see envy and division stirred up between 'a part of an army in opposition to that army whereof it is part'. He pointed out also the military differences between the situations at Reading and Hereford, probably repeating what he had heard the old soldiers say as they puffed their clay pipes. But Puritan readers would not be misled. It seemed plain that God marched with Waller, 'The Night Owl' as the Royalists now called him, and not with Essex.

Several contemporaries mention that Hampden urged Essex to advance upon Oxford in May, but to no avail. The arrest and trial of Colonel Richard Feilding had produced animosity and then disunity among the Cavalier officers in Oxford, as some sided with him and some against. The King's cause stood at a low ebb. Upon a false report in early May that Essex had started out for Oxford, the King at once resolved to march away towards the North. 'And if the Earl of Essex had at that time made any show of moving with his whole body that way,' concluded Clarendon, 'I do verily persuade myself Oxford itself and all the other garrisons of those parts had been quitted to them.' Hearing that Essex made no such move, the King resolved to remain at Oxford and give him battle about Oxford if he advanced.

Elsewhere the war had burst into life. The Fairfaxes, father and son, kept the Earl of Newcastle in play in the north, but they could not prevent some Royalist incursions into the northern borders of the Eastern Association nor stop the Royalists from building up their forces at Newark in Nottinghamshire. In order to counter this new threat, Essex sent orders to Lord Grey of Wark and Colonel Oliver Cromwell to meet Sir John Gell and his Nottinghamshire Parliamentarians at Stamford in Lincolnshire. Fearing an attack on Leicester, Lord Grey did not obey the command. On 9 May, however, Lord Willoughby of Parham, Sir John Hotham, and Cromwell brought their regiments to a rendezvous at Sleaford in south Lincolnshire, some eighteen miles east of Newark. Cromwell led a successful cavalry charge during a skirmish in Grantham on 13 May, but the Parliamentarian commanders wisely made no attempt to storm the stronghold of Newark itself.

On 16 May Sir Ralph Hopton changed the entire military situation in the west by decisively defeating the Earl of Stamford's Parliamentarian army at the Battle of Stratton in Cornwall. Within the next few days all of Devon except for the beleagured towns of Plymouth, Exeter, Bideford and Barnstaple passed into his hands. Knowing that Hopton still lacked sufficient cavalry, the King dispatched the Marquess of Hertford and Prince Maurice with a strong body of Cavaliers to meet him in Somerset. Waller began to concentrate the Parliamentarian forces in the region at Bath to meet the Royalists, but resolved to secure his rear by the capture of Worcester first. He arrived there on 29 May, but news of the Royalist advance in the southwest sent him marching back to Bath by way of Gloucester and Bristol.

Meanwhile Edmund Waller, a kinsman of both Sir William Waller and John Hampden, had tried his hand at treachery. The silver-tongued orator would have done better to stick to poetry, wherein he excelled even in an age of poets, with such verses as:

> *Go, lovely Rose!*
> *Tell her, that wastes her time and me,*
> *That now she knows,*
> *When I resemble her to thee,*
> *How sweet and fair she seems to be.*

Many of Waller's poems, such as his 'Of his Majesty's receiving the News of the Duke of Buckingham's Death', should have warned his contemporaries that here walked a born courtier. With intellectual pretensions, Waller became a close friend of Viscount Falkland and a member, along with Hyde, of the circle which met at Falkland's country house at Great Tew. He sat in the Long Parliament for a Buckinghamshire borough. As his name appears in Hampden's will, he must have been on good terms with his cousin. He acquired a reputation as a maker of speeches in the House of Commons, crying up the cause and denouncing the King's party. Possibly with his intransigent words ringing in their ears, the Commons chose him, despite his 'carnal eye', to speak with the King at Oxford as one of the peace commissioners in February. There his old friends soon played on his vanity and in no time converted this empty poet into a Trojan Horse.

Thus when Edmund Waller returned to London his head was full of the plans of a hare-brained Royalist plot with himself in the key position. The Tower of London would be seized, as well as other forts around the City. Parties would arrest Saye, Wharton, Pym, Stapleton, Hampden and Strode. Meanwhile the King would approach at the head of three thousand men towards London. Yet Edmund Waller, the poet and orator, could not stop talking. As the details of the plot leaked out, he found himself under arrest by the end of May.

Parliament handed the traitor over to the Earl of Essex for trial by court martial. Waller used his tongue and pen with good effect upon his acquaintances in order to lengthen his life. In June he chose the inopportune time when Hampden lay gravely ill after Chalgrove to seek Arthur Goodwin's support. Writing to Goodwin some weeks later, Waller referred to their conversation thus: 'Be not offended (I beseech you) if I put you in mind of what you were pleased to say to your servant, when the life of that worthy person was in danger as any is now in the country. You asked me then if I were content my kinsman's blood should be spilt . . .' Waller argued that he had preserved Hampden's life in earlier days by voting that the London trained-bands should be asked to protect the House of Commons. 'As then you were pleased to remember I was of his blood, so I beseech you forget it not now, and then I shall have some hopes of your favour.' After the court martial had pronounced him worthy of death, Essex showed clemency.

By allowing the garrison of Reading to march off with colours unfurled, drums beating and match alight, Essex had lowered the morale of his army. He may have thought that the men were dissatisfied because they had not been allowed to storm the town and win some booty for themselves, but the causes lay deeper. The Puritan officers and soldiers in the army probably felt a sense of spiritual anti-climax. The Lord God had shielded their regiments to what purpose? The surrender of Reading upon terms gave Him no glory.

For a month after the capitulation, Essex made matters worse by putting the army into quarters in Reading. Young soldiers live for action; boredom breeds discontent. Moreover, the lack of long marches on the open road reduced the army's fitness. Over-crowded houses and inns, insanitary habits and polluted water, and the poor quality of food did the rest: sickness spread as fast as the lice. To complete their plight, the soldiers had received no pay for several weeks. On 12 May Essex pointed out to Parliament that without a prompt dispatch of money his army would 'be forced still to live on hopes'. In this soil the tares of mutiny took root.

When their officers received orders to draw their men out to a rendezvous in the park near Caversham bridge on 27 May, many regiments refused to march until they were paid their wages. The two regiments most infected with this mutinous spirit were the Lord General's own Regiment of Horse and Hampden's Greencoats. Not without difficulty, Essex drew out his regiment to Caversham park that evening. But Hampden's regiment remained behind in their quarters. Hampden went himself to speak to them. According to Sir Samuel Luke, the Scout-Master-General, Hampden 'with good words and fair language, wrought so upon them that he made them ashamed of their actions, and they marched cheerfully to Caversham the next morning.'

Perhaps the long-awaited great battle would now take place. Probably Hampden had appealed to the deeper Puritan faith of his men, as well as both praising and chiding them like a father for their behaviour. Hampden's own spirit as he rode forth upon his last campaign might have been expressed in a similar prayer to that which Lord Brooke, the first really prominent Puritan leader to sacrifice his life in the war, had concluded his noble Warwick speech:

Lord, we are but a handful in consideration of thine and our enemies. Therefore, O Lord, fight thou our battles: go out as thou didst in the time of David before the hosts of thy servants; and strengthen and give us hearts, that we may show ourselves men, for the defence of thy true religion, and our own and the King and Kingdom's safety.

Chapter Twelve

CHALGROVE FIGHT

How died he? Death to life is crown or shame.

JOHN MILTON

While the Greencoats trudged through the rain towards Oxford with the army of the Earl of Essex in the first week of June, some stirring events were gathering momentum in the west. On 4 June the Marquess of Hertford and Prince Maurice from Oxford and Sir Ralph Hopton from Cornwall jubilantly joined forces at Chard in Somerset, making a combined army of 4,000 horse, 2,000 foot, 300 dragoons and 16 field pieces. Meanwhile Waller reached Bath during that same week and, in a mood of mounting spiritual excitement, he made ready his Western Association army for the coming battle.

During this time Hopton proposed a meeting with his old friend. Waller replied on 16 June with a letter which expressed perfectly the feelings of a Puritan gentleman caught up in a civil war against his kinsmen and countrymen:

> That great God which is the searcher of my heart, knows with what a sad sense I go upon this service, and with what a perfect hatred I detest this war without an enemy, but I look upon it as *opus domini*, which is enough to silence all passion in me. The God of peace in his good time send us peace, and in the mean time fit us to receive it. We are both upon the stage and must act those parts that are assigned us in this tragedy. Let us do it in a way of honour, and without personal animosities . . .

Like Hampden, Waller sought victory in the field. To that end he expected some support from the Earl of Essex: at the least a move against Oxford to keep the attention of the King's main army occupied. But Essex could not interpose his forces between Oxford and Bath, for that would have left the western approaches to London undefended. Neither could he play into the hands of his Puritan critics in London and Westminster by doing nothing. Thus he resolved upon a march to the eastern environs of Oxford. Clarendon may have read the motives of Essex accurately when he wrote: 'In the end, there being no other way to quiet the city of London, he marched towards Oxford, but in truth rather to secure Buckinghamshire, which was now infested by the King's horse, than to disquiet that place.'

Essex had a second reason for seeking to cut off Oxford from the midlands. Queen Henrietta Maria was bringing a great convoy of arms and ammunition towards the city from the north in early June. He had sent orders to the Parliamentarian commanders in the area of the convoy's route to seize it. Like Waller in the west, however, they either could not or would not obey his dispatches, much to the Lord General's chagrin. Therefore he may have decided to attempt the interception himself somewhere immediately north of Oxford.

In order to march at all the Lord General left behind him in Reading some three thousand sick soldiers. He took with him two thousand horse, less than half the size of Waller's cavalry at Bath. But his three thousand pikemen and musketeers still constituted the largest and finest body of Parliamentarian infantry in the country, with the exception of the untried London trained-bands. With these depleted but not insignificant forces, Essex entered the town of Wallingford on 6 June. Lord Grey of Wark, the general of the Eastern Association, had already brought his four or five thousand men three days earlier to Nettlebed, some seven miles south-east of Wallingford.

For creating a diversion or intercepting a convoy, an army of five thousand men might have been sufficient. But Parliament probably expected the Lord General to draw the King out of Oxford and defeat him in the field. Therefore his army must be made larger. To that end, Essex had issued orders to effect a concentration of a large Parliamentarian army in east Oxfordshire. Sussex and Bedfordshire, for example, both sent soldiers: Colonel Morley's Regiment of Horse and some dragoon companies for Sir Samuel Luke. One Parliamentarian account gives his strength as thirty thousand men, but it was probably half that number by the middle of June.

Hampden laboured to build up this army in preparation for the expected great battle. On 9 June he wrote a letter – the last to survive from his pen – to his kinsman Sir Thomas Barrington, the most influential Puritan gentleman in the wealthy county of Essex and a member of the House of Commons for Colchester, in support of the Lord General's request for more soldiers. Doubtless he wrote many others in a similar vein that have not survived.

> SIR–My Lord General hath written to the county of Essex to call in the well-affected people to his assistance, and hath entreated the help of the Deputy Lieutenants in it. The work is so necessary and so hopeful that I cannot but improve the interest I have in yourself for the promoting of it.
>
> The power of Essex is great, a place of most life of religion in the land, and your power in the county is great too. The difficulties of this war needs the utmost of both. Our army wants both men and money, and therefore their help in this way proposed would be very seasonable.
>
> I know you need not to be moved to a thing that you apprehend for the good of the cause. Such I conceive this business for the good of the kingdom in general, and so of Essex in particular. Consider of it, and you will find it deserves your serious and hearty endeavours. It will be a service acceptable to my Lord General, and you shall further engage
>
> > Your affectionate cousin and servant,
> > JOHN HAMPDEN
>
> Stokenchurch, June 9th, 1643

On 10 June the advance guard of the Parliamentarian army marched towards Thame, where the Lord General established his headquarters. The rain had fallen steadily for two weeks, turning the roads into deep mud. Every small town, village and hamlet around Thame now held a regiment or troop of soldiers. While he waited for reinforcements to arrive, Essex gave his permission for a raid upon the Royalists quartered in Islip.

On Saturday 17 June a strong party of about two and a half thousand Parliamentarian horse and foot set out for that

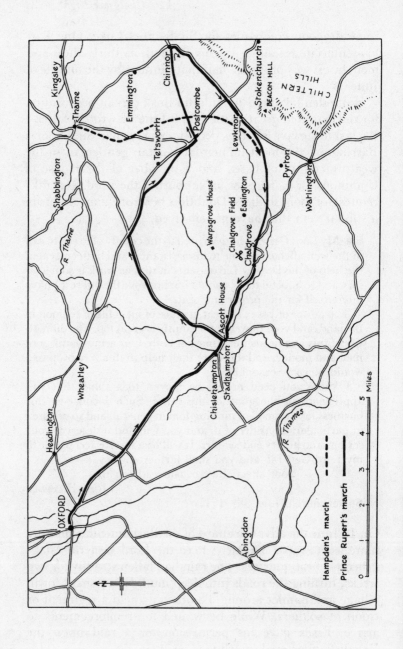

Prince Rupert's march to Chalgrove Field

village, which lay on the River Cherwell seven miles north of
the city. Cavaliers under Sir Arthur Aston, now Sergeant-
Major-General of Horse, occupied the quarter, with a still
larger force commanded by Lieutenant-General Wilmot
ensconced three miles further north at Bletchingdon. The
Royalist scouts gave Aston plenty of warning of the enemy's
approach, and he drew out some of his own and Wilmot's
troops to a good position east of the village on a rise of ground
along the road to Wheatley and Thame. One by one the
cavalry regiments of the Prince of Wales and Henry Percy,
who was General of the Ordnance, came into battle line,
followed by the rest of Aston's men and some hundred and
fifty dragoons from Lord Wentworth's regiment and others.
Seeing this Cavalier strength, and yet more regiments
appearing in the distance, the Parliamentarian commanders
drew rein. Then they gave orders for their forces to return to
Beckley Park, two miles away down the road, where they
made a halt and allowed the soldiers to make fires as if to
prepare a meal. But they thought better of it, and marched
back to their quarters without firing a shot or drawing a
sword.

A Parliamentarian spy from Oxford reported that night to
Sir Samuel Luke, Scout-Master-General in Essex's army.
Besides recounting the consternation in the military ant-
heap of Oxford caused by the sudden approach march, this
spy John Lane told Luke that the Queen's convoy was now
expected there the following week. News of a repulse given
by Prince Maurice's troops to some regiments of Waller's
army at Chewton Mendip on 12 June had also occasioned
much rejoicing on Friday evening. The Royalists had set all
the townsfolk and scholars to work digging and building
fortifications, such as a mound behind Christ Church for two
great pieces of ordnance which lay in the magazine. Some
students boasted that if the King deserted the town they
would keep it 'for they say they have swords that have not
seen the sun these seven years'. At least their spirits were not
as rusty as their blades.

His Excellency the Earl of Essex had made the first 'courtesy
call', and His Highness Prince Rupert determined to repay

the compliment promptly. To show that the Royalists in Oxford did not regard Essex as an enemy to be reckoned with, the arrogant Prince resolved to march that night through the middle of the Parliamentarian quarters and fall upon the furthest away of them. To do this he would pass within a mile or two of Thame, the Earl's own headquarters. Thus on that same day, Saturday, 17 June, at about four o'clock in the afternoon, Prince Rupert rode out of Oxford across the River Cherwell at the head of a column of soldiers.

Major William Legge of Prince Rupert's regiment led the way with a vanguard of a hundred troopers and fifty dragoons, riding out a good distance before the main column, like a forlorn hope. Prince Rupert followed with one thousand troopers under the colours of three regiments of horse. Lieutenant-Colonel O'Neal headed Rupert's own excellent regiment, accompanied by his troop of Life-guards under Sir Richard Crane. Major Thomas Daniel, a Yorkshireman, commanded the equally fine regiment of the Prince of Wales. General Percy and his own Regiment of Horse brought up the rear. Lord Wentworth, Sergeant-Major-General of Dragoons, led the three hundred and fifty dragoons, drawn from four different regiments. Colonel Henry Lunsford's four or five hundred foot completed the flying column. As they belonged to a variety of regiments in Oxford they carried no colours.

With Prince Rupert rode Colonel John Urry, a Scots soldier of great reputation as an excellent commander of horse, who as a result of the differences between the English and Scots officers in the army of Essex, had recently deserted to the King. This proud and imperious Scotsman still possessed knowledge of where the Parliamentarian horse were quartered, and so he served as guide to the expedition. For his treachery that night Urry would receive a knighthood and a regiment of horse from King Charles. (Later both sides grew tired of this double turncoat and he received his just deserts on the scaffold in 1651.)

By one o'clock next morning, having ordered some halts on the way to refresh both man and beast, Prince Rupert reached the area south of Tetsworth, a Parliamentarian quarter twelve miles from Oxford on the highway from that city to Wycombe and London. An alert sentry outside the village sighted the Royalist party and fired his pistol, and then his carbine, to give the alarm. Several other shots rang out from the main guard by the side of the road. The Cavaliers, standing still and silent, saw pin-pricks of light like fireflies in the dark as the Parliamentarian musketeers lit their long matches ready for action. The Prince would not allow his men to answer these shots; he intended to march on further and he did not want to waste more time or give the alarm to the other quarters. Nevertheless that warning pistol shot at Tetsworth triggered off the train of events which would lead to Hampden's death. For Tetsworth lay three miles south of Thame and a trooper galloped into that town and informed Sir Philip Stapleton, the officer in command of the court of guard, that a large body of Cavaliers had been sighted moving eastwards. By this time Stapleton would have been able to hear for himself the sounds of fighting at Postcombe.

After the alarm had thus sounded in Thame, several troops of horse were chosen to sally forth against this expedition. According to the authors of *A True Relation*, the main Parliamentary account of these events:

> amongst those Colonels and Commanders that were at an instant willing to hazard their lives upon this design, Colonel Hampden (who is a gentleman that hath never been wanting to adventure his life and fortunes for the good and welfare of his King and Country, may not be forgotten), who finding of a good troop of Horse (whose Captain was at that time willing) desired to know whether they would be commanded by him upon this design: whereupon the officers and common soldiers freely and unanimously consented, and proffered to adventure their lives with this noble Gentleman, and shewed much cheerfulnesse that they could have the honour to be led by so noble a Captain.

This troop belonged to Captain Crosse.

The Royalist column drew near to Postcombe, a hamlet in the parish of Lewknor three miles from Tetsworth where a troop of Colonel Herbert Morley's Sussex Regiment of Horse was quartered. Having heard shots in the night, the Sussex men were saddling their horses when they espied

Wentworth's dragoons alighting from their nags at the street's end. Thus most of the troop made their escape. Besides some pistols, swords, carbines, and horses, the raiders took the troop's colour and nine sleepy troopers caught in the houses at the end of the street.

After resting for about thirty minutes, Prince Rupert mounted again and marched north-east under the ledge of the Chilterns towards Chinnor, four miles beyond Thame and the furthest quarter towards London. Major Legge and his advance guard immediately entered the village while the remaining forces surrounded it. Within it lay some two hundred dragoons of Sir Samuel Luke's new Bedfordshire Regiment under command of Major Edwards. These raw soldiers had taken part in the march against Islip the day before, and in consequence had returned completely weary to their quarters. Several bold lads who snatched up their swords or carbines were cut down by the Cavaliers. Some sixty more surrendered in the barns and cottages without offering any resistance. The captain and other officers did make a fighting stand in a house at the village's end, firing their pistols and muskets from the windows. The Cavaliers put a torch to the thatched roof and shot down the defenders as they ran out at the back. Besides more horses and arms they collected three of Luke's dragoon colours: black swallow-tail flags with small embossed open Bibles painted on them in the place of the customary spots to distinguish one company from another.

Leaving Chinnor in flames, the Royalists began searching in the roads and lanes nearby for a convoy – said to contain chests of money worth £21,000 – which they knew had set out from London for Thame. But the wagon-master, hearing the alarm, had sensibly hidden the carts in a wood.

The action in Chinnor had taken about one and a half hours. Thus Sunday had dawned when Prince Rupert turned his horse's head homewards. Marching slowly, the exhausted men rode and marched back along the line of the Chiltern escarpment south-eastwards. Between seven and eight o'clock their outriding scouts brought word of an enemy party in the village upon their left hand. Shortly afterwards the Cavaliers caught sight of about ten Parliamentarian scouts on the side of Beacon Hill close to Lewknor.

Meanwhile Hampden and his borrowed troop, together with those of Major John Gunter and Captain James Sheffield belonging to the Earl of Essex's Regiment of Horse, began to close upon the rear of the Royalist column. In some panic the Prince's troop of Life-guards over-marched the Prince's Regiment of Horse and Percy's regiment, who formed the rear-guard. The Parliamentarian troops worried the rear, like hounds snapping at the heels of a stag. Once or twice Percy and O'Neal swung around their regiments and faced them, winning time to catch up with the main body, which had halted in Chalgrove cornfield, three miles from the bridge at Chislehampton over the River Thame.

It was now about nine o'clock in the morning and the sun grew very hot as it climbed ever higher in a clear blue sky. The Royalists standing in Chalgrove Field watched as some Parliamentarian horse and dragoons came into view on the gentle slope of Golder Hill a mile or so away. Eventually these forces drew down to a great close or pasture, and began to get into battle order among the trees, beyond a large hedge which separated their ground from Chalgrove Field itself. Beside Hampden's three troops there now stood the troop of Captain Sanders, Captain Buller with fifty commanded horsemen, Captain Dundosse's company of dragoons, and a few of Colonel Mills' Regiment of Dragoons, not more than four hundred soldiers in all. Probably they regarded themselves as the forlorn hope of the much larger forces already on the road from Thame not seven miles away.

Prince Rupert, who could not see behind Golder Hill, probably thought that a great body of enemy were waiting out of sight there until their dragoons, supported by a few troops of horse, had succeeded in lining the hedge. Consequently he took good care to secure his line of retreat over Chislehampton bridge. To this end he sent Colonels Lunsford and Washington with all the foot to guard both ends of the bridge. Then he laid an ambush by ordering his dragoons to line the hedgerows along each side of the long lane leading from Chalgrove to the bridge's mouth.

To entice the enemy into this ambush, so the Royalist

account claims, Prince Rupert made a show of retreating. Whereupon the Parliamentarian horse advanced cheerfully, doubling their march for very eagerness, and thus came up much closer to the Cavaliers. A Royalist account of the fight gives their numbers as eight troops of horse, about a hundred commanded horse and as many dragoons of Colonel Mills' regiment, now led by the redoubtable young Scot, Captain. John Middleton.

It was Sunday morning; soon the bells would be ringing for morning service. The Puritans paused and made ready in their hearts for a more costly sacrifice that day than psalms of praise and thanksgiving. For the Parliamentarians had resolved to fight. Clarendon asserts that Hampden 'was the principal cause of their precipitation, contrary to his natural temper, which, though full of courage, was usually very wary; but now, carried on by his fate, he would by no means expect the General's coming up; and he was of that universal authority that no officer paused to obey him.'

Prince Rupert's experienced eyes surveyed the scene. His move towards the bridge had drawn some eight rebel troops out into the open. He could now see three other troops in reserve in their former ground, that close among the trees by Warpsgrove House, and also two more troops just emerging from the woods higher up on the hillside. There was no time to lose. If he left the rebels alone they would snap at his heels all the way to Oxford, or possibly force him to fight at a disadvantage elsewhere, when his men and horses were even more weary than now. Yet what other enemy forces were hastening towards him? Should it be flight or fight?

A long hedge and ditch divided the ground between the two opposing sides. The Parliamentarian dragoons had dismounted and lined the centre, while the forlorn hope of commanded horse came to the end of it. The eight troops faced Prince Rupert's regiment and his Life-guards, and made a front so much too large for them that two troops from the Prince of Wales' regiment had to be ordered forward to make the lines even. General Percy's regiment stood further back on the right wing and the remainder of the Prince of Wales' men took up a similar position in reserve on the left. The Cavaliers wore red sashes or scarves tied around their waists.

At this juncture some senior commanders counselled Rupert to continue the retreat, but his judgment overswayed them. He told them that the rebels being so near would bring their rear into confusion even before they could entice them into the ambush in the lane leading up to Chislehampton bridge. Moreover, the brave bearing of Hampden's small force, outnumbered by more than four to one, galled the Prince. Some of the dragoons in the hedgerow may also have recognized his tall figure and sallow face, and opened fire at his party. Suddenly the Prince shouted, 'Yea, their insolency is not to be endured!' Pulling his horse about he plunged his spurs into its sides and tore towards the hedge. His horse rose up and crashed through the thick green hawthorn hedge, scattering dragoons from left to right like startled partridges. Sir Richard Crane and the Life-guard caught their breath and they also set off after their leader. About fifteen lifeguardsmen had jumbled through or over the hedge and Rupert made them form a front. Behind this shield the other lifeguardsmen forced their jaded mounts to leap the bushes. The Parliamentarian dragoons, who emptied some saddles with their first volley, had fallen back.

Meanwhile Lieutenant-Colonel O'Neal had taken the Prince's regiment around the end of the hedge on the left hand. He advanced at their head towards the enemy's eight troops, who had also withdrawn at a trot several hundred yards when the hedge came under attack. Facing them about once more, the Parliamentarian captains arrayed their men in good order. Sitting his horse before the front rank of the troop of Captain Crosse, Hampden made ready his two pistols and loosened his sword in its sheath. The troopers behind him drew out their short carbines.

The colours of O'Neal's six troops of horse fluttered in the breeze as they came into line and drew nearer their quarry. At perhaps eight paces away a volley of carbine fire rang out from the close-ordered ranks of the Parliamentarian horse. The troopers then drew and fired their first pistols. They just had time to discharge their second pistols before spurring forward to take the full force of a Cavalier charge. Prince Rupert's regiment felt the clash as much as their opponents, for this time the Parliamentarians withstood the onslaught. Not since the fight at Powick Bridge, wrote one Cavalier, had they encountered such spirited opposition. Prince Rupert rallied his Life-guard and led them in a fierce charge home upon the exposed flank of the troops in the Parliamentarian left wing, which caused them to give ground. By this time also General Percy, with several of his troops, had found a way over the hedge and rode up to second the charge. Meanwhile Major Daniel and the five hundred men of the Prince of Wales' regiment hurled themselves against the other flank of the Parliamentarians. Miraculously they stood their ground.

By this time Hampden had suffered his fatal wound. A Cavalier trooper had ridden up and shot him from behind with a double-loaded carbine or pistol. The two balls bit deep into the flesh behind his shoulder blade. Shocked and growing weaker as his blood stained his shirt and buff-coat, Hampden found it difficult to stay upright on his horse. A Parliamentarian trooper, taken prisoner later that day, told his captors 'that he was confident Mr Hampden was hurt, for he saw him ride off the field before the action was done, which he never used to do, and with his head hanging down, and resting his hands upon the neck of his horse, by which he concluded he was hurt.' By tradition Hampden rode towards his father-in-law's house, Pyrton Manor, three miles away. As it lay anyway in his natural line of retreat over Golder Hill, it is a doubtful story, for he must have known that he would not be safe there. He turned north-wards and rode five miles to the security of Thame.

Behind him the battle raged on, as the soldiers fought hand-to-hand with sword and pistol amid the smoke, noise and dust. At one point in the fight three troops of the Round-head horse wheeled about, as if they intended either to get between the Royalists and Chislehampton bridge or to charge them in the rear. Lieutenant-Colonel O'Neal promptly borrowed two troops from Percy's regiment and made after them. Seeing their line of march blocked, the Parliamentarians turned bridles and made haste back to their fellows.

One daring fellow thrust hard at Prince Rupert 'and had

the honour to die by his pistol'. General Percy also shot one Parliamentarian commander, probably Major Gunter who commanded the two or three troops of the Earl of Essex's Regiment present at the fight under their orange colours. Colonel Urry, who charged in the very left hand of the Prince of Wales' Regiment, was recognized and offered quarter, but bought himself off by his sword cheaper. O'Neal offered quarter to 'a proper young gentleman' who refused it with a reproach and thereby lost his life. Both Major Legge and Major Daniel found themselves prisoners for a brief spell. Before that Daniel had shot down a cornet and taken his colour (therefore regaining for the troop of the Prince of Wales the precious right to bear a colour which they had forfeited by the loss of their own at Hopton Heath). Some Royalists claimed afterwards that they overheard Dalbier shouting out to his people 'to retreat, lest they were hemm'd in by us'. Sir Samuel Luke found himself taken prisoner thrice and rescued each time. Captain Crosse had his horse shot under him, but one of his troopers mounted him again. A pistol ball struck Captain Buller in the neck.

The Parliamentarian troopers had fought well with sword and pistol, but they were hopelessly outnumbered. Their officers somehow extricated them from the confusion, and drew them back towards three troops or dragoon companies in the close by Warpsgrove House. There the officers rallied the men and they faced about to confront their pursuers. But the elated Cavaliers had scented victory and they pressed the attack. The brave Parliamentarians broke ranks and scattered pell-mell over Golder Hill, streaming past the hamlet of Easington on its southern slopes.

Two or three miles from Chalgrove Field the fugitives caught sight of the rest of the Earl of Essex's Regiment of Horse about two miles away from the battlefield, marching resolutely under the command of Sir Philip Stapleton. Some regiments of foot may have also set out from Thame. But why did these reinforcements not arrive sooner? Had the soldiers been mustered shortly after dawn they should have covered the five miles from Thame to Chalgrove by nine o'clock. In his published letter, the Earl of Essex merely says: 'When I heard that our men marched in the rear of the

The Prince of Wales's Regt.

Prince Rupert's Regt.

The Life Guard

Prince Rupert's Regt.

General Percy's Regt.

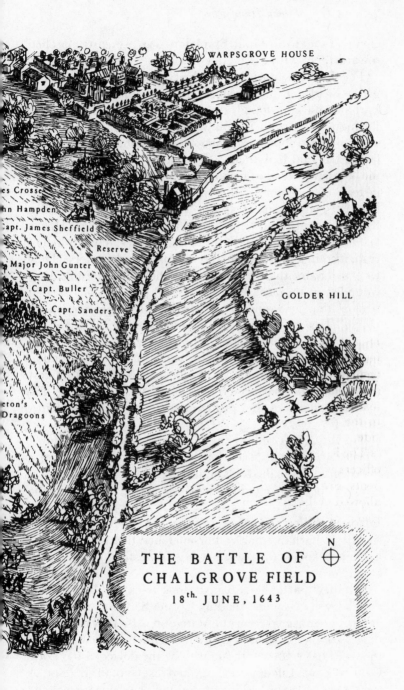

WARPSGROVE HOUSE

es Crosse

hn Hampden

apt. James Sheffield

Reserve

Major John Gunter

Capt. Buller

Capt. Sanders

ton's
Dragoons

GOLDER HILL

THE BATTLE OF
CHALGROVE FIELD
18th. JUNE, 1643

N

enemy, I sent to Sir Philip Stapleton, who presently marched toward them with his regiment.'

The Parliamentarians left thirty dead bodies on Chalgrove Field and fifteen more in Easington. Ten wounded Parliamentarians found shelter in Mr Stevens' house at Easington, where their wounds were dressed. Four of these unfortunate troopers or dragoons succumbed in the jolting farm carts that took them to Thame. Apparently several of the Parliamentarian troops had also worn red scarves instead of the more common orange sashes. Indeed two Royalist gentlemen – Captain Thomas Gardner of Prince Rupert's regiment and the Earl of Berkshire's son Mr Henry Howard – who followed those red sashes too far before realizing their mistake, found themselves prisoners. They were at Thame that day, where they heard Captain Buller – wounded in the neck by a shot – tell the Earl of Essex in person 'that he would not give a fig for all his Lordship's Horse'. His remark is understandable in the heat of the moment, but it was not true. With good leadership, the Lord General's cavalry had fought well. Indeed, Clarendon described the encounter as 'the best, fiercest, and longest maintained that has been by the horse during the war', due to the presence of the 'prime gentlemen' on Parliament's side.

The Royalists combing the field found two badly wounded officers who had been left for dead: Cornet Sheffield and a Scots dragoon called Captain Berkeley. Prince Rupert allowed them to remain behind on parole. Yet when the coach of Colonel Sir Lewis Dyve arrived next day from Oxford to collect them they declined to enter it. On Tuesday a party of Parliamentarian horse fetched them away, pausing first to knock down a stone cross that stood in the centre of Chalgrove village.

For their part, the Royalists took back to Oxford with them eleven prisoners, sending Cornet Sanders and several others under armed escort to Abingdon. Also they carried off the two orange cornets of Gunter and Sheffield, one bearing the word CAVE ADSUM, thought to be the device of the Lord General's own Life-guard. They had lost Captain Jackson of the Prince of Wales' regiment and ten or twelve men slain.

Their surgeons counted between sixteen and twenty wounded men. Having left a strong guard on Chislehampton bridge, Prince Rupert rode into Oxford early that afternoon where he received a warm welcome from King Charles.

In Thame, John Hampden lay in bed. By tradition again his quarters were in the 'Greyhound' Inn on the north side of the main street; it has been long since converted into a chemist's shop, although the arched window of the room where Hampden is said to have died can still be seen. At first it seemed as if all would be well. *A True Relation,* the account of the great fight printed in London within a day or two of it, reported: 'it is certain that Colonell Hampden that noble and valiant Gentleman, received a shot with a Bullet behind in the shoulder, which stuck between the bone and the flesh, but is since drawne forth, and himselfe very cheerfull and hearty, and it (through Gods mercy) more likely to be a badge of honour, than any danger of life.' Having extricated the two balls, the chirurgeons probably poured oil and balsam into the wounds, pressing them out afterwards.

Almost certainly, however, Hampden's shoulder or arm had been shattered. Within a day or two complications developed. Inflammations and spasms, or possibly gangrene, caused serious concern to the doctors. On 22 June a letter-writer noted that three physicians went from London to Hampden's bedside.

Dr Giles, the parson of Chinnor, met Sir Philip Warwick by accident in an Oxford street and told him the sad news of Hampden's fever. Warwick blamed the fever on the poor quality of Hampden's blood, which 'in its temper was acrimonious, as the scurf on his face showed'. Being a gentleman volunteer in the King's Life-guard, he had no difficulty in bringing Dr Giles to the King:

> The Doctor was a near neighbour and friend of Mr Hampden's, and being an opulent man, he had built himself a very good Parsonage-house, in the contrivance of which structure Mr Hampden had used his skill. The King required the Doctor, as from himself, to send to see him, for I found the King would have sent him over any surgeon of his, if any had been wanting; for he looked upon his interest, if he could gain his affection, as a powerful means of begetting a right understanding betwixt him

and his two Houses.

I remember how the Doctor regretted the King's command; for, says he, 'I have seemed unlucky to him in several conjunctions of time, when I made addresses to him in my own behalf: for he having been formerly so kindly my friend, before I came to Oxford, we the Prebendaries of Windsor being all turned out of our houses, in the carrying off of my goods my wagons were robbed and plundered, though warranted by passport, and I addressing to him for release, my messenger came in that very instant in which the news of his eldest son's death came to him; and some good time after, falling into a like calamity, though I failed of the fruit of his intended release the first time, yet I hoped to have found it the second; but my messenger unfortunately met then with another, that brought the news of his beloved daughter, Mrs Knightley's death; so I seemed to scritch-owl him.' However, the Doctor sent, and when he heard of a messenger from him, this poor gentleman, though he was in a high fever and not very sensible, was much amazed at it.

Hampden did not regain his full senses. He died on Saturday, 24 June, his wedding anniversary. On the following day his body was borne ten miles to Great Hampden for burial in the parish church at the side of Elizabeth, beneath the chancel. Probably the Greencoats accompanied their slain leader, marching before and behind the cart bearing the coffin. They would have marched with heads uncovered and weapons reversed. Black ribbon hung like tears upon the colours, while the muffled drums beat out a slow tread. Before him they carried his helmet, armour and sword.

Hampden's friend Arthur Goodwin had stood by his bedside at Thame. On the day after the funeral, Goodwin wrote to his daughter Lady Wharton as follows:

Dear Jenny,

I am here at Hampden in doing the last duty for the deceased owner of it, of whom every honest man hath a share in the loss, and therefore will likewise in the sorrow. In the loss of such a friend to my own particular, I have no cause of discontent, but rather to bless God that he hath not according to my deserts bereft me of you and all the comforts dearest to me. All his thoughts and endeavours of his life was zealously in this cause of God's, which he continued in all his sickness, even to his death. For all I can hear the last words he spake was to me, though he lived six or seven hours after I came away as in a sleep. Truly, Jenny, (and I know you may easily be persuaded to it), he was a gallant man, an honest man, an able man, and take all, I know not to any man living second. God now in mercy hath rewarded him. I have writ to London for a black suit, I pray let me beg of you a broad black ribbon to hang about my standard. I would we all lay it to heart, that God takes away the best amongst us. I pray the Lord to bless you. Your ever, dear Jenny, most affectionate father,

ARTHUR GOODWIN

Hampden, June 26th, 1643

HAMPDEN IN RETROSPECT

Farewell then honour'd Hampden (heav'nly Jem)
Adorning now the new Jerusalem
Farewell belov'd in Parliament and Field,
Farewell thy soldiers faithful broken shield.

Thus wrote John Leicester in an *Elegiacal Epitaph* published in London on 27 July 1643. In October further *Elegies on the Death of that Worthy and Accomplished Gentleman, Colonel John Hampden, Esquire* appeared in print, including the verse of Captain John Stiles of the Greencoats. Many less formal tributes appear in the letters and journals of the day. Robert Goodwin, for example, a future member of Cromwell's Council of State, bewailed to Sir Thomas Barrington the 'sad tidings of Colonel Hampden's death . . . a cause to all men of much reluctation and sorrow'. In *The Kingdome's Weekly Intelligencer* published in London a week after his death, the editor declared that 'the loss of Colonel Hampden goeth near the heart of every man that loves the good of his king and country, and makes some conceive little content to be at the army now he is gone . . . The memory of this deceased colonel is such that in no age to come but it will more and more be had in honour and esteem; a man so religious, and of that prudence, judgment, temper, valour, and integrity, that he hath left few like behind him.'

Even those who stood far off from the centre of events mourned his passing. 'I am very sorry for Mr Hampden', wrote Lady Sussex to Sir Ralph Verney, 'I do not know him but I haye heard he is a discreet good man.' But those who counted themselves friends and colleagues of Hampden felt a much deeper grief. 'Poor Hampden is dead . . . I have scarce strength to pronounce that word,' wrote Anthony Nichol, a member of the House of Commons. 'Never kingdom received a greater loss in one subject, never man a truer and faithful friend.' Certainly Nichol's reaction is echoed by Clarendon's more considered judgment on the death of Hampden: 'Never was there such consternation and sorrow at one man's death, as when the tidings thereof did reach London, in the Parliament and the people throughout the land; as if their whole army had been defeated: his private loss is unspeakable.'

Anthony Nichol was the son of Pym's half-sister and a member of Pym's inner circle of friends. Pym himself seems to have reacted more with anger than grief. On 25 June Colonel Urry led another raid, defeating Stapleton's horse and plundering Wycombe. The City stood to arms in the general mood of alarm. Pym wrote a sharp letter to Essex telling him that men were safer under the King's protection than his, and asking him to tender another covenant to his soldiers. On 28 June Essex replied to the House of Commons by offering to resign his commission, but Pym hastily wrote to say that he had not intended any reflections upon the Lord General's honour, and the matter rested there. For, in Clarendon's words, Essex was 'yet the soul of the army' and the leaders of the House of Commons could not dispense with him. The death of Hampden removed the main link between the House of Commons and the army of Essex. Sir Philip Stapleton and Arthur Goodwin (until his death in August 1643) spoke up for Essex at Westminster, but they could not personify the Puritan House of Commons in the army as Hampden had done. Thenceforth the army lacked any inner political direction, and it became increasingly erratic. In the summer of 1644 Essex even wandered down to Cornwall, and his humiliating surrender at Lostwithiel spelt the virtual end of his army.

The Royalist newspaper *Mercurius Aulicus* had reported rumours that Hampden would shortly replace the Earl of Essex in command of the army. Historians have tended to dismiss this idea, emphasizing Hampden's careful loyalty to the Lord General. Hampden had probably learned much about the art of generalship since August 1642; certainly he possessed many of the essential soldierly qualities for command, such as courage, leadership, initiative, boldness and caution. Above all, he manifested the will to win, the spirit that makes a general seek out the enemy's forces and attempt to defeat them in battle. Bullets broke the shoulders of both Sir Thomas Fairfax and Hampden in 1643; the former survived and the latter did not. It is tempting to speculate on the outcomes in English history had the reverse happened.

Clarendon reported jubilation in Oxford at the news of Hampden's death, saying that the Puritan party had come to rely more on him than Essex himself. Moreover, his combination of talents made him an enemy to be feared. 'In a word, he had a head to contrive, and a tongue to persuade, and a hand to execute, any mischief. His death therefore seemed to be a great deliverance to the nation.'

We can only speculate on whether or not Hampden would have made a commander-in-chief. Certainly, however, he was a consummate politician, whose background and style suited him admirably to be a 'first among equals' among men such as Vane, St John, Sir William Waller, Heselrige and Cromwell. Besides his character and reputation, he displayed a mastery of parliamentary tactics. 'He was certainly a person of the greatest abilities of any of that party', wrote Sir Philip Warwick. 'He had a great knowledge both on Scholarship and in the Law. He was of a concise and significant language, and the mildest, yet subtillest, speaker of any man in the House; and had a dexterity, when a question was going to be put, which agreed not with his sense, to draw it over to it by adding some equivocal or sly word, which would enervate the meaning of it, as first put.'

Hampden's habit of listening clearly surprised people. It was an age of great talkers and orators, who sought to sway others in public or private by lengthy speeches full of references to authorities. By contrast Hampden excelled in personal conversation, drawing out the other man's inner thoughts and seeking a common ground with his own views. Some suspected that the ignorance he professed continually in the discussions, and the deprecations of his own knowledge, which all men knew to be considerable, smacked of dissimulation if not cunning, but those who knew him better sensed the presence of a genuine humility, that rare grace of a great mind. By questioning, and then sowing seeds of ideas in opened minds, Hampden guided men perhaps without either party being fully aware of it. He was a teacher by natural vocation. Like a patient and loving university tutor, he encouraged others and flattered them by treating them as his intellectual equals.

Pym died of cancer in the lower bowel on 8 December 1643. Had Hampden lived he would have probably inherited Pym's mantle as the recognized leader of the House of Commons. Had the King negotiated with Hampden after the Civil War and not with a Parliament bereft of him, still less with an Army dominated by separatists and radicals, the chances of a negotiated settlement would have been greater. Thus the King (or his advisers) may have shown some foresight in attempting to save Hampden's life.

The tale of Hampden's immediate descendants can soon be told. His twelve-year-old son Richard succeeded him as his chief heir. In 1656 Richard sat for Buckinghamshire in Cromwell's second Parliament. According to a contemporary pamphlet, the Protector made him a member of the new House of Lords in order 'to settle and secure him to the interest of the new court, and wholly take him off from the thoughts of following his father's steps or inheriting his noble virtues'. After the restoration of the Church of England with that of King Charles II in 1660, Richard Hampden befriended those Puritan ministers ejected from their livings. During the plague of 1665, for example, Richard Baxter found refuge at Great Hampden, and describes his host as 'the true heir of his famous father's sincerity, piety, and devotedness to God'.

Baxter had served as a chaplain in the Parliamentarian army in the Civil War. He possessed a human curiosity which led him to ride over the field of Edgehill the morning after the battle, and he was among the first to observe the religious temper of Cromwell's troopers, some of whom he knew personally. In the earlier editions of His *Saints' Everlasting Rest* before 1659 he wrote that he thought heaven would be more enjoyable because he would meet there Lord

Brooke and Pym and Hampden. Later he omitted this passage. 'But I must tell the reader', he added, 'that I did blot it out, not as changing my opinion of the person . . . . Mr John Hampden was one that friends and enemies acknowledged to be most eminent for prudence, piety, and peaceable counsels, having the most universal praise of any gentleman that I remember of that age. I remember a moderate, prudent, aged gentleman, far from him but acquainted with him, who I have heard saying, that if he might choose what person he would be then in the world, he would be John Hampden.'

Richard Hampden zealously advocated the Exclusion Bill to prevent the Duke of York from ascending the throne as a Catholic. In 1690 after the accession of William and Mary, he became Chancellor of the Exchequer. Four years later he retired, and it is reported that he replied to the offers of a peerage or pension by declaring 'that he would die a country gentleman of ancient family as he was, which was honour enough for him; that he had always spoken against giving pensions to other, and at such a time it was oppression; whilst he had a roll or a can of beer he would not accept sixpence of the money of the nation.'

Bishop Burnet describes Richard's son, John Hampden the younger, as 'a young man of great parts, one of the learnedest gentlemen I ever knew; for he was a critic both in Latin, Greek and Hebrew; he was a man of great wit and vivacity, but too unequal in his temper.' Unfortunately John went to live in Paris, where he fell under the unsettling influence of a prominent free-thinker. Some time after his return home he was sentenced to death for his part in the Duke of Monmouth's rising, but he bought his life by paying a £6,000 fine. He failed to get a parliamentary seat in 1690 as he had fallen out of favour with the Whig oligarchy who dominated the county. In December 1696 he committed suicide by cutting his throat with a razor.

Hampden's mother Elizabeth had left the unexpired lease of Hampden House in London to her four grandchildren. The lease ran out in 1682, and it was then acquired by Sir George Downing. Son of parents who had sailed with him to the New World in 1638, Downing had the distinction of being the second graduate of the new university at Harvard.

He began the process of pulling down the ramshackle
medieval buildings and erecting new houses along a widened
street. Number 10 Downing Street, stands on the site of the
original garden of Hampden House. It is not unfitting that
the official residence of England's Prime Minister should
have an association with John Hampden.

John Hampden's great-grandson Richard became lord of
Great Hampden, and was succeeded on his death in 1728 by
his half-brother, John, who died without issue in 1754. The
estates then passed to the Trevor family, descendants of
Hampden's eldest surviving daughter Ruth. The Trevor of
the day took Hampden as an additional name, and became
Viscount Hampden. That line and title became extinct in
1824, and the manor-house became the property of the
Hobarts, descendants of Hampden's daughter Mary. The
Hobarts also coupled their name with that of Hampden, and
acquired the Earldom of Buckinghamshire. The predecessor
of the present Earl of Buckinghamshire conveyed Hampden
House to a trust which established a girls' public school
there. Despite his hesitations on the wisdom of sending girls
to boarding schools, John Hampden would probably have
been delighted with this use of his home.

Hampden's place in history depends in part upon the per-
ceptions of historians. Much as the Tories contemplated the
memory of King Charles as a Blessed Martyr, so their opponents the Whigs – those political heirs to the 'Good Old
Cause' – looked back upon a Hampden bathed in celestial
light. For them his name became an image, standing for the
long struggle for the liberty of Parliament and the subject
against royal despotism. Still more, the word 'Hampden'
entered the language as a symbol for patriotism. The poet
Thomas Gray traps this use of it like a fly in amber in his
immortal 'Elegy Written in a Country Church-yard':

> *Some village-Hampden, that with dauntless breast*
> *The little tyrant of his fields withstood.*
> *Some mute inglorious Milton here may rest,*
> *Some Cromwell, guiltless of his country's blood.*

Stoke Poges in Buckinghamshire, where he wrote the poem,

lies at the edge of the Chilterns and is an apt setting for this reference to Hampden. There is a brass portrait of one of Hampden's forefathers on the chancel floor. In the manor-house next to the church where Gray stayed during his summer vacations from Cambridge, that prominent figure of Hampden's youth, the famous parliamentarian and lawyer Sir Edward Coke, had once lived. King Charles lodged there briefly as a prisoner after the Civil War in 1647. Thus Gray breathed the very air of Hampden's country.

The first Whig historian to write Hampden's biography was also steeped in the Buckinghamshire scene. In 1831 George Grenville, Lord Nugent, published his *Memorials of John Hampden,* a work which enjoyed a reception that exceeded his expectations; it ran into four editions. Nugent took his title from his mother's side of the family, being born in 1789 the second son of the second Earl Temple, who became Marquess of Buckingham five years earlier. Nugent served under Wellington in the Peninsular War and then sat in Parliament for Aylesbury from 1812 onwards with interruptions until his death in 1850. In politics a resolute Whig, Nugent assured the Aylesbury electors in 1847 that he had been 'the resister of oppression, the advocate of religious freedom . . . the unflinching promoter, according to the best means God may give me, of the greatest of His gifts to man, after reason – Liberty!'

Lord Nugent's book evoked a celebrated review from the pen of Lord Macaulay. Besides underscoring Nugent's eulogy of Hampden as the true Whig hero of the Civil War, Macaulay neatly encapsulated the Whig myth of Hampden:

> The celebrated Puritan leader is an almost solitary instance of a great man who neither sought nor shunned greatness, who found glory only because glory lay in the plain path of duty. During more than forty years he was known to his country neighbours as a gentleman of cultivated mind, of high princi-ples, of polished address, happy in his family, and active in the discharge of local duties; and to political men as an honest, industrious, and sensible member of Parliament, not eager to display his talents, staunch to his party, and attentive to the interests of his constituents. A great and terrible crisis came. A direct attack was made by an arbitrary government on a sacred right of Englishmen, on a right which was the chief security for

all their other rights. The nation looked round for a defender. Calmly and unostentatiously the plain Buckinghamshire Esquire placed himself at the head of his countrymen, and right before the face and across the path of tyranny.

The second centenary of the Long Parliament in 1840 provided Lord Nugent and his friends with an occasion to drink Hampden's health in the hall of Hampden House. As the wine flowed freely, Lord Nugent hit upon the idea of erecting a monument on Chalgrove Field on the second centenary of Hampden's death in 1843. Subscriptions poured in. Mindful of the old Whig toast 'The cause for which Hampden bled on the field, and Sidney and Russell on the scaffold!' the Duke of Bedford donated twenty pounds. Many thousands of people attended the ceremony on Monday, 19 June 1843 (the actual anniversary falling on a Sunday), and that evening two hundred and fifty sat down to a large dinner. Subsequently Nugent raised another memorial in the parish of Stoke Mandeville to commemorate Hampden's refusal to pay Ship-Money, while a fine statue of him stands in the market-place of Aylesbury, pointing imperiously towards London.

From this pinnacle of fame the name of Hampden slipped into a country obscurity. Thomas Carlyle in *Cromwell's Letters and Speeches*, published in 1845, displays a contempt for him. The Cromwell band-wagon had begun to roll. Reflecting Carlyle's assumption that history is made by a few great men, biography after biography of Oliver Cromwell appeared, extolling his contribution above all others. Thus a new myth grew up, namely that Cromwell had conceived and led the opposition to King Charles from the start and won the Civil War single-handed. In broadcasting this myth, the film *Cromwell* (1970) even made him one of the five members. Thus Hampden's name became relegated to a bare mention or as a footnote in a school-books, usually in connection with Ship-Money.

The political historians of the Long Parliament, especially Professor J.R. Hexter in his pioneering book *The Reign of King Pym* (1941), have done much to change this picture. Hexter and others have tended to confirm Clarendon's view that the

Long Parliament was guided in its early stages by a 'select junta' of eight or nine members. In this loose group the names of Pym and Hampden stand out, the one a consummate and tireless business manager and the other the best-loved man in the House. Among the members of this 'great and ruffling' Parliament who had no concept of party leadership or discipline but saw themselves as a whole – as equals in a body conscious of corporate dignity – the self-effacing and intelligent personality of Hampden suddenly seems highly appropriate and effective for the work of higher political direction. For the House of Commons, then as now, could not be dominated: it could only be led.

In the Civil War itself, Hampden indeed drew his sword and threw away the scabbard. His active spirit sought a clear victory in the field. Yet his fellow countrymen may have lost at Chalgrove Field that wise physician who could have dressed the wounds and nursed England back to health through the fevers and distempers of a troubled peace.

SELECT BIBLIOGRAPHY

Reliquiae Baxterianae, or . . . Baxter's narrative of the most memorable passages of his life and times. Ed. by M. Sylvester. 1696.

Sir Richard Bulstrode. *Memoirs and Reflections upon the Reign and Government of King Charles the Ist and King Charles the IId*. 1721.

Calendar of State Papers, Domestic Series.

C. Coates. *The History and Antiquities of Reading*. 1802.

A Cowley. *The Civil War*. ed. by A. Pritchard. Toronto, 1973.

The Journal of Sir Simonds D'Ewes. Ed. by W. Notestein. New Haven, 1923.

J. Drinkwater. *John Hampden's England*. 1933.

The Journeys of Celia Fiennes. Ed. by C. Morris, 1947.

Hampden's Will, in *Wills from Doctors' Commons*. Ed. by J.G. Nichols and J Bruce. Camden Society. Old Series, 83.

The Tryal of Mr. Hampden. 1719.

C. Hill. *Puritanism and Revolution: Studies in Interpretation of the English Revolution of the Seventeenth Century*. 1958.
Society and Puritanism in Pre-Revolutionary England. 1964.
Intellectual Origins of the English Revolution. 1965.

J. Hexter. *The Reign of King Pym*. Cambridge, Mass., 1941.

Lucy Hutchinson. *Memoirs of the Life of Colonel Hutchinson*. (ed). London, 1965.

E. Hyde, Earl of Clarendon. *History of the Rebellion and Civil Wars in England*. Ed. by W.D. Macray, 6 vols. Oxford, 1888.

A.M. Johnson. 'Buckinghamshire 1640-60: A Study in County Politics'. M.A. Thesis. London University Library.

M.F. Keeler. *The Long Parliament, 1640-41*. Philadelphia, 1954.

F.G. Lee. *The History . . . of the Church of Thame*. 1883.

G. Lipscomb. *The History and Antiquities of the County of Buckinghamshire*. 4 Vols. 1831-47.

C.E. Lucas-Phillips. *Cromwell's Captains*. London and Toronto, 1938.

A.P. Newton. *The Colonizing Activities of the English Puritans*. New Haven, 1914.

George Grenville, Lord Nugent. *Some Memorials of John Hampden, his Party and his Times*. 2 vols. 1831. Macaulay's review appeared in *Edinburgh Review*, 54 (1831).

V. Pearl. *London and the Outbreak of the Puritan Revolution*. 1961.

J.L. Sanford. *Studies and Illustrations of the Great Rebellion*. 1858.

R. Spalding. *The Improbable Puritan: A Life of Bulstrode Whitelocke, 1605-1675*. 1975.

Lady Frances Parthenhope Verney. *Memoirs of the Verney Family during the Civil War*. 2 vols. 1892.

E.G.B. Warburton. *Memoirs of Prince Rupert and the Cavaliers*. 3 vols. 1849.

Sir Philip Warwick. *Memoirs of the Reigne of King Charles I . . . with a continuation to the happy restauration of King Charles II*. 1701.

H.R. Williamson. *John Hampden*. 1933.

R.H. Whitelocke. *Memoirs, Biographical and Historical, of Bulstrode Whitelocke*. 1860.

C.V. Wedgwood. *The King's Peace*. 1955.
The King's War. 1958.

P. Young. *Edgehill 1642: The Campaign and the Battle*. 1967.

NOTE ON HAMPDEN'S LETTERS
Hampden's letters to Eliot are in the Eliot MSS at Port Eliot, with the exception of the letter dated 21 March 1632 which is in the British Museum. Other letters by Hampden are to be found in the British Museum (Stowe MSS, 142 ff, 39, 40 and 188, ff. 3, 5; Additional MSS, 15858 f.8; Egerton MSS, 2643, f.7), the Bodleian Library at Oxford (Tanner MSS, 62ff. 85, 115, and 63 f. 153; Carte MSS, 103 ff. 121, 123) and Hull University Library (the Hotham MSS).

INDEX